Beyond the Green Transformation

Until very recently, the climate crisis was considered the most serious and urgent challenge facing contemporary societies. There was widespread agreement that a comprehensive green transformation is necessary to address the planetary emergency, secure the survival of humanity and facilitate a good life for all. Yet, suddenly, ecological issues have slipped down the political agenda. Conservatives welcome 'the end of the green hegemony', the far-right rallies against eco-emancipatory policies, and an authoritarian turn that once again champions fossil fuels is gaining momentum across the world.

This book examines the causes of this dramatic change of course. It reminds us that in environmental politics, social norms and cultural values are as important as biophysical facts. Even if the scientific evidence on climate change and the collapse of biophysical systems is clear, the supposedly categorical imperatives presented by ecologists ultimately express a particular worldview.

Ingolfur Blühdorn argues that the emancipatory logic itself is a key driver of the current collapse of the green project. He shows how this counter-cultural project was fraught with inherent contradictions. Eco-emancipatory movements themselves contributed to mainstreaming values, lifestyles and notions of self-determination that ultimately blocked the green transformation and propelled a postliberal turn. To many, eco-political ideals today appear more like a threat than a promise. A renaissance of fossil fuels, autocratic leadership, and strict policies of exclusion seem to offer a better future, beyond eco-emancipatory values and the scenarios of ecological collapse.

But the transition to a postliberal modernity will benefit very few and make life brutish, nasty and short for many.

Ingolfur Blühdorn is Professor of Social Sustainability and head of the Institute for Social Change and Sustainability (IGN) at the Vienna University of Economics and Business.

Beyond the Green Transformation

On the Way to a Postliberal Modernity

Ingolfur Blühdorn

polity

First published in German as *Unhaltbarkeit. Auf dem Weg in eine andere Moderne* by Suhrkamp Verlag, 2024

This English edition published in 2026 by Polity Press

Polity Press Ltd.
65 Bridge Street
Cambridge CB2 1UR, UK

Polity Press Ltd.
111 River Street
Hoboken, NJ 07030, USA

ISBN-13: 978-1-5095-7103-1
ISBN-13: 978-1-5095-7104-8(pb)

A catalogue record for this book is available from the British Library.

Library of Congress Control Number: 2025949649

Typeset in 10.5 on 12 pt Sabon by
Cheshire Typesetting Ltd, Cuddington, Cheshire
Printed and bound in Great Britain by Ashford Colour Ltd

The publisher has used its best endeavours to ensure that the URLs for external websites referred to in this book are correct and active at the time of going to press. However, the publisher has no responsibility for the websites and can make no guarantee that a site will remain live or that the content is or will remain appropriate.

Every effort has been made to trace all copyright holders, but if any have been overlooked the publisher will be pleased to include any necessary credits in any subsequent reprint or edition.

For further information on Polity, visit our website:
politybooks.com

CONTENTS

UNTENABILITY

Introduction to the English Edition

Unhaltbarkeit, the title of the original German edition of this book, is a term that does not easily translate into English. *Untenability* comes close, yet this word is not easy to grasp, nor is it very commonly used. Admittedly, this also applies to the German term *Unhaltbarkeit*. And in the present context, this may actually be a strength rather than a weakness: an unusual term aiming to capture an exceptional condition, in fact, the *syndrome* of contemporary Western societies – which is the topic of this book. Until very recently these societies have conceived of themselves as the most progressive and advanced worldwide. Yet, suddenly they find themselves in deep trouble. They are accused of having taken not only themselves to the brink of disaster, but the entire world. Progressive movements and intellectual avant-gardes had long since criticized Western societies and modern consumption trends for their social and ecological impact and had self-confidently presented themselves as the spearheads of a great societal transformation that would cure these problems and fully realize progressive values and promises. But now they are as con-founded as anyone else. Climate scientists are warning of a *planetary emergency*; political intellectuals in the Marxist tradition see *capitalism at the limit*; right-wing populists are talking of a *broken society*; sociologists diagnose a *crisis of late modernity*; others again call it a *polycrisis* – and promising solutions are nowhere in sight.

The term *untenability* captures this syndrome more succinctly than any of the above. For a book on eco-politics, the term *unsustainability* might have been a better translation of *Unhaltbarkeit*. But this book is about more than ecological issues narrowly defined. Advanced modern societies find themselves in crisis in a much more comprehensive sense. Their established arrangements, institutions, self-perceptions, practices, values and beliefs have, in a whole range of respects, become literally untenable; and in a manner unlike that which the term *unsustainability* tends to suggest, this is not just a vague warning of a point or threshold in the more or less distant future beyond which they can probably no longer be upheld. They are crumbling and collapsing right now in the present – public infrastructures, systems of social provisioning, industrial supply chains, societal cohesion, liberal democracy, international law, human rights, to name but a few. A wide spectrum of systems, biophysical and social, are hopelessly overstrained and, whether we admit and like it or not, are simply no longer tenable.

Apart from being less restricted to ecological issues and far more definitive than *unsustainability*, the term *untenability* is also much richer, semantically. It has at least three different meanings which in the present context help us to grasp the actual dimension(s) of the issue: untenable in a *temporal* sense of outdated, obsolete or anachronistic; untenable in the *epistemic*, truth-related sense of unconvincing, unsound or indefensible; and untenable in the moral, *normative* sense of unethical, reprehensible or irresponsible. In a temporal sense, for example, the notions of alienation, liberation, civic duty or collective reason which once underpinned progressive thinking and politics have become untenable. In contemporary Western societies, the prevailing understandings of freedom or rationality are very different from those assumed by progressives. In the second sense, the self-description of Western societies as open, liberal and democratic is an example of their untenability. Both their migration policies and the autocratic-authoritarian turn that we see even in the most established democracies speak an entirely different language. And normatively, the constantly repeated entreaties to hope, for instance, and the reassurances that technological innovation and market-based solutions will cure ecological problems, are untenable because it is well established by now that these policies at best displace these problems and often actually aggravate them. Very often, these different meanings of untenability blend into each other, but to describe the syndrome of contemporary Western societies they are all equally constitutive. Thus, *untenability* is a very powerful concept indeed. And, in particular, it may be applied not only to the established societal order of Western societies, which environmental movements and many scientists have long criticized for its ecological and social unsustainability, but also to the narratives and promises of these movements themselves. All this, however, remains hidden in an unusual term until careful exegesis reveals it. As a title for the English edition, I therefore opted for something much more intuitively accessible: *Beyond the Green Transformation*.

In the past two years, since I completed the manuscript for the German edition of this book, the syndrome it investigates has become ever more evident. Political, technological and ecological developments have accelerated rapidly. In the USA, in particular, so far the heartland of Western values, the authoritarian turn has progressed rapidly, with Donald Trump incessantly attacking democratic institutions, the rule of law, the separation of powers and the freedom of speech and the press. His deliberate incitement of hatred and violence render ever more obvious that MAGA, Make America Great Again, is a revolt against all values and agendas that had been central to progressives and eco-emancipatory movements, in particular. And, curiously, while ecologists are traumatized by the prospect of populist denialism further accelerating ecological disaster, the far right has succeeded in creating a new project and perspective, a new narrative of a Turning Point towards a better future, and a new belief in political efficacy. But it is not the purpose of this introduction to provide a commentary on global political developments. Such updates might further illustrate the argument of this book, but they would not meaningfully add to its substance. Instead, with the benefit of some distance from the original writing process, and drawing on many instructive debates on the German edition, I want to reflect, once again, on my agenda, strategic approach and main arguments in this book. And it may also help readers if I address upfront some misunderstandings and objections that have arisen in many debates about the German edition. As regards the main body of the book, I have left the text largely unchanged. I have placed a bit more emphasis on the term *postliberal* – also in the book's subtitle – but apart from that, this introduction is followed by a fairly direct translation of the German edition.

Perspectives on a syndrome

In public discourse, until recently, the climate crisis has been the dominant framing of the syndrome. It was widely presented as the most serious and urgent challenge that contemporary societies have to confront. This frame puts the focus on the socio-natural metabolism and the transgression of *planetary boundaries*, which, sustainability researchers warn, leads to the collapse of biophysical systems and, by implication, of social systems, arrangements and institutions. For environmental movements and climate scientists, the remedy is a *socio-ecological transformation* (SET) or, more recently, the decarbonization of societies built on fossil fuels. Perceptions of ecological crisis and the understandings of the required societal transformation have themselves gone through a striking transformation. In the 1970s and 1980s, emancipatory issues figured very prominently in environmental debates. At the time, political ecologists wanted to liberate and fully realize what capitalist industrial modernity was seen to alienate, oppress and enslave: the authenticity, dignity and integrity of the human subject and its claim to autonomy. Today, these subjective, emancipatory aspects are playing a rather subordinate role. Instead, concepts like planetary boundaries and CO_2 emissions have moved to the fore. The focus is on supposedly objective problems, whereby the normative standards by which they are diagnosed as problematic and categorized as more or less urgent remain largely obscure – veiled by scenarios of apocalypse, the uninhabitability of the Earth and the extinction of the human species. Yet, this objectification neglects and denies the significance, indeed centrality, of the subjective – of predominant social norms which always remain the yardstick by which empirical phenomena and changes are perceived as problematic and become political concerns.

Of course, ecological movements and ecologically committed scientists have always pursued strategies of objectification. They were convinced that, in the name of avoiding disaster, they had to bring their fellow citizens, society and humanity at large to ecological reason, that they had to break through their *apocalypse blindness* and their *persistent denial of reality*. Theirs was a mission of public education and enlightenment. Until the present day, they are battling the delusion, the denial, the obstruction, against which they defend the *reality principle*. Yet it is exactly this approach that far-right movements are employing now, too. They position *common sense* against the supposedly objective problems and the eco-movements' *universal reason* – which, conversely, they now portray as ideology, madness and delusion. In doing so, these movements challenge the political left's established monopoly on defining progressive and emancipatory values, and call to mind the inescapable dependence of the supposedly objective problem diagnoses by environmental movements and sustainability scientists on values, ideals and beliefs which – although they may be deeply rooted in the Western tradition – are, nevertheless, contingent and today increasingly untenable in the multiple senses of the term.

Sociologists in the tradition of post-Marxist critical theory have often framed the current crisis and transformation of Western society as the collapse of neoliberal ideology and the logic of capitalism in general. Following the banking and financial crisis of 2008/9, in particular, they believed that Occupy Wall Street and the diverse movements it sparked in Europe would finally fulfil the promise that *another world is possible*. However, the transformative energy of these movements soon became exhausted. Their ideals of degrowth and collective self-limitation remained incompatible with the reality of contemporary societies and the aspirations of their citizens – which, in fact, emancipatory movements had themselves helped to shape.

When it comes to the climate crisis, sociology had long been considered as a latecomer. This was not least due to its analytical commitment. Sociologists want to solve problems and change society, of course, but they tend to be cautious about simply accepting given problem diagnoses. Rather, they see it as part of their business to explore the perspective from which, and the norms on the basis of which, something is perceived as a problem in the first place. Accordingly, they are aware that ecological problems – and the climate crisis – are not actually *out there*, but to a significant extent a matter of social perception and social norms. More recently, however, sociologists have increasingly jumped on the bandwagon of objectification. The polycrisis, the planetary emergency, suggests that action is required immediately. And in this constellation, the commitment to change, to initiate a societal transformation now, often gets in the way of the commitment to analysis. The desire for change trumps, conditions or even obstructs the analysis of how and why supposedly objective problems, emergencies, perceptions of abysses, etc., have become hegemonic – or untenable – under what conditions contemporary societies can – or cannot – respond to these emergencies, and which parameters shape their actual responses.

Still, critical sociology now increasingly buys into the notion of a planetary emergency and tacitly assumes that the goals and values which signpost the required transformation are self-evident. In view of the amassed scientific data on climate change and the human impact on biophysical systems more generally, this conflation of facts and problems is perfectly understandable. It is also a response to the tide of right-wing narratives of denial, conspiracy theories and the spread of so-called 'alternative facts'. Furthermore, this tendency to objectify problems and crises and discount their dependence on social norms – which are always changeable, essentially contingent – probably reflects the fact that the normative foundations on which critical sociology itself used to rely for its diagnoses and progressive agendas are increasingly contested, too. Against this backdrop, the supposedly objective diagnoses presented by climate science and sustainability research, and their demands for immediate determined action, are proving useful for sociological responses. They provide a new foundation and give new impetus to the critical project, beyond the traditional critique of capitalism. They facilitate a straightforward distinction between what is required, that is, effective action, and what is to be rejected, that is, denial or obstruction; and they sideline any uncomfortable reflection that the supposedly objective problems are problematic only from a specific perspective and measured against particular norms – which are, ultimately, contingent.

For environmental movements and sustainability research, this acceptance by sociologists of their objectifications may seem like a major achievement. Yet, the tide of science scepticism, climate denial and 'alternative facts' signals that this is a false and unhelpful victory. At a point when the unexpected side effects of several decades of progressive, eco-emancipatory activism and politics – such as the spread of notions of freedom and self-realization which are socially and ecologically destructive, or the rise of societal complexity to a level that exceeds the capacities of democratic institutions – are increasingly well researched, when democratic elections reveal the extent to which the eco-emancipatory project has actually lost its appeal, and even in Western societies significant parts of the citizenry are welcoming what is now dubbed the *end of the green hegemony* and the new era beyond the *liberal ideology of wokeness*, an urgent task for sociology would be to investigate how this change came about, and whether, from a different perspective, the practices which environmental movements and climate researchers perceive as denial and obstruction might actually appear as perfectly appropriate. A critical sociology, in contrast, that simply puts itself at the service of given problem diagnoses, forfeits its critical ambition and becomes affirmative. And if it clings to traditional *progressive* positions that have become detached from factually prevailing aspirations, if it remains trapped in its established but ultimately contingent normativity, it loses all access to the new and distinctive features of contemporary Western societies. This sociology can no longer provide relevant social analyses and diagnoses. In fact, it then turns into an intellectual and discursive space for the reassuring experience of certain values or beliefs which, nevertheless, obstruct a fuller understanding of the syndrome of these societies, of the metamorphosis they are experiencing and of the new kind of society that is emerging. This kind of sociology then might be perceived as normatively right but may well become empirically irrelevant.

Social theorists who, in light of the uncertainty of critical theory's normative foundations, focus on the analytical dimension frame the syndrome of contemporary Western societies as the *crisis of late modernity* (Reckwitz & Rosa 2023). They place the emphasis not on the logic of capitalism but on the logic of modernization, which in the post-war decades, in particular, had been imagined as producing linear progress and social improvement. Theorists of the crisis of late modernity call to mind that this logic has, in fact, always been ambiguous. Given their analysis of this ambivalence, these theorists are much more cautious about possible solutions to the perceived problems, which – if they are to be successful – would have to unhinge this underlying dynamic and logic. Instead of the normatively desired transformation demanded by environmental activists and traditional critical theorists, these theorists focus on the factual transformation of late-modern societies, on the triggers and drivers of this metamorphosis and on the question of what kind of society might emerge beyond the current crisis of late modernity. However, a purely analytical social theory that only describes and seeks to explain a transformation, but cannot suggest any solutions to perceived problems, runs the risk of being purely affirmative and, ultimately, only playing into the hands of those who oppose progressive policy agendas. As such, it may be empirically convincing, but may well be accused of being normatively wrong.

Finally, from the perspective of the far right, that is, for populist movements and right-wing intellectuals describing themselves as postliberals, the syndrome of contemporary Western societies is their moral decay and cultural exhaustion. For populist movements and their leaders, the main causes of the problem are immigration, left-wing identity politics and what they call the *elitist ideology of wokeness*. Furthermore, they see climate and sustainability policies as an unacceptable intervention into private matters and as impairing the prosperity and strength of local and national communities. Accordingly, the tight control of immigration, an end to policies of diversity, equity and inclusion (DEI), and the termination of climate and sustainability policies are their favoured solutions. For postliberal intellectuals, in turn, the cause of the problem is that liberalism has undermined and destroyed its own foundations and those of communal life. For them, the solution is a *regime change* (Deneen 2023), which is supposed to reinstate traditional family values, some kind of religious framework as the basis of communal life and the authority of supposedly *natural* elites.

In contemporary Western societies, these narratives of the far right find considerable resonance, not only because of the simplicity of populist arguments, but also because of their criticism of excessive individualism, on the one hand, and of universalism and cosmopolitanism, on the other. From a sociological perspective, however, these narratives are just as implausible as those of the eco-emancipatory left – with which they actually have some common ground. For example, the eco-emancipatory left, too, aimed for a fundamental change in societal values and culture; it also opposed liberal individualism and liberal democracy and, just like today's populist right, it encouraged citizens to *take back control* from the established elites. What separates them is, inter alia, that the left demanded and believed in *collective self-limitation* to secure a good life for all, whereas the far right believes in the *limitation of the collective* by means of strict demarcation and exclusion to secure a good life for some. Yet, the progressive left fails to account for the inherent contradictions and the unexpected side effects of their emancipatory project, and the far right simply denies the biophysical realities as well as the social impacts of its blend of radical exclusion and the liberation from eco-political regulation. There is nothing to suggest that this could restore the foundations of communal life, but there is much evidence that the reinstatement of the law and rule of the strongest will lead to severe conflict, violence and suffering worldwide.

Thus, there is broad agreement on the profound destabilization and transformation of the established order of so-called advanced modern societies. Yet there are no promising solutions. In fact, as noted above, a very important characteristic, a constitutive dimension, of the syndrome that this book examines is that *untenability* no longer refers only to the established practices, arrangements and institutions of the existing order that environmental movements, social theorists and the far right all diagnose from their respective perspectives, but also to the framings of the problem and the proposed solutions that each of them offer. They all agree that the established societal order is untenable, but their respective framings of the problem and suggested solutions are untenable, too. They all retreat into their self-reassuring bubbles, deny rather than confront the reality of late-modern hypercomplexity, insist on the exclusive validity of their own normativities – and thus escalate societal polarization and conflict.

Access routes

My aim in this book is explicitly not to address or even try to resolve the ecological crisis and the climate emergency, even though these are often referred to as the most serious and most urgent challenges for contemporary societies. Many readers of the German edition found this difficult to understand. Rather, the objective here is to theorize the particular condition or syndrome of Western societies, of which the *climate emergency* is only one perception and framing. How may this particular condition of the supposedly most advanced and progressive societies be conceptualized? How might we explain the obvious inability of these societies to resolve their polycrisis? How, in particular, do we explain the failure of progressive thinking and the self-proclaimed avant-garde to really initiate a societal transformation that fully implements progressive values? What do we make of the relief that significant parts of society feel about the *end of the green hegemony* and the *liberation from the ideology of wokeness*? How do we theorize the metamorphosis of these societies that is occurring instead of the projected green transformation? What can we say about the *next society* that is emerging beyond this project? All these are sociological rather than ecological or eco-political questions. And they also include the question for the future of sociology itself: what is the role of sociology in the next society beyond the project of the green transformation? What contribution can it make beyond its traditional commitment to furthering what it considered as the *progressive* agenda? Adopting this sociological perspective does not mean, as eco-political activists might suspect, to belittle any problem or deny scientific facts. Rather, the objective is to understand the syndrome, as sociologists do, in its dependence on social parameters, that is, as a social phenomenon rather than a purely biophysical one; or more precisely: to regard it neither as a purely biophysical problem, as the notions of *planetary boundaries* and the *climate emergency* suggest, nor as purely cultural, as far-right notions of *moral decay* and the *broken society* suggest.

To explore these questions, I draw on political sociology, eco-political theory, social theory, the theory of democracy and other social science subdisciplines. Centrally important for my approach in this book are the concepts of the *silent revolution*, the *participatory revolution* and the ambitious *new politics* project of the new social movements (NSM) of the 1970s and early 1980s – concepts which are all very familiar from social movement research and from research on the transformation of values and culture in Western societies at the transition from the traditional industrial to the *post-industrial* era (Touraine 1971; Bell 1974). For the syndrome of contemporary Western societies can, arguably, only be understood adequately against the backdrop of the NSM and what I call their *eco-emancipatory project* (EEP). In the wake of the *silent revolution* (Inglehart 1977), the claim to personal and political self-determination, to autonomy and political efficacy, which in traditional industrial societies had still been reserved for a fairly small bourgeois elite, was fully democratized and at the same time ecologically rebranded. The *participatory revolution* (Kaase 1984), in turn, was the assertive articulation of the citizens' new belief in their political maturity and their ability to effectively manage their own lives, develop their own self-determined identity, self-organize their own community, collectively shape politics and forge a better society. It is precisely this overwhelming optimism and self-confidence, I am suggesting, that is the backdrop against which the crisis of contemporary Western societies must be seen and which makes it understandable in the first place. For underneath the diverse framings of the current crisis of these societies lies, arguably, the radical discrepancy between the ideal of the self-determined citizen, the *autonomous subject*, which the eco-emancipatory movements – assisted by progressive intellectuals and critical social theorists – once managed to make hegemonic, and today's experience of comprehensive disempowerment, disabling hyper-complexity and effective ungovernability.

Put differently, the catastrophe, the unbearable state of supposedly advanced modern societies, is to a significant extent that the narratives of political efficacy, of the citizens' own ability to change things and transform society, to become the masters of their individual and collective destiny, indeed the very notion of the *autonomous subject*, have become untenable. In so-called advanced modern societies, the *existential crisis* to which climate movements and sustainability scientists often refer in an objectifying manner is not primarily about physical survival – although in these countries, too, there are ever more victims of weather extremes and environmental catastrophes. Above all, it is about the survival of the emancipatory self-descriptions and self-perceptions mainstreamed by the NSM. In the face of looming ecological and nuclear disaster, they had been convinced that reason, responsibility and civic maturity would prevail over *madness* and the forces of destruction. Today, however, after decades of eco-emancipatory socialization and political education, the untenability of these very beliefs is a traumatic experience.

From a more narrowly eco-political perspective, the perceived crisis is the present resubjectification of the problems that eco-emancipatory movements and intellectuals have, for decades, been trying to objectify. Niklas Luhmann, Ulrich Beck and many others were all too aware of the dependence of all crisis diagnoses on subjective norms, but, as outlined above, more recently, ecological issues have been successfully objectified. And what is widely experienced as a planetary emergency today is the coincidence of the evident biophysical unsustainability of advanced modern societies, on the one hand, and the repoliticization of the particular notions of reason, maturity and responsibility which had underpinned the eco-emancipatory diagnoses and transformation project, on the other. These norms are challenged today by revised conceptions of freedom and a good life which directly contradict those of the EEP. Especially in light of mounting biophysical pressures and the widespread perception of an existential imperative to act, this repoliticization is fatal. At a point when determined transformative action seems more urgent than ever, it further aggravates a condition I conceptualize as *ecological ungovernability*. This ecological ungovernability is the radical counterpart to the modernist claim to personal and collective self-determination and political efficacy, which the NSM had democratized and framed as the categorical moral-cum-rational imperative for an ecological transformation. Set against this categorical imperative, the diagnosis of ecological ungovernability is catastrophic and unbearable – not least because it plays directly into the hands of the far right's practices of eco-political denial and obstruction.

From social theory I adopt, inter alia, the concepts of *late modernity* and the *crisis of late modernity*. By implication, I also take up the approach of exploring the syndrome of contemporary Western societies from the perspective of modernity and modernization rather than that of capitalism and its logic of growth and profitability. The notion of *late modernity* has often been criticized as being unduly vague and not clearly distinct from what precedes and what follows this phase, especially since the term *postmodernity* has fallen out of fashion (e.g. Inglis 2024). The perspective of modernization, in turn, is still burdened by the legacy of traditional modernization theory which believed in linear progress towards the full realization of specific ideals of modernity, in a uniform development path common to all societies worldwide and in the guise of Western societies as the avant-garde of this development. Hence, many have preferred to investigate the syndrome of contemporary Western societies from the perspective of capitalism, which incessantly colonized the biophysical world and pervaded all dimensions of society and private life. From this perspective, today's condition of Western societies is understood as the long-predicted, perhaps final, crisis of capitalism – which now 'cannibalizes' its own preconditions (Fraser 2022) and may then be superseded by a post-capitalist degrowth society.

However, an end of capitalism is not really in sight, nor is a post-capitalist society. Also, the diagnosis of a *crisis* of capitalism is weak in terms of its normative foundations, since its reference norms cannot be derived from the theory of capitalism itself. For this purpose, the critique of capitalism must resort to the philosophy of modernity, which established the ideals that capitalism is felt to violate. Furthermore, these normative standards are subject to ongoing contestation and reinterpretation – which the narratives of the crisis of capitalism do not adequately reflect in either its causes or its effects. In this regard, the modernization perspective is much more helpful. It recognizes that the ongoing reinterpretation of prevailing social norms is not induced and determined by the logic and pressures of capitalism alone but also by the emancipatory logic itself. If stripped of the untenable assumptions of traditional modernization theory, the modernization perspective actually facilitates a much fuller understanding of the continuous transformation of prevailing social norms and helps to shed light on the shifts in prevailing social value preferences – which shape the social perception of capitalism and its consequences, set the framework for the current repoliticization of the EEP's normative foundations, and condition the ongoing metamorphosis of Western societies into the next society and modernity beyond the project of the green transformation. In addition, the modernization perspective also draws attention to the new political actors who at the end of classical industrial society and modernity reframed the earlier meaning of progressive politics and took over as its political subject. It highlights the emergence of a new sociocultural class and elite which, in the decades thereafter, was to set the political agenda – until, eventually, it became the primary target of the populist right.

From recent debates on the far right, finally, I adopt the term *postliberalism*, which I use as a label for what is emerging beyond the EEP and the crisis of late modernity: *postliberal* society and modernity. Since this term has been appropriated by the far right, it carries a heavy ideological burden which for present purposes is unhelpful. Hence, building on Ulrich Beck's distinction between a *first*, linear, and a *second*, reflexive modernity, I initially refer to the newly emerging era, simply as *third modernity*. Yet this term is rather bland. The label *postliberal modernity* is stronger because the relevant literature – though referring to liberalism rather than the EEP – rehearses an argument that is similar to my analysis of the demise of the eco-emancipatory project. Indeed, I am suggesting that the EEP has not simply *failed* because the logic of capitalism and the power of capitalist elites have suppressed and blocked it – in which case it might still be reactivated – but that it has become *exhausted* because the eco-emancipatory logic itself persistently chipped away at the EEP's foundations and, in doing so, unknowingly paved the way for a very different societal transformation. In other words: the eco-emancipatory logic itself made a significant contribution to today's ecological ungovernability and to the emergence of a society and modernity that radically depart from eco-emancipatory values and, more generally, from the values and institutions of liberal modernity so far. The far-right literature quite clearly signals what a postliberal society and modernity implies in practical terms. At the same time, however, this concept remains open and itself provisional: it does not preclude that, despite all evidence of a new era of radical exclusion, conflict, violence and the rule of the strongest, a full-blown turn towards authoritarianism and tyranny can, perhaps, still be averted. Indeed, some postliberal thinkers explicitly hope for a *renewal* of liberalism (Pabst 2021).

Thus, in this book, a range of different academic subdisciplines and diagnoses of so-called advanced modern societies provide the toolbox for analysing and conceptualizing the syndrome of these societies. At the same time, the weaknesses and deficits of these concepts and diagnoses signal the pitfalls that such an analysis ought to avoid. Arguably, the synthesis of these different perspectives and the refinement of their respective concepts allows for a much fuller understanding of the syndrome of untenability than, as yet, any of them have provided individually.

Trauma and normalization

This syndrome is traumatic (a) for those whose belief in the absolute necessity of transformative action and whose commitment to actually initiating such action radically clash with a societal reality of comprehensive political disability; (b) for emancipatory movements who fail to deliver to their own demanding standards of political efficacy, duty and responsibility, and – even worse – have to confront the fact that their emancipatory logic itself, unintendedly, has undermined the eco-emancipatory project and become one cause of what I call *ecological ungovernability*; (c) for the *losers of modernization* who feel they have not gained but lost control over their lives and destiny and now invest their hope in authoritarian leaders; and (d) for critical social theory, which loses its normative foundations and gets caught up in the problem that it either holds on to its established normativity, but then systematically fails to grasp the logic and reality of contemporary Western societies or, alternatively, surrenders its traditional norms and critical ambitions, but then runs the risk of becoming purely affirmative and further reinforcing the dynamics which it has always sought to unhinge. Two generations of political activists and critical social scientists see their dearest beliefs, assumptions, claims and hopes melt away: civic maturity, citizen empowerment, participatory governance, deliberative democracy, environmental education, ecological duty, categorical imperatives, and so forth. The whole normative order collapses; the basic distinction between good, moral, rational, progressive, emancipatory, participatory eco-movements, on the one hand, and evil, irrational, reactionary, denialist, anti-democratic, anti-ecological, anti-egalitarian right-wing populists, on the other, becomes untenable. In the face of 'alternative facts', conspiracy theories and authoritarian structures, the Kantian belief in reason, responsibility, the cosmopolitan community and *perpetual peace* lies in tatters.

Reactions to the German edition of this book confirmed this trauma. In line with the considerations above, many readers categorically insisted: you are normatively wrong; this cannot be empirically right! My earlier work on *simulative democracy, sustained unsustainability* and *second-order emancipation* had triggered similar responses. They articulate unwillingness to even contemplate what might challenge established normative certainties and disrupt the protective comfort zone. In order to prove their point, these critics stressed that there has never been a singular, homogeneous *eco-emancipatory project* and not a *green hegemony* either. Accordingly, they argued, there also has never been a second modernity, nor a late-modern metamorphosis of the latter into a third, postliberal modernity. Yet, the concept of the EEP is explicitly presented in the book as a heuristic device rather than an empirical claim; and the term *green hegemony* is not a concept I suggested myself, but a proverbial skittle set up by conservatives in order to knock it down and then celebrate its *end.* Contesting the concept of the EEP and the term *green hegemony* disproves neither the societal mainstreaming of entirely new value orientations, civic self-understandings and political expectations in the wake of the silent or participatory revolution, nor today's syndrome of the polycrisis, the autocratic-authoritarian turn and the popular revolt against policies for an SET. Other readers were more conciliatory and conceded: you may be empirically right, but you are normatively wrong! But again, this response signals that the need for self-confirmation and reassurance is prioritized over the commitment to sociological analysis that might yield unsettling results.

This said, in public debate the initial horror at the 'fossil-authoritarian' backlash faded rather quickly, much facilitated by the second presidency of Donald Trump – who is not the cause of this change, of course, but whose election was a powerful indicator of the extent to which ideas had already become widespread, ideas which for eco-emancipatory movements and the critical social sciences were still entirely unthinkable. Within just a short time, the diagnosis of major setbacks, if not a collapse of the SET policy agenda, became largely uncontested. The dominance of right-wing rhetoric in political discourse, the shift in political priorities and the general dismantling of ecological policies and DEI agendas are now well documented and undeniable. The same applies with regard to the demise of liberal democracy, the rise of oligarchy and the autocratic-authoritarian turn, as well as the decline of international law and international institutions, and the transition to the law and rule of the strongest. Politically promising resistance to Donald Trump's policies has not yet emerged, nor to Benjamin Netanyahu's genocidal agenda in Gaza and the West Bank. Alternative visions and perspectives, which after the financial crisis of 2008/9 seemed to be gaining traction, no longer exist or find no significant resonance. Instead, the discursive normalization of what eco-emancipatory movements had always fought against prevails, and their vision of a good life for all within ecological boundaries is discredited as outdated and illusory. The remains of the progressive movements may keep trying to defend the *reality principle* against the *tide of denial* and obstruction, but many others – by no means just on the populist right – welcome *the return to common sense* and, by implication, declare the order of unsustainability the norm. The deviation from normality is now the attempt to achieve an SET and realize the underlying ideals and promises of the Enlightenment and liberal modernity.

This swift and frictionless normalization of the previously unthinkable signals far more than just widespread helplessness in the face of the obvious metamorphosis of politics: it must be read as a form of affirmation, consent or even tacit complicity. It reveals that far-right populists, contrary to their portrayal by *progressive* critics, are by no means regressive forces but rather the avant-garde of a new society that emancipates itself from the duties, imperatives and commitments entailed in the EEP and liberal modernity at large. And the traditional progressive avant-garde has not simply been overwhelmed by the right or crushed by capitalism: it has rendered itself untenable. In the early 1970s, German Social Democrat Erhard Eppler, referring to a full-blown transformation of Western societies, still avowed the *feasibility of the necessary* (Eppler 1975). Today, former British Prime Minister Tony Blair regards even the technocratic project of climate neutrality and Net Zero as 'irrational and doomed to fail'. Policies that 'limit fossil fuels' or seek to reduce air travel are 'riven with irrationality', he declared, 'unaffordable, ineffective and politically toxic'.[1] Instead, domestic as well as international policy aim to organize and secure what, only recently, progressive intellectuals had tried to scandalize us into conceiving as *living at the expense of others* (Lessenich 2019a) and the *imperial mode of living* (Brand & Wissen 2021). In the emerging new modernity, this is no longer offensive, problematic or even dystopian; just as the departure from democracy, which Colin Crouch once characterized with the alarmist term *post-democracy* (Crouch 2004), is now perceived in a far less uniformly negative way. In fact, all this is now portrayed as reasonable and liberating; as pragmatic preparation for an expected condition marked, firstly, by political lawlessness, moral disinhibition and post-factuality and, secondly, by the non-negotiability of values and demands whose realization depends on radical social inequality and exclusion.

Escape routes and lifebuoys

Empirically speaking, the untenability of the EEP and the metamorphosis of late-modern societies to a new postliberal era are now widely uncontested. Yet, the suggestion that the EEP falls victim to its own inherent contradictions, that it undermines its own normative foundations and renders itself untenable, remains, for many, hard to accept. Similarly, the argument that the eco-emancipatory logic itself has contributed to the condition of *ecological ungovernability* and is one driver of the transition to postliberal society and modernity is still unpalatable. These issues concern the third of the three dimensions distinguished above, that is, the normative untenability of the EEP. Three of the most common objections which were raised in many debates on the German edition of this book are outlined below:

(a) given the urgency of effective action and the wide range of attitudes of denial and obstruction, a primarily analytical social-theory approach which does not offer any practical solutions is not particularly helpful or desirable;

---

[1] 'UK's net zero policy is irrational and doomed to fail, says former PM Blair'. *The Guardian*, 30 April 2025.

(b) the suggested analysis is overly pessimistic and deterministic. Most probably, what late-modern societies are currently experiencing is but a temporary phase that in due course will be superseded by a new counter-movement, with the pendulum swinging in the opposite direction again.

(c) in view of the autocratic-authoritarian turn, the unprecedented power of billionaire alpha males and tech-oligarchs, and the rapidly unfolding AI revolution, an actor- and power-centred approach exploring the condition of late capitalism would be much more appropriate than an analysis inspired by modernization theory and focusing on unintended side effects of eco-emancipatory agendas and the dynamic of an unrecognized dialectic.

Overall, the quest for solutions was the most prominent concern: if this is the syndrome, politically committed readers kept asking, how do we cure it? How do we get out of this mess? Effective action is required immediately, or else . . .! For many, this fixation on solutions displaces all other considerations. But these questions, while being perfectly understandable, miss – or deny – the very diagnosis provided here: that in postliberal modernity these questions are rapidly losing their relevance; for, once the caterpillar has metamorphosed into a butterfly – if this metaphor is really suitable here – its values, interests and needs are entirely different. This is what the concept of untenability is all about; and it is what eco-activists and critical sociologists alike are finding extremely difficult to accept – but still have to confront. The quest for solutions, in contrast, clutches on to modernist values and visions. What is considered a solution is meant to reconfirm, save and reinstate these values. Yet, it is the hallmark of late modernity that this is no longer possible, that these attempts have become untenable. Holding on or seeking to return to the ideals of social equality, the open society, liberal democracy, ecological sustainability or the good life for all is not a viable option any longer because societal complexity renders governability in the eco-emancipatory sense impossible; because prevailing value orientations make such ideals counterproductive; because dominant problem perceptions and political priorities turn proposed eco-emancipatory solutions themselves into a problem; and because such solutions would invariably reinforce the unexpected side effects which have rendered the EEP questionable and untenable.

But there are countless initiatives, many readers continued to insist, that are already experimenting with convivialist ways of life, practising collective self-limitation and creating degrowth communities! And ever more people worldwide recognize the absolute urgency and inevitability of an SET! Rather than more books and articles that provide analyses of the contemporary situation, one indignant reviewer wrote, we must take concrete steps! Further books will not save a single endangered species, enfranchise or ameliorate the life of a single impoverished or alienated citizen, or safeguard a single civil liberty! They only undermine, actively or tacitly, the life of political action! Undoubtedly, there are many initiatives experimenting with convivialist values and degrowth practices. And there is a long tradition of anti-intellectualism on both the left and the right. But rather than disproving the EEP's untenability and reversing the metamorphosis of late-modern societies to a postliberal modernity, such responses, arguably, mainly illustrate the ways in which late-modern societies are seeking to cope with their trauma.

Similarly, the objection that the current cultural and political shift is only temporary and the tide will soon go in the other direction again is nothing but a lifebuoy for the EEP and traditional-style critical thinking. At first sight, this objection may seem plausible. After all, traditional theories of linear modernization are now widely rejected, and in this book, too, unexpected side effects and dialectic processes figure very prominently. Thus, any determinism is ill-conceived; the trajectory of history remains open. Also, the Trump presidency has in some countries triggered a resurgence of parties in the political centre and on the left. Yet, this does not resolve the underlying causes of the syndrome that is distinctive of late-modern societies. Sociologically, the hope for a counter-movement that will reinstate the EEP is naïve and untenable because this project was firmly rooted in particular societal conditions which have long since fundamentally changed. Since the beginning of Trump's second presidency alone, the authoritarian right has taken giant strides, rapidly, and without significant resistance, destroying democratic institutions, pushing a fossil-authoritarian turn, dismantling the international order, rule-based politics and its institutions, and asserting the law and power of the strongest. A global system of autocrats is rapidly emerging, and the restructuring of institutions that the right is currently implementing will not be easily reversed.

Furthermore, the narrative of the pendulum soon swinging in the *opposite* direction again fails to recognize that the right-wing rebellion against the established elites and their liberal *ideology of wokeness*, though in a sense being a counter-movement to the EEP, in fact further extends at least one of its most entrenched constructs – given that, in certain respects, conservatives and right-wing populists adamantly defend notions of freedom, self-realization and a good life which eco-emancipatory movements – perhaps unintendedly – have helped to make hegemonic. Furthermore, the right-wing agenda of social inequality and exclusion further pursues the liberation from earlier ideals of equality, justice, ecological responsibility and moral duty which is well known from eco-progressive movements, too, whose emancipatory achievements have, in fact, always been socially exclusive and *at the expense of others*. Hence, rather than holding on to unwarranted hopes for the pendulum to swing back and reinstate the EEP, the objective should now be to explore why and how the late-modern condition of untenability reconfigures the parameters that shape what is newly emerging.

Finally, the objection that the focus of analysis should be shifted to power structures, actors and the logic of capitalism is another attempt to dodge the syndrome of untenability. Admittedly, in view of the decline of democratic capitalism and rule-based politics, and given the power of billionaires and oligarchs and the centrality of populist, autocratic leaders, the focus on an unrecognized and essentially depersonalized dynamic as a driver of the metamorphosis of late-modern societies to a new postliberal modernity may seem strangely out of touch with political reality. The emphasis on the unforeseen side effects of the EEP seems to ignore – or even deny – the much more tangible impact of Donald Trump and others who are ruling by decree and throwing the whole world into turmoil. I am far from suggesting that power structures, actors and the logic of capitalism are irrelevant! There already exists a vast and ever-growing literature on these aspects. The significance of the NSM for the contemporary perceptions of an emergency, in contrast, and the relevance of what I conceptualize as the EEP and its dialectic or of the curious interplay between so-called *progressive* and *regressive* agendas, have received much less attention.

As regards the prevailing power structures, exploring these latter parameters helps to explain why authoritarian structures are flourishing in late-modern societies, while democratic movements are finding it difficult to make attractive offers and gain transformative force. With regard to political actors, the approach chosen here extends the perspective to include emancipatory movements and investigates why in the late-modern condition these actors of new politics are losing rather than gaining strength. And when it comes to capitalism and the critique of its logic of destruction, it helps to explain why in late modernity this logic can unfold more unrestrictedly than ever before without triggering any significant counter-movements or visions of an alternative societal order. Hence, the relationship between more traditional approaches focusing on power structures and the logic of capitalism and the approach I am taking in this book is explicitly not a matter of either/or. Rather, my analysis is located at a different level and explores how the traditional approaches of the critical social sciences may be refined, supplemented and revised so as to make them more suitable for the late-modern condition and sensitive to the syndrome of late modernity.

A sociology of untenability

For critical sociology itself, the particular challenge of my approach is that it does not just attempt – as traditional activist social science does – to break through the *widespread denial of reality* in public discourse, assuming that the desired SET will then occur automatically, but that it aims, just as much, for the *denial of reality* by significant parts of the sociological literature on late modernity and its crises. It pushes a transformation of established critical sociology and the sociology of sustainability into a *sociology of untenability*. In view of the unforeseen side effects of progressive movements and politics, this kind of sociology will need to move away from the untenable project of bringing society and the world to ecological reason. It needs to surrender its claimed monopoly on determining the meaning of progressiveness, emancipation and truth. As its earlier normative certainty has disappeared, as the notion of ecological reason itself has become entirely uncertain, it pursues – much more modestly – a project of sociological enlightenment in Niklas Luhmann's sense of sociological *self-enlightenment.* Eco-activists and their academic companions have always called for an *adequate response to the challenges of late modernity.* At least for sociology itself, such a sociology of untenability is, arguably, a far more *adequate response* than the array of *solutions* suggested elsewhere and the persistent renewal of moralizing appeals for transformative action and false promises of hope.

A sociology of untenability is not simply a *sociology of loss* – which is what bourgeois cultural criticism and pessimism have always been concerned with. As such, it would remain backward-looking and within the normativity of an exhausted modernity. Rather, it explores why just this normativity has become untenable and what this may imply both for society at large – and for sociology itself. Its objective is not simply to shed light on the *flip side of progress*, as Andreas Reckwitz put it, that is, on the *experiences and practices of loss* (Reckwitz 2023). This is an affirmative exercise. Rather, it seeks to illuminate the contingency of the perspective from which this loss appears as such – and postliberalism appears as regressive. Thus, the sociology of untenability helps to understand why to some observers, including myself, the current journey to postliberal modernity appears as an abyss, an emergency and an apocalypse, while others perceive it as a promise, as emancipatory progress and the beginning of a great new era. It will continue to be driven by the concern that the fossil-authoritarian turn and postliberal modernity – contrary to the hopes many invest in them – will benefit very few, but make life *nasty, brutish and short* again for many, and further aggravate the conflict and violence that come with the rule of the strongest. Yet, rather than continuing the well-established forms of mobilization, it will help eco-activists to recognize that they have manoeuvred themselves into a trap: with their dualism of *socio-ecological transformation vs apocalypse* they have conjured up a constellation where, in view of the untenability of their own project, there now seems to be no future, 'except perhaps memory of a time when there was a future' (Delanty 2024: 154). Their discourse has constructed a reality so bleak and unbearable that it could hardly be more favourable for those seeking to sell new narratives of hope – however self-serving, short-sighted and implausible these may in fact be.

But the future is not just 'an empty space in which waste and trivia is preserved for ever, and sustained by nostalgia for what has been irrevocably lost' (ibid.). A sociology of untenability sees the present conjuncture not simply as the end point of a trajectory of decline but as the beginning of something new that ecologists have themselves helped to shape. It will help ecologists to remember that – although the science about climate change and the collapse of ecological systems is unambiguous – their reading of these empirical facts, their truth and their categorical imperatives are indeed only a *worldview*. And if political opponents refer to it as an *ideology*, they do actually have a point. In fact, it was not so long ago that ecologists themselves proudly announced that their thinking had now established itself as an 'ideology in its own right' (Dobson 1990) on a par with other ideologies.

The present volume ought to be read as a contribution to such a sociology of untenability. I am grateful to all who have attended the numerous presentations and contributed to the lively debates since the publication of the German edition. Their comments have been invaluable for further reflecting on the syndrome of late modernity and the core ideas presented here. I would also like to thank Zoë Großbötzl for her committed contribution to preparing the English edition.

Vienna, September 2025

— 1 —

AFTER THE END OF HUMANITY

'Five minutes to midnight!', 'U-turn or apocalypse!', 'Socio-ecological transformation or uninhabitability of the Earth!' These and similar formulas have dominated eco-political discourse since the early days of the environmental movement, and they are still very much present today. 'Humanity has a choice', UN Secretary-General António Guterres said at the COP27 climate summit in Egypt: 'Cooperate or perish. It is either a Climate Solidarity Pact – or a Collective Suicide Pact' (Guterres 2022). But this rhetoric has become old and dull. It misses the reality of late-modern societies. The threats today are undoubtedly greater and more acute than ever. But this kind of thinking obscures more than it illuminates. It is time to break out of the dualism of insight or doom.

Around the turn of the 1980s, eco-apocalyptic visions first gained significant, broadly based mobilization power in Western societies. In addition to accelerating environmental change, new technologies such as nuclear power, genetic engineering, the introduction of home computers and the Cold War arms race were important triggers. Against this backdrop, the project of a socio-ecological restructuring of capitalist industrial and consumer society, organized by civil society, obtained widespread societal support. It was to be a democratic-emancipatory transformation that would facilitate a self-determined and good life for all in a sound natural environment. It would address manifold issues at the local and national levels but, ultimately, the project aimed for a socially and ecologically pacified world society. In the decades that followed, occasionally the impression arose that this project was running out of steam. The change in societal value preferences, which was crucial to it, seemed to be coming to a standstill. In the early 2000s, some researchers believed

23

there was a new turning point: 'The doggedness has disappeared', they noted, 'the end of the world is not happening' (Noelle-Neumann & Petersen 2001: 22; cf. also Hradil 2002). There was even talk of an 'uprising against the 1970s and 1980s', of a 'pent-up counter-revolt' (Beck & Beck-Gernsheim 1994: 33f). But the protests against the ongoing destruction, against the socio-ecological effects of rapid economic growth and mass consumption, continued. The awareness of an escalating crisis and the realization that industrial societies cannot go on like this, that 'business as usual is not an option', became ever more widespread.

Today, the belief in the absolute necessity of a profound transformation has become almost hegemonic, even if the pathway to its practical implementation remains unclear. A social consensus seems to have been reached that a fundamental structural change is indispensable and urgent, especially in the rich countries of the Global North. 'System change, not climate change!' is no longer just a slogan of climate activists – but one that is echoed by the European Union, the United Nations, even some heads of industry. CO_2 neutrality has become the big mantra. Companies, municipalities, regions, nation states, the EU – all now have clearly declared target years by which they want to be CO_2 neutral. For decades, philosophers, citizens' initiatives, social movements, green parties, international NGOs, critical social scientists and many other actors had been at the vanguard of this struggle for a great transformation. But just as there seems to be more consensus than ever before, and at a point in time when the ecological and social urgency seems greater than ever, the eco-emancipatory project itself has suddenly slipped into a profound crisis.

In respect of climate, environmental, social and security policy-making, the situation today is even more explosive than it was in the 1980s. With the digital revolution and the rapid development of artificial intelligence, technological progress, too, is no less a cause for concern than it was in the 1980s. But in late-modern societies, a feeling of political powerlessness and loss of influence is spreading. The optimism of civil society and the confidence of environmental movements in their ability to organize and shape a societal transformation have much diminished. The protests of groups such as Extinction Rebellion or Last Generation seem utterly helpless – but trigger considerable public fury, despite the declared commitment on all sides to the goal of sustainability. In fact, the consensus that a fundamental structural transformation of modern societies is absolutely necessary and the most pressing challenge these societies need to confront is itself being challenged with verve, irrespective of the mass of climate and sustainability data that is evidenced to corroborate this urgency. Organic agriculture, renewable energy, post-fossil transport systems, species protection, climate targets – all of these would certainly be nice to have, but in the face of acute crises – pandemic, inflation, war, terrorism, migration, geopolitics – other things seem more urgent.

Priorities are shifting; ecological agendas are being put on the back burner. Nuclear power, a symbolic issue for the environmental movement like no other, was classified as 'sustainable' by the EU in January 2023, and related financial investment thus became 'climate-friendly'. In the wake of Western sanctions against Russia and its war in Ukraine, coal is experiencing a global renaissance. Climate targets are not only being subordinated in the field of transport policy, where they are particularly hard to achieve. In many countries, European agreements on nature conservation are being delayed and incompletely implemented. Animal welfare, land protection and organic farming would appear to be of secondary importance. Instead, the attempt to secure existing levels of prosperity and the fear of censure from potential right-wing voters take priority. In 2023, US President Joe Biden approved another gigantic new oil drilling project in Alaska, Willow. In Europe, liberal and conservative parties resisted efforts to impose within the next decade a ban on new cars with combustion engines. Investment in the energy efficiency of urban dwellings will drive up rents and propel gentrification, critics say. Tightened standards for animal welfare will force farmers into bankruptcy and make schnitzels a privilege of the rich. The costs of renewable energy threaten the competitiveness of local, regional and national industries, they argue. Socially and ecologically produced textiles or electronic goods would be unaffordable for many people. Indeed, the argument of social justice and inclusion is now used very commonly in attempts to block ecological agendas. And the mass of those who cannot afford to pay for high ecological and social standards is mobilized against the more privileged sections of society and their eco-emancipatory project. And anyway, 'there is no evidence for any doomsday apocalypse', some political leaders insist, 'we can learn to deal with rising sea levels'.[1]

While critical observers had just diagnosed a comprehensive 'depoliticization' and an era of 'post-politics' (e.g. Wilson & Swyngedouw 2014) driven by the ideology of market liberalism, there is suddenly a striking repoliticization with increasingly polarized positions

---

[1] Then Austrian Chancellor Karl Nehammer in his speech on the Future of the Nation, Vienna, 10 March 2023.

(e.g. Jäger 2023), especially in climate and sustainability policy. The coordinates and lines of conflict are shifting: unlike in traditional industrial society, it is no longer labour versus capital. And unlike in the 1970s and early 1980s, the conflict lines do not run between the NSM of post-industrial society and traditional politics and its institutions. Instead, the conflict has shifted to the centre of the middle class: while wealth and poverty in the upper part of the wealth pyramid and at its base continue to stabilize and appear unchangeable, the active political conflict line runs between those who fear for their middle-class prosperity and lifestyle and those whose demands for a 'socio-ecological transformation' (SET) are perceived as a threat to exactly that. Against this backdrop, the 'pent-up counter-revolt' now actually seems to have become real: the champions of this transformation project suddenly find themselves confronted with accusations that they are self-righteous elites, that, ultimately, they have always been much more concerned with their own identity and diversity interests than with social equality and redistribution, and that they themselves are the social class that has benefited most from the participatory revolution of the 1970s. For these eco-activist groups, such accusations are traumatic. They radically contradict their self-perception as the avant-garde, providing leadership – intellectually, morally and in their own everyday practices – for the great transformation of society at large. And the global political context reinforces this irritation: the self-identification of the supposedly most civilized and progressive societies in the world is crumbling. Their sense of moral superiority and economic and political supremacy is becoming untenable. The self-declared 'free West' and its 'open societies' are losing ground to authoritarian regimes – and are becoming increasingly post-democratic themselves. It is precisely this, and not simply the steep rise in the military defence budget, that is at the core of the turn to a new era, the *Zeitenwende*,[2] which has been much debated since Russia's attack on Ukraine in February 2022. In the social sciences this crisis of the self-perception of Western societies had already been debated for some time. But with the war in Ukraine it also reached the broad political debate.

'End or turnaround!', 'We are on the brink of disaster!', 'Business as usual is not an option!'; these formulas must now be interpreted in a radically different way: a turning point has undoubtedly arrived, a turning point that, as yet, is still difficult to define. What is abundantly

---

[2] Announced by then German Federal Chancellor Olaf Scholz in his speech to the Bundestag on 27 February 2022.

clear, however, is that it is not the turning point that German Social Democrat and intellectual Erhard Eppler once envisioned, when he wrote the booklet *Ende oder Wende* (End or Turnaround) (Eppler 1975), nor is it what in the social sciences and in activist circles much later became known as the 'socio-ecological transformation'. And an end is clearly recognizable, too. But it is not the end of humanity or the uninhabitability of the planet that activists have been warning about for decades. These are possible scenarios, but neither of them seems immediately acute. Instead, the boom of eco-emancipatory mobilization seems to have come to an end, and the belief in 'the feasibility of the necessary', once invoked by Eppler (1975), too. A decade after sociologists first spoke of the 'end of sustainability' (e.g. Foster 2015; Benson & Craig 2017; see also Chapter 5), they now diagnose a shift in the environmental debate away from apocalyptic discourse aimed at preventing major socio-ecological disaster towards 'post-apocalyptic' discourse that assumes it is already too late for prevention and, instead, late-modern societies are already in the process of coming to terms with the catastrophe and settling into the ecological and social ruins of capitalism and the liberal world (e.g. Tsing 2016; Latour 2017; Wakefield 2018; Cassegard & Thörn 2018; Blühdorn 2020a; Wainwright & Mann 2020; de Moor 2022; Staab 2022). Or put differently: just as, at the end of the 1980s, the idea of the socialist transformation of capitalist industrial society was abandoned, today we are saying goodbye to the utopia of the SET.

This does not mean, of course, that environmental, climate and sustainability issues are suddenly irrelevant. They remain important, and they may well become even more so. But they are now framed and negotiated very differently than before. The underlying parameters have changed. As the eco-political consensus that had been achieved is being repoliticized, 'business as usual is not an option' no longer only refers to the established order of modern societies, their relationship to nature and the way they deal with their biophysical foundations, but also to the way in which eco-progressives frame and address environmental policy issues. What only recently was still widely described, at least on a declaratory level, as a categorical imperative – climate protection, human rights, democracy, biodiversity, planetary boundaries, a good life for all – is now being openly questioned because it threatens prevailing understandings of freedom, jeopardizes the prosperity that Western societies have achieved and brings tangible disadvantages for their economic competitiveness, while the promised benefits of these ideals are long-term, at best, tend to benefit distant countries and foreign people and are by no means certain, anyway.

Exactly this is what this book is about: the simultaneity of the deep crisis of Western societies or indeed civilization and the crisis of the eco-emancipatory project that sought to transform these societies. Especially in the affluent consumer societies of the Global North, the untenability of the former, the social order of sustained unsustainability, coincides with a crisis of the latter, the project of SET. And this is not simply caused by the power and logic of the capitalist system. Rather, as I will explain in greater detail later on (see Chapter 3, in particular), the eco-emancipatory project falls victim to its own logic and its internal contradictions. In a sense, it is overtaken in an emancipatory manner; the emancipatory logic itself renders it obsolete. Especially for the large generation of those who have been socialized in and with the NSM since the late 1960s and who once launched this project, this dual untenability or exhaustion implies the traumatic collapse of their self-understandings, their constructions of meaning and their view of the world. But the end of *their world* does not imply the uninhabitability of the planet nor the end of humanity. Rather, it opens up the prospect of a new modernity, a 'next society', beyond (the narrative of) the end of humanity. There is no promise and no comfort in this. The extent to which this is perceived as a threat remains to be seen. In any case, it is not an option that can be chosen or rejected, but something inevitable, a compelling dynamic. In fact, the dual untenability – precisely because the end of humanity is not acute – is forcing Western societies (and their social sciences) onto the path to a different modernity.

1.1 The eco-emancipatory project

So, what is this eco-emancipatory project that I have mentioned already more than once, and which is supposedly in a fundamental crisis? First of all, it is a rather unwieldy term, which for the sake of simplicity I will abbreviate to EEP. I should also make clear, of course, that there has never been a singular, unified, clearly defined, internally consistent and stable ecological project, nor an eco-emancipatory one, either. Environmental discourses and agendas have always been multidimensional, contradictory and full of conflict. They have also always been unstable and in a continuous process of change. Their normative foundations, problem perceptions, solution strategies and so on have always been diverse and have been continuously adapted.

There always have been anti-modernist, conservative, nationalist, liberal, progressive-reformist and radical-revolutionary currents, and those who regard themselves as decidedly apolitical. As Ulrich Beck once put it, the environmental issue is a 'political chameleon which changes its appearance'; 'there is probably no political tendency that could not draw honey' from it (Beck 1998: 160f). Thus, instability and crisis are neither new nor unusual in eco-politics; in a sense, they are part of the DNA of environmental movements and the ecological debate.

When, nevertheless, I talk about the crisis of the EEP, I am not taking a romanticizing look back at a supposedly better past when environmental movements were still united and all pulling in the same direction. There never was such a time. What I am aiming at is rather the steady demise of a very specific way of thinking, formulating and politicizing environmental issues, problems and demands. In fact, it makes sense to think of the EEP more as a social science construction, not directly as an agenda that could be attributed to a specific and unified political actor. Just as the NSM since the 1970s have not been so named by these movements themselves, but by sociological observers who recognized commonalities between different move-ments from the distance of an outside perspective, the EEP, too, can best be defined from the outside as something coherent, even though comprising quite different ways of thinking and practical approaches. To a certain extent, the EEP is an idealization, an abstraction, an ideal type to which no specific actor, no singular political subject can be assigned.

To clarify the term, it is first of all important to make a fundamental distinction between the EEP and eco-conservative, eco-nationalist, eco-authoritarian and other movements, which have also always existed since the beginnings of the environmental movement in the nineteenth century. During the 1970s, Western, so-called post-industrial socie-ties began to view environmental issues and societal relationships with nature from the perspective of emancipatory values such as freedom, equality, dignity, self-determination, reason and universal human rights. Following the tradition of early critical theory, this new way of thinking made a direct connection between the oppres-sion, exploitation and enslavement of nature and the oppression, exploitation and enslavement of human beings – women and social minorities, in particular. Just like human beings, nature, too, was from this perspective widely recognized as having a certain subjectiv-ity, an intrinsic value, inviolable dignity and integrity. Accordingly, in the struggle for nature and the environment, great importance was attached to their liberation from human domination, exploitation and instrumentalization. And even if the protection of nature was not demanded for its own sake, but ultimately remained instrumental and subordinate to anthropocentric interests, environmental issues were clearly thought of from the perspective of liberation and the values of political self-determination, the empowerment of responsible citizens, self-organized civil society, the development of democratic institutions and a cosmopolitan, integrated world society. The German Green Party's basic programme of 1980, for example, iconically articulates core elements of the EEP (Die Grünen 1980). The project that emerged in the context of the great transformative spirit and optimism of the early 1970s was the ecological renewal, expansion and correction of the much older emancipatory project that had its bourgeois-liberal origins in European Enlightenment philosophy and is still the normative foundation of Western modernity today: freedom, equality, reason, democratic self-determination and the collective responsibility of mature citizens.

The profound culture change that began in the late 1960s and has been described as the 'silent revolution' (Inglehart 1977) made these emancipatory values hegemonic in Western societies far beyond the NSM; and they became constitutive for the EEP. Inter alia, this strengthened the belief in the possibility – even the necessity – to actively reconfigure societal institutions and reorganize society's relationship to nature. In an effort to move beyond any predetermination by tradition, religion or social class, citizens now insisted on the right and their ability to control their own lives and identity. This, in particular, was the emancipatory dimension of the EEP, which is, therefore, not just an ecological project but, very importantly, also one of self-determination and self-realization. The openness of the future and the ability to actively shape it were key prerequisites for the EEP. The crucial questions it raised – and which activists continue to raise to the present day – are: 'How do we want to live?', and 'What kind of world do we want to live in?' Their basic assumption and starting point is that people and communities can themselves decide, determine and control, that they are not simply at the mercy of fate, but can shape their lives, their community and their relationship with nature. And this self-determination was not only regarded as an individual and collective right, but also as a moral duty, especially in the face of growing ecological threats. In fact, the ecological crisis turned the task of responsible self-government into a new categorical imperative. In eco-emancipatory thinking, the belief in empirically grounded 'ecological reason' became the functional equivalent of Kant's transcendental reason. The societal mainstreaming of this self-confident belief in the right to – and the capability of – rational and responsible self-determination was the great achievement of the emancipatory social movements. It was the centrepiece of the societal awakening since the late 1960s. Instead of placing their fate in the hands of political elites, citizens now held these very elites responsible for the massive social, ecological, political and economic problems that had become increasingly visible since the 1970s.

It is just this perspective, this framing, this basic normative position defined by the points tentatively summarized in Table 1, that I am referring to as the EEP. This project was – and to some extent still is – supported by diverse social movements, countless NGOs, green parties, critical scientists, progressive administrations, committed church groups, institutions of political education, socially and ecologically oriented commercial enterprises and many other societal actors, each with their own thematic emphases, weightings of particular issues and concretizations of individual aspects. With the intention of expanding and updating the agenda of the older social movements which had mainly focused on issues of material production and distribution, eco-emancipatory movements and mobilizations always aimed at the *socio-ecological transformation* of modern industrial societies – another cumbersome term, which from now on I will abbreviate as SET. Some currents pursued radical, fundamentalist and revolutionary strategies, others focused on more reformist approaches and incremental change. But the guiding principle, the underlying commitment and vision of these actors, was the ecological and social restructuring of society as a whole, which would ultimately ensure a good life for all in an ecologically intact environment: another world is possible! The goal was a democratically negotiated, controlled, responsible transformation, not one forced by catastrophes and emergencies; a transformation by rational and responsible design, not by disaster.

Again, this notion of the SET is not about conjuring up a golden age that never really existed. Just like the EEP, the SET is a social science abstraction, a regulative ideal. But today, this vision, too, is widely pulled into doubt again, at a point in time when it seemed to have gained broader societal support than ever before. The belief and hope that the new, transformed, socially, militarily and ecologically pacified (global) society can actually be realized has essentially collapsed. In fact, some of its most central values such as democracy, equality and universal rights are themselves up for discussion. It is evident that business as usual is no longer an option, that the established order is not only ecologically and socially unsustainable, but has become

Table 1. Key features of the eco-emancipatory project

Historical conjuncture (emergence)
➢ transition from industrial to post-industrial society; ➢ *great acceleration*: ecological and social impact of industrial modernity and the rise of mass consumerism; ➢ *silent revolution*: values of self-determination and self-expression as mainstreamed in post-industrial societies in the 1970s and early 1980s

Geographical location/socio-structural base
➢ post-industrial societies in the liberal-democratic, capitalist Global North; ➢ primarily younger generation born in the 1960s; educated middle class

Core values
➢ autonomy of the subject (human and ecological); ➢ inalienable dignity and universal rights; ➢ moral freedom and responsibility; ➢ moral-cum-rational duty/categorical imperatives of reason; ➢ rational argument and collective reason; ➢ cosmopolitan orientation and horizon

Political agenda		
Ecologization of industrial society	Authentic self-determination	Democratization of democracy
➢ integrity, dignity, autonomy of nature; ➢ critique of domination and exploitation of nature; ➢ belief in non-negotiable ecological imperatives, reason and responsibility; ➢ concern about the compatibility of ecology and capitalist economy; ➢ critique of the logic of growth and material accumulation; ➢ critique of large-scale technology; ➢ needs- rather than profit-oriented economy	➢ liberation from the rule of tradition, religion and secular authorities; ➢ autonomous self-development and self-realization; ➢ critique of social inequality and injustice; ➢ protection of minority rights; ➢ understanding of the citizen as *citoyen*; ➢ information, education and the development of critical abilities for the development of civic maturity and responsibility	➢ critique of liberal representative democracy; ➢ belief in authentic empowerment of the citizenry; ➢ radical expansion and deepening of democratic participation; ➢ claim to political maturity and ability to take collective responsibility for the common good; ➢ confidence in self-organization of civil society and democratic self-governance

Self-perception of activists
➢ vanguard of an ecologically, economically, politically and culturally transformed world society allowing for a good life for all within ecological limits

untenable in a much more comprehensive sense. Yet, contrary to all eco-emancipatory hopes and expectations, what is falling apart today is not the destructive order of growth, waste, exploitation and inequality, but the eco-emancipatory framing of climate and sustainability issues. And the new society, the new world that is emerging, is a far cry from what the movements had imagined. In view of biophysical and social tipping points, beyond which the dynamics of change can no longer be slowed down or influenced, little remains of the openness of the future assumed in the EEP. Indeed, against the backdrop of the supremacy of global corporations, the overwhelming dependence of Western societies on authoritarian systems, the pace of the autocratic-authoritarian turn within these societies themselves, and the development of digital technologies and artificial intelligence, the belief in the democratic ability to shape and control the future seems downright naïve. Given the tension between the ever-rising demands for individual freedom and self-realization, on the one hand, and planetary boundaries, on the other, a good life for all – or what is now widely perceived as such – is simply impossible. And in view of the geopolitical competition between the global superpowers and the mounting problems of transnational and international institutions such as the EU or the UN, the vision of a cosmopolitan global society seems illusory and strangely anachronistic.

So, what has fallen into crisis is the fusion of ecological and emancipatory values, which conceived of the ecological transformation of society as an emancipatory one and assumed that the liberation of nature and that of human beings were two dimensions of the same idea. What is faltering is the belief in the utopia, the vision, that has guided the forward-looking eco-emancipatory movements since the 1970s, and the conviction of the movements that they themselves are the avant-garde, the pioneers of a socially and ecologically pacified world society. In his book *Buying Time*, Wolfgang Streeck (2014) described the crisis of democratic capitalism as the collapse of the highly improbable connection between democratic and capitalist values. What I am exploring here is the crisis and disintegration of the no less improbable liaison between emancipatory and ecological values – the eco-emancipatory project. But what follows this disintegration is not the apocalypse, the end of humanity and the uninhabitability of the planet, but the repoliticization and reframing of environmental, climate and sustainability issues, and the transformation of contemporary societies into a different modernity beyond the eco-emancipatory imagination. This is the central concern of this book.

1.2 Guiding questions and lines of continuity

Difficult books may need to be written more than once. Or rather: large topics that go far beyond the politics of the day can only be penetrated incrementally in repeated attempts, at different times and from different perspectives – while they continue to unfold. After *Post-Ecologist Politics*, *Simulative Democracy* and *Sustained Unsustainability*, this is my fourth book-length attempt (Blühdorn 2000a, 2013, 2020a). Again, it is about the disintegration of the European Enlightenment perspective on the ecological question and on the world, more generally. Once again, I am concerned with the emergence of a new modernity that is abandoning assumptions and norms that previously seemed unquestionable. Once again, the focus is specifically on the central modernist ideal, the 'autonomous subject', which is also at the very core of the EEP. And once again, I try to separate social science analysis and political campaign as strictly as possible. A brief look at some lines of continuity may help to further explain my approach and the objectives of this book.

Taking a perspective of normative certainty and full confidence in their ability to shape and control, the champions of the EEP ask: 'How do we want to live?'; 'What kind of world do we want to live in?'. Their questions are rhetorical, since their answers arise directly from the normative foundation on which they operate and which they consider to be unassailable. The social sciences examine the question from a different perspective. If they take their task seriously, they are less ambitious in transformative terms and less certain in normative terms. It is not their primary business to save the world. First and foremost, it is their task to describe the world, make diagnoses and offer possible explanations for these diagnoses – while always reflecting on the contingency of the norms on which these diagnoses and explanations are based. Only then, the social sciences may set out to make suggestions for changing the world – which, however, is not so easy given this normative contingency. In this sense, this book is neither about predictions of doom nor attempts to save the world but, above all, about grasping what is special about the current constellation – the SET is not taking place, but neither is the end of humanity – and illuminating the parameters that condition whatever will emerge from this constellation. In doing so, it is important to avoid the doomsday sentiments and cultural pessimism as well as the appeals and narratives of hope that are commonplace in the more activist literature. Of course, the fundamental crises of late-modern societies and the profound transformation they are undergoing must not be down-played or glossed over. But in order to obtain a fuller understanding of these crises and transformations, it may well be necessary to move beyond the established perspective on them – and the established norms of assessing them. In late modernity, the sociology of sustainability walks a fine line between the effort to provide new descriptions and analyses – which given its normative uncertainty always run the risk of appearing affirmative – and the traditional approaches of critical sociology, whose established normative perspective necessarily remains blind to the particularities of late modernity.

In *Post-Ecologist Politics*, I first dealt in detail with the crisis of the EEP. Drawing on critical theory and Niklas Luhmann's system-theoretical view on modern societies, I explored the question whether it is actually conceivable that the ecological problem will not be solved but may, instead, *dissolve* in the course of the ongoing reconfiguration of the societal apparatus for its perception and processing. Already back then, I was driven by a thought that was probably also on Ulrich Beck's mind when he wrote somewhat cryptically: 'The ecological crisis is in crisis. Someday someone will attempt to establish a career by demonstrating that it only ever existed in people's minds' (Beck 1998: 155). I described the modernist ideal of the 'autonomous subject' – something that, being a regulative ideal, has indeed only ever existed in people's minds – as the normative foundation, the normative point of reference, of political ecology and then pursued the idea that the supposedly objective problem diagnoses of political ecology, as well as its categorical imperatives, might simply dissolve in the course of ongoing modernization if, or to the extent that, this normative foundation loses its strength and viability. This is a thesis that, today, has gained rather than lost in relevance. A good twenty-five years later, precisely what I was concerned with at the time can be seen very clearly: 'The de-problematization of human autonomy', say social theorists Katharina Block and her co-author Sascha Dickel, 'is no longer a possible scenario of the future but, given the observable dismantling of autonomy, an empirical reality that requires a theoretical explanation', and one 'that does not merely understand the phenomenon as a problem to be corrected' (Block & Dickel 2020: 109).[3]

In *Simulative Democracy*, I then posed the question whether it is actually conceivable that the highest political good, the highest political achievement of modern societies, democracy, could one day

---

[3] Unless official English translations are available, citations from German language publications have been translated, throughout this book, by the author.

become outdated (Blühdorn 2013). There, too, the modernist norm of the autonomous subject was at the centre of my analysis. With the theorem of 'second-order emancipation', I offered an explanation for the observation that in late-modern societies democratic participation and civic self-determination are by no means only withheld from citizens by those in power – or taken away from them again by the new autocrats – but that in the wake of emancipatory progress itself, these ideals have actually become impractical and a burden in several respects, for many citizens, which leads them to rethink their democratic expectations, to voluntarily delegate some democratic rights, or even relinquish them. At the time, many observers found my considerations entirely unacceptable. Today, however, the fundamental crisis and the demystification of democracy are undisputed. The comforting and by no means unfounded narrative of capitalism expropriating democratic rights is, of course, still very present in the social science literature. Yet, there is also a consensus now that in late-modern societies, very different social groups – each for their own reasons – develop a particularly ambivalent relationship to democratic institutions and procedures (cf. Blühdorn 2018). I proposed the concept of 'simulative democracy' in order to account for the paradox that, while democratic self-determination continues to be demanded with vehemence, and democratic values continue to be widely accepted in principle, doubts are spreading as to whether in highly complex, accelerated and internationally interdependent societies, democracy is really still the best – and a practicable – form of government. I suggested that in advanced modern societies, democratic institutions and procedures can be described as 'simulative' insofar as they allow for the articulation and experience of democratic values to which modern citizens and societies feel deeply committed and which are an indispensable part of their identity and self-understanding, but which are also perceived as increasingly unsuitable for solving the problems of today's societies with the necessary efficiency and effectiveness, and which can no longer do justice to the prevailing understandings of individual freedom and self-determination (cf. Chapters 3.3 and 5.3). Practices of simulation, I argued, allow for the simultaneity of commitments which are mutually exclusive (see also Blühdorn 2007a, 2007b, 2011).

After *Simulative Democracy*, I increasingly focused on the peculiar durability of the established social order, the unsustainability of which has actually been undisputed for decades. I understood sustainability and unsustainability not only in an ecological sense, but in a much broader way that also includes the political, economic, social and cultural dimensions. In this context, I indirectly posed the question whether it is actually conceivable that the SET will not succeed and what that would mean. Extending my thesis beyond the narrower project of conceptualizing democracy in advanced modern societies, I outlined a diagnosis of society at large: the society of unsustainability (e.g. Blühdorn 2020b). Strictly speaking, I did not just ask whether it might be possible that the SET does not succeed. Rather, by drawing on the analyses on which the concept of simulative democracy is based, I tried to explain why an SET in the sense outlined in the previous section is very unlikely to occur. I developed the thesis that, contrary to the assertion that 'business as usual is not an option', precisely this 'business as usual' is not just an option, but the priority project that advanced modern societies are pursuing with utmost determination – while they continue to cultivate the EEP and the idea of the SET as a practice of simulation. In my work on both simulative democracy and the society of unsustainability, I have always been at pains to make clear that these concepts do not articulate normative claims, but are attempts to conceptualize, interpret and explain empirically observable phenomena or changes. Secondly, I have always emphasized that both simulative democracy and sustained unsustainability are transitional phenomena, interludes that cannot be made permanent. So, both these concepts raised the question of what comes afterwards: transitional phenomena to where?

This is the question which the present book focuses on – and not by way of speculating about the as yet unknown, but by trying to shed light on the path on which late-modern societies are moving, and by pointing to cornerstones that are already recognizable, contours that are already emerging. In doing so, I am now replacing the concept of sustainability or unsustainability with that of untenability. 'Sustainability' and 'unsustainability' have several weaknesses: firstly, in everyday language they are still understood primarily in the ecological sense, and other dimensions of sustainability – the social, the political, the cultural, the economic – are at best given incidental consideration. Secondly, there is something optional about sustainability in the everyday understanding: sustainability is certainly absolutely desirable, yet unsustainability does not mean that the corresponding practices or structures cannot be held on to regardless – at least temporarily. This is precisely what modern societies have always done with great determination – often with the explicit statement: 'whatever it takes'[4] – and there is no indication, right now,

---

[4] For example, the then European Central Bank President Mario Draghi during the financial crisis from 2009 or the German Chancellor Olaf Scholz during the coronavirus crisis.

that this might change. Thirdly, there has been a certain consensus in the literature for some time that the concept of sustainability, which in the late 1980s and early 1990s had provided a strong political impetus, has become largely exhausted in late-modern societies and is no longer suitable as a vision for eco-political mobilization and transformation (e.g. Foster 2015; Folkers 2022; Blühdorn 2016, 2022a; see also Chapter 6.2). If we switch from sustainability and unsustainability to the term untenability, these weaknesses are at least partially circumvented. This concept shifts the perspective from the desirable to the factual. And it better captures what is at stake in late modernity: the narratives of the EEP as well as the social arrangements, self-descriptions and self-images of modernity as a whole have become exhausted. The expiry of their shelf life means that they disintegrate and transform, regardless of whether late-modern societies want, like or admit to it.

So, in comparison to my earlier books, the perspective has, once again, widened: from the crisis of democracy to the fivefold sustainability crisis, to the crisis of the EEP and on to the untenability of Western modernity at large. The question now is: is it actually conceivable that the EEP and the model of Western modernity as a whole will one day be exhausted without this implying the end of the world – either literally or figuratively? Ultimately, of course, this question has always been behind the questions that guided me in earlier books. The term 'late modernity' has become firmly established, as has the realization that late modernity is in crisis (e.g. Reckwitz & Rosa 2023). The abandonment of the idea of the autonomous subject – as the central norm of social theory – which Luhmann had already vehemently called for, but which was still an unbearable provocation at the time (e.g. Blühdorn 2000b), has now become mainstream in significant parts of the social sciences. 'In the broader discussion in the humanities and cultural studies', write Block and Dickel, 'decidedly post-humanist interpretations have been emerging for some years, which affirm the end of the autonomous subject or have accepted it as a realistic possibility' (Block & Dickel 2020: 110).

Previously, in *Post-Ecologist Politics*, in *Simulative Democracy* and in *Sustained Unsustainability*, I attached great importance to understanding the phenomena described not simply as showing signs of decay, nor as regressive in nature. Instead, I sought to argue that these phenomena result from the consistent implementation of modernity, not from its suspension or from the violation of its logic. As paradoxical as this may seem, my argument has always been that these phenomena must at least *also* be understood as emancipatory achievements. Following the same logic, the disintegration of the EEP and the crisis of late modernity are not understood in this book as a final stage and farewell to modernity (even though prima facie the term 'late modernity' seems to suggest otherwise), but as its dialectical further development. This is signalled by the subtitle of this book, which adapts that of Ulrich Beck's *Risk Society: Auf dem Weg in eine andere Moderne* [On the Way to a Different Modernity] (1986).

1.3 The unthinkable

Thus, looking beyond the crisis of the EEP, the key question in this book is whether it is conceivable that Western modernity and its fundamental norms of freedom, the self-determined subject, human rights, democracy, the open society, etc. will one day become outdated. Until very recently, this has been inconceivable. The West had found it so difficult to imagine the end of its own project that it tended to equate this idea with the end of humanity. The *end of history*, according to Western thinking, was to be the global rule of the European-Western ideals of the Enlightenment, which were considered to be universally valid and which, ever since Kant, it was hoped would lead to a *cosmopolitan society* and *perpetual peace* (Kant 1784/1970, 1795/1970). The eco-emancipatory movements, too, believed in this equation – if only for strategic reasons, that is, in order to mobilize popular support. On the one hand, these movements were critical of bourgeois ideals, traditional beliefs, liberal democracy and Western modernity as a whole. They were highly sceptical of the modernist obsession with domination, control and the instrumental appropriation of nature. At the same time, however, these movements and their project were firmly rooted in the tradition of modernity. They firmly believed in the ability to shape and control, and in the myth of rational politics. They were determined to repair the weaknesses, side effects and dark sides of modernity to date – and to this end they insisted on their right and ability to reorganize and steer things in a self-determined manner. And even if they were increasingly critical of the ideas of Kantian reason, they remained committed to the project of modernity, which they wanted to liberate from its own pitfalls. In this respect, contrary to its frequent (self-) portrayal, the EEP was never really an alternative to, but rather a renewing extension of the bourgeois-liberal project. This is still true today, when emancipatory movements are seeking to grapple with the colonialist and racist legacy of modernity to date.

However, the possibility of the exhaustion of their project, its becoming anachronistic and its emancipatory abandonment, was something the pioneers of the EEP could not – and did not want to – imagine. Not until today. From their perspective, that is, within their normative horizon, this possibility was and is literally unthinkable. It is not least for this reason that the possible failure to achieve an SET has always been thought of as catastrophic, as the apocalypse, as the end of humanity. As such, it is the dystopian antithesis to the envisaged 'end of history' in the perpetual socio-ecological peace of cosmopolitan society. This thinking still reverberates in the rhetoric of today's climate activists, for example, when they refer to themselves as the 'last generation'. It is also reflected in the warnings by Earth system scientists that crossing the non-negotiable planetary boundaries could lead to the uninhabitability of the planet and endanger the survival of the human species (Steffen et al. 2015, 2018; Rockström et al. 2009a, 2009b, 2021). But this is a very Western idea and concern. It is not shared in other parts of the world where, instead, people see themselves at the beginning of a new golden age. And even in Western countries, narratives of a new golden age beyond the eco-emancipatory warnings of doom are gaining popularity fast.

In fact, the scenarios depicting the demise of humanity – despite all theoretical possibilities and the comprehensively documented destruction of biophysical systems – is, in a sense, the left-wing activist counterpart to the right-wing populist denial of global warming and the sustainability crisis. 'End or turnaround' and 'business as usual is not an option' are the TINA (there is no alternative) of the emancipatory climate movement and critical environmental sociology. What this emancipatory-critical TINA-thinking and the thinking of climate change deniers have in common is that they both – from their respective perspectives – ignore a scenario that is in fact the most realistic, but which for both would cause their respective worlds to collapse and is therefore intolerable. However, there is an alternative, and 'business as usual' is certainly an option – but it means that late-modern societies (have to) abandon the norms and social self-descriptions that Western societies – and the pioneers of the EEP and the SET, in particular – have so far proudly proclaimed as the very core of their identity. This is exactly the price that must be paid when the motto is 'whatever it takes'. Accordingly, the activists of the group that has given itself this name are probably not the 'Last Generation' that can still limit global warming to the level of less than 1.5 degrees Celsius as defined in the Paris Climate Agreement (this would be or is a fatal overestimation of their own efficacy); and they are certainly not the last generation before the climate-induced demise of humanity. Rather, they may well be the last generation that, in the modernist spirit and in the tradition of the eco-emancipatory movements since the 1970s, is still holding on to the belief that global warming can be limited to 1.5 degrees Celsius and that the project of an SET can – and ought to – be practically implemented. For, although late modernity is not at the end of history, it is at the end of *this story* or narrative.

From an ecological and activist perspective, the excluded third scenario is 'not an option' in the sense that it is 'not at all desirable'. For the social sciences, however, an exclusive focus on the desirable and the corresponding narrowing of the diagnostic-analytical perspective are hardly acceptable. When, in the 1980s, Niklas Luhmann stated that functionally differentiated societies are hardly in a position to overcome their ecological crisis because the internal logics of their diverse function systems are mutually incompatible (Luhmann 1989), this was entirely unacceptable for emancipatory eco-movements and for critical sociology. However, Luhmann made an important contribution to understanding the lasting unsustainability of modern societies and the obstacles to an SET. Luhmann dared to think what for classical sociology was unthinkable. The eco-activist TINA, on the other hand, is a kind of immunization not only against the idea that the EEP could one day become outdated, but also against the suspicion and possibility that eco-emancipatory thinking and the social actors who have promoted it, might – without noticing and certainly without intending this – themselves have become part of the problem. From the perspective of the EEP this, too, is unthinkable. It would be traumatic. And yet, today, exactly this seems to be the case, for example, insofar as its champions have ultimately always placed their identity- and self-actualization-related agenda above their equality- and redistribution-related goals, or insofar as they have never succeeded in supplementing their agenda of emancipatory boundary-transgression by an equally powerful agenda of ecological boundary-setting and self-limitation.

Part of the unthinkable, part of the traumatic nature of late modernity is, furthermore, the above suggestions that the EEP and modern society are becoming exhausted and breaking down, not least because of their own inherent logic and dynamic. This means that the EEP and modern, open, democratic society at large are experiencing exactly what Marxist theory has always said about capitalism: namely, that its own inherent contradictions make it increasingly susceptible to crises and destabilizing forces until, eventually, it will break down and thus clear the way for a radically different and fully liberated society.

In late modernity, capitalism continues to prove astonishingly resilient, but the foundations of the EEP are breaking down. The crisis of the EEP is therefore about much more than just the post-apocalyptic realization that the window of opportunity for certain climate targets and an SET has now closed, and that certain consequences, which climate and sustainability science had always warned about, can no longer be prevented (cf. Cassegard & Thörn 2018; de Moor 2022). It is about the progressive normalization and de-problematization of the previously apocalyptic and unthinkable. This process, too, is opening up the perspective for a radically different and fully liberated society – but in a sense diametrically opposed to the tradition of post-Marxist critical theory.

For the sociology of late modernity, the exploration of modernity beyond its traditional normative foundations is so difficult exactly because the EEP and Western modernity as a whole are not simply blocked by powers hostile to modernization, emancipation and ecology, but have destabilized themselves. The objective of this book is to shed light on this unthinkable. This does not mean to normatively call for, that is, to affirm a modernity that distances itself from the values of the EEP. Nor does it mean to abandon the ideal of a good life for all. Both would be fundamentally wrong. Rather, the aim is to correct the often distorted relationship between the diagnostic-analytical and the normative-transformative agenda of critical sociology, especially in the environmental and sustainability literature. The critical sociology of sustainability must break out of its overly narrow normative horizon, since the emancipatory diagnoses of problems and therapeutic proposals that it has offered to date have always facilitated – probably unintentionally and unconsciously – the continuation of the status quo rather than its radical change, and thus, the seamless transition to a new form of modernity beyond autonomy, maturity, dignity, human rights and democratic self-determination. Freeing itself from this complicity must be a fundamental concern for critical sociology. Accordingly, it is time for it to shift its attention from the normative demands for an SET and from the mobilization narratives of the end of humanity towards the next society and the other modernity, which are already unfolding in the shadow of the doomsday discourses.

1.4 Roadmap

These introductory thoughts have drawn attention to the completely new constellation 'after the end of humanity'. They mark out the sociological space that will be explored in more detail throughout this book. This constellation and this space only become visible when we look beyond the activist dualism of 'end or turnaround', and when we leave the normativity of this narrative behind. Just as the NSM and early green parties once wanted to move the debate into a new discursive and political space 'beyond left and right', that is, beyond the dualism that had determined political thinking and activism until then, just as these movements and their intellectuals saw the urgent need to do so because this was the only way to explore the specific characteristics and challenges of their time and society, it is now necessary to explore the discursive and political space beyond the dualism of 'U-turn or catastrophe'.

The next chapter further explores the implications of 'standing at the abyss' and 'being at the brink of disaster' (Guterres 2021). It reconsiders the activist promise that the socio-ecological crisis, however serious it may become, always entails new opportunities for an SET. It points to the paralysing dilemmas in which late-modern eco-politics gets caught up. And it flags up exhausted illusions of activist movements and untenable orthodoxies of critical sociology. Chapter 3 focuses on a number of 'great transformations' in late modernity – the much-debated crisis of capitalism, the arrival of a new geological era, the Anthropocene, the digital revolution, the autocratic-authoritarian turn, and the rise of China as a new geopolitical superpower – which all signal just how profoundly late-modern societies are, indeed, changing. In the literature, each of these transformations has been at the centre of specific diagnoses of the present and of contemporary society (e.g. Brand & Wissen 2021; Zuboff 2019). For present purposes they are significant in that, taken together, they all signal the abandonment of core ideals that now appear increasingly anachronistic and thus point to the end of a particular phase of modernity. Collectively, these transformations are shifting the parameters under which climate and sustainability issues are addressed today. They shape the parameters of the late-modern repoliticization of the EEP, and they condition the metamorphosis of contemporary societies beyond the late-modern era.

In Chapters 4 and 5, the crisis of the EEP and this metamorphosis are then framed in terms of modernization theory. To this end, I take up the theoretical propositions that Ulrich Beck developed since the 1980s. When Beck described modern societies as 'risk societies' and pointed to the unforeseen side effects of industrial modernity which, he believed, catapulted these societies 'onto the path to a different modernity', he meant, among other things, that new political actors and their 'new politics' would now eliminate these unforeseen side effects – such as environmental damage, social inequalities, unemployment and famines. He believed that by politicizing the traditional, still pre-modern elements of modern society, this 'new politics' would ensure that the promises of modernity – self-determination, inclusion, equality, universal human rights, etc. – which had only been partially fulfilled up to that point, would be completely fulfilled in a second attempt. In this sense, Beck's agenda of the 'second modernity' corresponds quite closely to what I have described here as the EEP and what is referred to in social movements and the relevant literature today as the SET. However, his theory of the risk society and the second modernity not only captures the overwhelming optimism of this project, but with his concept of 'reflexive modernization' Beck also helps to explain how and why this SET could never succeed. Although this was by no means his intention, his model thus anticipated the untenability of the second modernity and the EEP and showed how and why this second modernity itself triggers a transformation into another, a *third* modernity. Building on Beck and my earlier experiments with this approach (e.g. Blühdorn 2013: 50–56, 149), Chapter 5 thus offers a model of a first, a second and a third modernity that helps to understand the crisis, exhaustion and metamorphosis of late modernity and the EEP.

Focusing on the three main dimensions of the EEP – the ecological, the emancipatory and the democratic – Chapter 6 further explores how this project is not only blocked by a counter-logic imposed on it from outside, but also undermines itself due to its own logic and internal contradictions. However, the primary focus in Chapter 6 is no longer on the untenability and disintegration of the EEP, but on the question of how the EEP itself has reconfigured the conditions under which questions of sustainability, emancipation and democratic self-determination are formulated and socially negotiated in late modernity and the 'next society'. I try to capture this unintended change, which occurs as an unnoticed side effect, with the terms 'dialectics of sustainability', 'dialectics of emancipation' and 'dialectics of democracy'.

Chapter 7 concludes by looking at the intermediate phase, in which the dual untenability of the established social order of unsustainability and the EEP is clearly recognizable and the contours of the new modernity are becoming increasingly visible, but in which, as Antonio Gramsci put it, although 'the old is dying, the new cannot yet be born' (Gramsci 1971: 276). Central themes here include the societal management of the tension between the fading norms and self-images of the second modernity and the new ones that are gradually asserting themselves, as well as the dilemmas that the double untenability poses for critical sociology, transformative sustainability research and political education. Also, this concluding chapter reflects on the relationship between the sociological diagnosis of a postliberal modernity presented in this book and recent debates on postliberal thinking.

Overall, this book pursues a threefold objective: firstly, it aims to contribute to consolidating the social-theoretical foundations of environmental and sustainability sociology. This is because a large part of the relevant literature is still primarily concerned with demands, wishes, hopes and appeals. But, today, we look back on more than five decades of such hopes and appeals, and their limits have become abundantly clear. In view of the worsening crises, the constant renewal of these well-established narratives is no longer a plausible counter-strategy. And in normative terms, too, these narratives have become untenable. After all, promises and hopes that are known to be unfounded and to come to nothing are likely to lead to experiences of disappointment and frustration which, in turn, fuel social conflicts that are becoming increasingly difficult to handle. As their unforeseen side effects have become blatantly obvious, holding on to these narratives thus becomes increasingly unacceptable. Hence, the objective here is to go beyond the endless feel-good literature that never tires of emphasizing that so much has already been achieved, that late-modern societies are actually already on the right path and that they now only need to make much more decisive progress. Yet, the objective is not to spread pessimism and conjure up 'the black hole of unsustainability' (K.W. Brand 2021). Rather, it is to shed light on the perspective and normative orientations that give rise to optimism and pessimism, hope and frustration. The further the EEP and Western modernity move beyond their best-before date, the more important will this approach become. Inter alia, it can help to understand, defuse and perhaps pacify the political conflicts, radicalizations and polarizations that are spreading like wildfire in late modernity and that may well lead to 'a new kind of barbarism', a new brutalized 'state of nature' governed, once again, by the rule of strongest (Horkheimer & Adorno 1994 [1944]: 16; see also Honneth 2012; Bauman 2017; Latour 2017).

Secondly, the book seeks to contribute – from the perspective of environmental and sustainability sociology – to a theory of late-modern societies. For, just as social theory is a blank space in much of the sustainability literature, the ecological theme is still a conspicuously weak or even blank space in current sociological theory (e.g. Reckwitz 2020, 2021; Nachtwey 2018; Amlinger & Nachtwey 2025; Nassehi 2021). And where it is taken into account, the authors usually remain caught up in the established categories and thought patterns of progressive vs regressive, emancipatory vs conservative or reactionary, and thus systematically fail to capture the specifically late-modern (e.g. Amlinger & Nachtwey 2025; Fraser 2022; Mouffe 2023). However, the untenability diagnosed in this book also pertains to the normativity of critical theory, which a theory of late-modern societies must transgress, if it does not want to miss its object.

Thirdly, this book works towards a theory of modern societies beyond late modernity, that is, a theory of the 'next' society and modernity beyond the current interregnum. With the concepts of postliberal society and modernity, it aims to go one step further than those approaches that attempt to free themselves from the normativity of critical theory, but ultimately still remain caught up in late modernity, in lamenting what has been lost, and that attempt to hold on to the untenable and, hence, do not really reach the other modernity (e.g. Nachtwey 2018; Amlinger & Nachtwey 2025; Staab 2022). In effect, then, this book deals with not just a double, but a triple exhaustion: that of the established arrangements of the society of unsustainability, that of the EEP and its activist narratives, and that of critical sociology and its normativity.

— 2 —

ON THE BRINK OF DISASTER

With the unprecedented climate protection movement initiated by Greta Thunberg in 2018, the Covid-19 pandemic of March 2020, the significant rise in inflation since mid-2021 and the outbreak of war in Ukraine in February 2022, the phenomenon of unsustainability suddenly became very tangible. Far beyond the ecological understanding of the term, *unsustainability* suddenly turned into *untenability*. Everyday things that were taken for granted became impossible and – unlike the many things that had long been known to be unsustainable – were actually restricted or suspended, whether through the collapse of certain systems of provisioning (such as international supply chains) or through lockdown (e.g. shopping, party or travel restrictions). This was new; and it affected not only certain sections of the population, but in many respects everyone – although of course the impact of the pandemic and its consequences were distributed unevenly across society.

Decades earlier, there had already been talk of *Limits to Growth* (Meadows et al. 1972), as well as, more recently, 'losers of modernization' and neoliberalism inducing 'social decline' (Nachtwey 2018). Thus, to some extent, new limits and factual deterioration had already become a social reality. But this had only ever affected and interested certain sections of society; for the majority, it had remained abstract. Terms such as self-limitation and voluntary simplicity had also been doing the rounds for a long time, and so had the argument that *less* – in terms of material possessions and consumption – is actually *more*, in terms of happiness and a good life (Jackson 2011; Paech 2012; Folkers & Paech 2020). However, this had not had any impact on the prevailing logic of growth and expansion, mobility, acceleration and ever wider horizons of life. In the pandemic, in

47

contrast, the experience of limits and restrictions suddenly gained a completely different quality, and the war in Ukraine once again heightened societal awareness of non-negotiable boundaries. After decades of growth, emancipatory movements and (market) liberalism, many citizens perceived the sudden suspension of everyday normality as unbearable and the state-imposed restrictions as an inacceptable encroachment on personal freedoms. Some liberals and right-wing populists, in particular, immediately denounced these measures as a 'corona dictatorship'. Against the backdrop of the great resonance of the new climate movement, they were portrayed as a foretaste of an impending 'eco-dictatorship' threatening 'our freedom, our values and our way of life'.

Indirectly, these concerns articulated a new reality: with the acute experience of limits, the task and project of limitation, of drawing boundaries, of exclusion and deportation become central in late-modern societies. When growth reaches its limits, but demands and expectations continue to rise, the question becomes urgent as to who may continue to participate in what, where the boundaries should be drawn, and who and what must be excluded. What the changed constellation made unmistakably clear was that, not *less*, but *more* is more – and in case of doubt, *more* also tends to be the better insurance. Moreover, if fewer are allowed to participate, more remains for those entitled! With their campaigns against 'immigration into the social systems', migration-related competition for housing, in the labour market or for daycare places, right-wing populists, in particular, made the issue of securing borders, fighting immigration and excluding the non-entitled the core of their political brand. But in late modernity, political actors of all persuasions have taken up the issue of limitation, and the politics of demarcation and exclusion has many faces: it appears as intensified identity politics from the left (cancel culture) and the right (nationalisms, conspiracy myths), as a neoliberal doctrine of self-responsibility, as the rediscovery of state regulation in the name of climate protection, as right-wing populist politics against migrants and minorities or as fundamentalist rigorism in religious communities. Border fences and border controls, which – one might have thought – fundamentally contradict the Western ideal of the open society, are suddenly becoming a priority project not only in the USA, but in Europe, too.

Since eco-emancipatory movements, which had taken up the issue early on, never succeeded in firmly anchoring the problem of ecological limits on the political agenda, nor in developing an effective concept of collective self-limitation, boundaries, borders and exclusion – as well as their organization and legitimization – have now, on their own, become a central concern of a wide variety of actors – as a side effect of the hegemonic logic of expansion. The continuous denial of limits, the unremitting transgression of boundaries and the sustained externalization of the social, ecological and future-related consequences have led to a situation where it is ever more difficult to find an 'outside' whose appropriation and exploitation could continue to secure 'our freedom, our values and our lifestyle', and into which the consequences of this practice can still be externalized.

2.1 The abyss

In the early 1970s, the British-French environmental activist, writer and philosopher Edward Goldsmith wrote in a text that became groundbreaking for the then emerging international environmental movement that the industrialized way of life and its ethos of expansion would inevitably collapse within the lifetime of then newborn children. Regardless of the level of prosperity and consumption they had already achieved, industrialized societies, he wrote, were dependent on ever-increasing growth. If this growth was too low or even failed to materialize, they would inevitably collapse. However, the attempt to secure this indispensable growth would not only destroy ecosystems but also create social inequality and tensions that would soon erupt into violent conflict. And in times of social stress and chaos, it would be more than likely that government power would fall into the hands of unscrupulous rogues who would not hesitate to threaten other states militarily (Goldsmith 1972: 2–5).

Goldsmith's analysis was nothing short of prophetic. Children who were newborns back then are now in their fifties, and the societies of the Global North are, it seems, at exactly the point Goldsmith predicted. Economic, ecological and social crises are coming to a head. Even the oldest and most established democracies are sliding steadily towards authoritarianism and autocracy. And even in Europe, where wars had long been assumed to be something of the past, military force is not just a threat but a cruel reality. Already before Russia's attack on Ukraine, António Guterres, had warned:

We are on the edge of an abyss – and moving in the wrong direction. Our world has never been more threatened. Or more divided. We face the greatest cascade of crises in our lifetimes. [. . .] A surge of mistrust and misinformation is polarizing people and paralyzing societies, and human rights are under fire. Science is under assault. [. . .] Peace. Human rights. Dignity for all. Equality. Justice. Solidarity. Like never before, core values are in the crosshairs. (Guterres 2021)

In modern acceleration- and distraction-societies, everything is perfectly geared towards ensuring that, ideally, moments of reflection and larger concerns do not occur at all. But where the ever-faster rat race of everyday life and the narcotic strategies of the entertainment industry fail, it becomes ominously clear that something very fundamental is happening at present that goes far beyond earlier discussions of *post-democracy* or the *great regression* (Crouch 2004; Geiselberger 2017). 'We are in the fight of our lives', said Guterres at the UN Climate Change Conference in Sharm El-Sheikh in the autumn of 2022, 'and we are losing. Greenhouse gas emissions keep growing. Global temperatures keep rising. And our planet is fast approaching tipping points that will make climate chaos irreversible. We are on a highway to climate hell with our foot still on the accelerator' (Guterres 2022).

In fact, it is by no means only with regard to climate change that there is a widely shared feeling of fundamental uncertainty, of decline, of the end, of subliminal panic. Many insist that it is not yet too late and urge rapid collective action for change. But it has long been clear that these narratives, first and foremost, have therapeutic value but hold limited potential for actually triggering significant change. Movements such as Extinction Rebellion or Last Generation, like Fridays for Future before them, articulate a sense of looming apocalypse that is widespread well beyond these groups, but which is more successfully suppressed and denied in other parts of society – or in other discourses. Occasionally, there is still reassuring talk of such perceptions being exaggerated – periodically occurring fears of doom, which also existed in earlier times (cf. for example Reckwitz 2021: 6f). But such appeasement is not convincing any more. The Intergovernmental Panel on Climate Change is calling for comprehensive, immediate measures and drastic changes in all areas of society. Sociologists diagnose 'the end of illusions', a notoriously 'overburdened society' and a 'society on the verge of a nervous breakdown' (Reckwitz 2021; Nassehi 2021; Lessenich 2022).

As regards the economy, where growth rates were already declining in the 1970s, the crisis was foreshadowed early on, and following the banking and financial crisis after 2008, the economic system almost collapsed. For decades, policies of public debt, privatization programmes, globalization strategies, deregulation initiatives, policies of low interest rates, public investment programmes and, most recently, government measures to ease the economic consequences of the Covid pandemic and the war in Ukraine managed to 'buy time', to 'delay the crisis of capitalism' and sustain confidence that the economy will soon recover again (e.g. Streeck 2014, 2016). But today, debt, inflation and even comparatively small interest rate hikes pose a considerable threat to the economy and social prosperity. The established ways of life are incompatible with ethical ecological and social standards. They depend on raw materials, energy and consumer goods from countries that categorically reject basic Western values and rights; and they also depend on the export of products to such countries. Thus, it is becoming increasingly clear that this economic system no longer works. Its shelf life has expired – or at least the shelf life of the democratic, social and ecological standards that modern Western societies expect it to meet (cf. Chapter 3.1).

In ecological terms, many long-invoked tipping points have been reached – and crossed – and politicians seem largely helpless. International climate summits do not lead to any significant results. So-called Green New Deals have little eco-transformative power. Major projects such as the sustainability transformation of the energy, transport or agricultural sectors are making slow progress, if that. There are a large number of local initiatives and experiments, but their transformative effect is low. Environmental regulations are being weakened or suspended in response to acute crises. Market-based instruments such as CO_2 pricing, which for decades were touted by many as the most promising strategy for an SET, have achieved little and are more likely to be suspended than seriously implemented in the face of inflation, rising energy prices and pressures for international competitiveness. Programmes of ecological modernization have brought improvements in air pollution control or water protection but often entailed the relocation of ecologically harmful processes to countries with less stringent requirements. They do little to alleviate crucial problems such as global warming, land consumption, habitat destruction or species extinction. In the meantime, the strategies of externalization – to the future, to other geographical regions or to the least resilient parts of society – are reaching their limits; ecological catastrophe seems inevitable.

Regarding societal integration and cohesion, the inequality crisis is steadily worsening. Both intra- and inter-societal divisions are deepening; the corresponding conflicts are becoming ever more polarized and irreconcilable. Questions of material distribution, on the one hand, and cultural identity and recognition, on the other, are closely interlinked, making social peace ever more fragile. The mechanisms of integration within societies have surpassed their limits, and this also applies to international cohesion.

And in terms of political culture, the decline, the regression, the recession of liberal democracy seems unstoppable (e.g. Levitsky & Ziblatt 2018; Manow 2020; Schäfer & Zürn 2021). A further democratization of democracy, that is, the further opening up of democratic institutions, seems to have little prospect of success in late-modern societies (see Chapters 3.3 and 6.4). Division and polarization are becoming more entrenched, and although election winners often assure citizens that they want to overcome the deep divisions in their respective societies, in practice it is completely unclear how this could succeed. Instead, sustained efforts to open democratic institutions to greater citizen participation have, actually, triggered new tendencies towards closure. The confidence of policymakers in the benefit of greater participation is waning. The optimism of civil society is turning into resignation and radicalism. Today, hope in the 'new politics' of social movements seems no less exhausted than trust in the institutions of traditional politics.

In all these respects, it is abundantly clear that a limit has been reached, even crossed, without alternative perspectives opening up. Much more so than in the 1980s, when Samuel Beckett's plays of hopelessness and apocalypse were performed in all theatres, late-modern societies today are in a very real *Endgame*. Even if the relevant actors never tire of repeating and renewing their narratives of hope, it is becoming increasingly difficult to believe that collective self-limitation in favour of a good life for all within ecological limits could actually succeed; that the social divisions and polarizations can be reconciled once more, or that the many small alternative initiatives and experiments of the much-cited 'pioneers of change' will actually one day grow into a major social transformation. The EU does promise to become climate neutral by 2050. But what significance do such announcements have? There is little to suggest that the fundamental tension between the commitment to ecology and human rights and the defence of Western prosperity and lifestyles can really be resolved. One would love to believe this, of course, but from a social science perspective, everything speaks against it. The societal framework conditions prerequisite for an SET are not in place.

Thus, late-modern societies are, one might say, *at their wit's end*. In practically all crucial respects (ecological, economic, democratic, cultural), these societies are beyond the point at which the momentum of the crises can be stopped. This loss of perspective and control is traumatic for Western societies, for whose self-image the ability to shape and control an open future has always been essential. In late modernity, however, the loss of confidence in this ability now also affects those who previously saw themselves as the pioneers, the avant-garde, the enlightened and knowledgeable. Loss of control has often been cited as an experience typical of the so-called 'losers of modernization and globalization' and as a major reason for their turning away from politics or drifting towards the populist right (e.g. Nachtwey 2018; Schäfer & Zürn 2021; Amlinger & Nachtwey 2025). However, even highly educated and politically informed citizens are no longer able to comprehend the current crises and transformations or make any promising proposals for the way forward. The climate crisis, the pandemic, the war in Ukraine, the conflict in the Middle East and the demise of liberal democracy are overwhelming even the intellectual elites. Many see a self-protective retreat into the private sphere, a process of deliberately ignoring the news and suppressing its alarming truths, as the only remaining strategy for coping with what is equally opaque and unbearable to them. The decades-long effort to acquire a clear understanding and offer a critical and progressive assessment, to participate and take responsibility, culminates in disillusionment and exhaustion (e.g. Friedrichs 2022). This, too, is a state of emergency, an experience at the edge of an abyss.

2.2 Crises as opportunities?

But isn't that far too pessimistic and deterministic an assessment, one might object? It is not only climate change deniers who point to the fact that there have always been crises – and solutions have always been found. Many *endgames* have been played, but they have never been the *end of the game*. So how can we justify the claim that the situation today is different and more serious than before? Isn't there also ample reason for hope? Are there not signs of great social solidarity, wherever crises and disaster hit? And are not crises, in any case, indispensable for breaking up established structures and routines so that they can then be reshaped? So, isn't there today good reason to believe even more strongly in the EEP and the SET? In this sense, Andreas Reckwitz, for example, strictly opposes any 'defeatist mood of catastrophe' and instead calls for an 'undogmatic and differentiated perspective' that makes the 'paradoxes and ambivalences' of the present visible (Reckwitz 2021: 6).

This demand is justified. And indeed, crises have always also been seen as an opportunity. In the environmental movement in particular, there have, in fact, always been voices that have been counting on a major catastrophe eventually becoming the driver for a real turning point that averts the ultimate catastrophe at the last opportunity (see also Chapters 4 and 5). At the beginning of the 1990s, Hans Jonas said: 'Perhaps man cannot be brought to his senses without serious warning shots and very painful reactions from tormented nature' (Jonas 1993: 11). At some point, it is also commonly argued, the objective pressure will become so great that it will render an SET inescapable and simply force it. Furthermore, there is a well-established tradition in critical social science that sees the increasing destabilization of the existing order – especially capitalism – as a growing opportunity, even a necessary precondition for emancipatory change and a better world (see also Chapter 6). Marx's argument that the oppressed and impoverished working class, ultimately, has nothing more to lose than its chains resonates to this day. In this tradition, Chantal Mouffe, for example, sees the current crises as an opportunity for 'a left populism' and a 'green democratic revolution' (Mouffe 2018, 2022). Nancy Fraser sees potential for a 'counter-hegemonic project' (Fraser 2019, 2022) to supersede the ideology of neoliberalism. And in popular literature and the feature pages, whenever the crisis is severe, there is renewed hope that perhaps this is the moment when everything will finally change, that the impetus will finally be strong enough to really initiate a fundamental structural change (e.g. Klein 2015; Göpel 2022).

These hopes are, of course, countered by the thesis that capitalism needs the regular crises that it generates itself in order to reproduce itself and strengthen its resilience. This would suggest that the current crises will not bring about a transformation beyond the established system, but rather a renewal and strengthening of capitalism. Moreover, the crisis and the state of emergency have repeatedly been described as instruments of power that legitimize political and economic measures that would not be easily conceivable, possible or enforceable under normal conditions (e.g. Agamben 2004, 2021). From this perspective, too, crises are investigated as opportunities to strengthen established power structures, not to transform them.

But if it is true that every crisis is also an opportunity for transformation, late-modern societies do indeed have more chances now than ever before. After all, the number of major crises is growing everywhere, and the intervals between them are getting shorter and shorter. And indeed, new waves of hope develop with great regularity in every crisis. This was the case after the banking and financial crisis of 2008/9, when the Occupy Wall Street movement and its European offshoots envisaged a new era of 'post-capitalism' and a 'post-growth society' (e.g. Paech 2012; Mason 2016; Dörre et al. 2019; Herrmann 2022). The refugee crisis of 2014/15 triggered an enormous willingness to help, and an impressive 'welcoming culture' was on display at many train stations in Europe. Great hopes were also associated with the Fridays for Future movement, whose pressure contributed, among other things, to the European Parliament declaring a 'climate emergency' in September 2019. During the Covid crisis, there were high hopes that people would suddenly remember 'buried values' such as solidarity and that underpaid but 'systemically relevant' professions would finally get the recognition they deserved. And the war in Ukraine, too, was associated with certain hopes, for example, for a strengthening of European and Western unity and a much accelerated transition to renewable energy.

So, just as there are tides or cycles of catastrophic moods, there are also those of hope. However, an 'undogmatic and differentiated perspective' is also required for these optimistic narratives. For, although crises certainly do create temporary scope for action, the hope for a major eco-emancipatory effect of these crises is ultimately mistaken. It has always been misguided, and now that the crises are occurring in ever faster succession, this is becoming increasingly obvious. This hope is little more than a comforting, nostalgic commitment to values and ideals that seem desirable, but which are at the same time incompatible with the rights, concepts of freedom and ways of life that Western societies regard as non-negotiable. From a socio-psychological perspective, these narratives of hope are an expression of a refusal to face up to the specificity of the late-modern constellation. They are a kind of self-illusionment (cf. Blühdorn 2006, 2007a, 2017, 2023; see also Chapter 7) that avoids the crucial question of why the current crisis should fulfil what has not yet been fulfilled since the beginning of the environmental movement. Or from a social science perspective: where exactly and in what respects have the parameters changed to justify the belief that the eco-emancipatory vision could now become reality?

In late-modern societies, the sense of end times, the awareness of the untenability of the established order – if one allows oneself such feelings at all – are, undoubtedly, more acute than ever. But the thesis of 'objective pressures' that will ultimately make an SET unavoidable has always been wrong. There is no objective pressure, only individual and collective limits to acceptability and to the capacity to cope with the phenomena and changes that scientific research flags up and that are widely perceived by society. Such limits are distinctly mutable and subject to continuous contestation. Furthermore, an SET could only be realized if there were a corresponding vision or utopia that mobilizes sufficient support across social boundaries and far beyond individual countries. However, despite all the crises facing us, such a vision is nowhere in sight. Rather, the most recent crises have illustrated impressively how the boundaries of what is socially acceptable and tolerable are shifting ever further in favour of safeguarding the status quo – and how society's ability to imagine genuine alternatives to the established order and its logic continues to erode.

Initially, there was great moral horror at the drowning of thousands of refugees crossing the Mediterranean and at the conditions in the refugee camps across Europe. However, this has done nothing to change the causes of migration and has not helped much towards an integrated EU refugee or migration policy. While qualified skilled workers continue to be recruited from less developed countries in a colonial manner, there is just as little willingness to take in economic and climate refugees as there is to help create conditions in their countries of origin that allow people to lead a decent life in dignity there. At the beginning of the Covid-19 pandemic, there was a lot of talk about 'systemically relevant' professions, solidarity and the state's regained ability to act. But then even relatively minor and temporary restrictions triggered considerable resistance in various parts of society, and the fastest possible and most complete 'return to normality' – rather than any kind of transformation – became the overriding guiding principle of pandemic policy. In the absence of gas supplies from Russia, there were high hopes for massive energy savings and an accelerated expansion of renewables. At the same time, the desire for greater independence from authoritarian regimes became central. However, the desire to defend established standards of living and social prosperity was even stronger. The expansion of renewables continues to lag well behind requirements, the potential for energy savings has been actively reduced through financial aid policies, and dependence on authoritarian states has merely been shifted from Russia to other countries in which democratic values, the rule of law and human rights are just as insignificant.

Thus, the recent crises can hardly be seen as a catalyst for a major transformation towards eco-emancipatory goals. Against the backdrop of the pandemic, the war and the autocratic-authoritarian turn, the narrative of crises as opportunities has reached its limits; it is exhausted. This, too, is a daunting prospect for late-modern societies at the brink of disaster. Of course, the crises have triggered specific reforms in various areas. But these do not represent an alternative to the prevailing logic, and certainly not a reversal of it. On the contrary, the recent crises have reinforced and strengthened the logic of acceleration, growth, competition, inequality and exclusion. This is because the public debt burden increases with every crisis, as does the pressure to 'grow out of debt' afterwards. This reduces the scope for any SET and leaves little room for post-growth and degrowth, in particular. And, as signalled above, this is further exacerbated by the fact that crises and disasters really *are* catalysts for transformation, just not only for the actors of the EEP, but also for those who are sceptical of the politics of equality, justice, inclusion, democratic self-determination and ecological integrity – or who openly reject it.

2.3 Transformation entrapped

In this respect, the late-modern constellation differs fundamentally from earlier phases of crisis. Its peculiarity cannot be dismissed by pointing out that there have always been troubling times and that a solution has always been found. Instead, an 'undogmatic and differentiated' view reveals that in late-modern societies the project of an SET is fundamentally trapped in several respects. The abyss that António Guterres spoke of in 2021, that is, the urgency of an SET that renegotiates the basic structures of modern societies and their natural relations, may be greater than ever, but the ability and willingness of late-modern societies to actually achieve this are effectively blocked by the interplay of a number of factors:

– These societies are caught in the vortex of multiple crises in which they can barely plan and navigate a more secure future but instead are forced to fixate on controlling the present and the immediate consequences of the most acute crises of today. In trying to achieve this, they have to weigh up ever more carefully whether it is worth investing available funds in long-term projects for an SET or in short-term measures to address the most urgent devastations of current disasters. In democratic systems, in particular, longer-term transformation projects are becoming increasingly difficult to implement, given that, in the face of immediate emergencies, democratic majorities for such projects are not easy to mobilize and even more difficult to sustain.
– An SET that ensures a good life for all would require a significant reduction in consumption, a restriction of demands and expectations in practically all areas of life, and a renunciation

of customary living standards, far beyond what today's citizens perceive as dispensable luxury – and by no means just for a small, privileged elite. For, 'even at minimum decent standards of living Northern consumers far exceed any global targets of emissions per head' (Gough 2020: 216). Yet late-modern societies are tied into infrastructures and committed to understandings of autonomy and patterns of self-realization that render any form of reduction extremely difficult. The triumph of neoliberalism, in particular, has engrained understandings of freedom and self-determination that regard any political regulation as unacceptable interference in the private sphere. This ideology of deregulation has placed enormous demands on planetary boundaries and at the same time considerably reduced the potential for collective self-limitation.

– Furthermore, after decades of market liberalism, social inequalities are so severe, even in generally affluent societies, that a sustainability transformation can no longer be achieved by means of 'honest prices', that is, through the internalization of previously externalized social and ecological costs. If the state intervenes with restrictive regulations, this invariably mobilizes those parts of society that reject such interventions and the project of an SET as a whole. However, the possibilities of the depoliticized market are just as limited, as ecologically and socially sustainable prices would no longer be affordable for significant sections of society and would mean a significant reduction in living standards and, conversely, an increase in social exclusion. This brings social organizations, right-wing populists and many other actors onto the scene. The recent conflicts over rising energy prices and inflation in general provide rich evidence. Even for higher earners, socio-ecological prices would mean a considerable drop in their accustomed standard of living. However, limitation and renunciation are taboo; beyond very marginalized groups, an absolute reduction in the need for mobility, electronics, housing or energy, for example, is not up for debate.

– For decades, social movements and scientific experts have relied on decentralized, participatory, consensus-oriented and flexible policy approaches as the most promising path to a sustainability transformation. *Governance* became the norm and *government*, that is, state regulation through legal rules and prohibitions, became a dirty word. Representatives of market liberalism took advantage of this trend and vehemently called for more individual responsibility. However, it is now clear that the capability of the new, decentralized, participatory forms of governance has been significantly

overestimated. Many climate activists and sustainability researchers are now once again calling for a strong proactive state. But
the state has been permanently weakened by neoliberal ideology.
Transnational organizations such as the EU, on the other hand, are
weakened by centrifugal forces and by member states prioritizing
their national interests.

– In addition, there is a structural mismatch in modern societies
between the idea of an SET and the possibilities of its practical
implementation. Transformative demands are formulated from
the perspective of citizens and their experience of the violation of
their socio-ecological values. In practice, however, such perceptions
and demands are primarily dealt with at the level of societal function systems – law, science, economy, media, etc. – each of which
is subject to its own logic, from which they cannot break out and
which are not synchronized with each other. This coordination is
generally expected of politics. Politics, however, remains trapped in
its own logic of gaining or maintaining power. Edward Goldsmith
had pointed to this difficulty already in the early seventies (1972:
5). Niklas Luhmann elaborated on it in the 1980s (1986a). More
recently, the pandemic has shown the extent to which modern societies are structurally overburdened with their crises: the diversity
and complexity of value preferences makes it difficult to define
problems by consensus and set stable priorities. The competition between the different logics of society's function systems is a
major obstacle to coordinated and consistent problem-solving (e.g.
Nassehi 2021). Attempts to accord the imperatives of SET greater
legitimacy by demanding, as Fridays for Future does, that policymakers 'listen to the science', seek to break out of this dilemma. But
science does not have a prominent position either. Also, science,
too, speaks with many voices, and in modern societies, scientific
scepticism, 'alternative facts' and post-rational worldviews are
flourishing.

– And finally, the attempts to overcome the multiple more limited
crises are also increasingly overshadowed by the new big geopolitical conflict between China and the West and the competition
between liberal-democratic and autocratic-authoritarian systems
(cf. Chapter 3.5). This once again increases the pressure of accelerated economic growth. Sustainability and transformation projects,
if they are to survive at all, must operate within this logic.

All this does not mean that in today's societies there is no scope for
ecological reforms at all. But there is indeed little room for suspending

the logic of growth, competition, exploitation and efficiency, for an absolute limitation and reduction of demands, expectations and needs, and for a decisive social redistribution that would enable a good life for all. Yet, precisely these parameters would be indispensable for an SET towards sustainability, which would have to go far beyond today's decarbonization efforts. Accordingly, such a transformation is not to be expected for structural reasons. António Guterres's warnings that our world has never been as threatened as it is today and that we are facing the greatest cascade of crises we have ever experienced are undoubtedly justified. However, as Luhmann noted decades ago, it is wrong to infer from the urgency and necessity of an SET articulated here to the societal possibility of such a transformation and the ability to actually implement it (Luhmann 1986a). The common appeals that in the face of the current crises 'we must go into action, immediately, collectively and with full determination' have primarily declaratory, experiential and reassuring character. They serve moral and psychological needs but are based on a rather inadequate understanding of late-modern societies. Back in the 1980s, Ulrich Beck described this dilemma as the 'system of organized irresponsibility', whose characteristic is the contradiction 'between system-immanently generated and system-immanently unattributable, unaccountable, unmanageable dangers' (Beck 1988: 104). And this contradiction does not only mean that such well-intended appeals have, more than anything, experiential value and a sedative function, but the constant repetition of these 'wake-up calls' and 'alarm soundings' actually generates syndromes of overload and exhaustion. For, in the late-modern constellation, the framework conditions for the SET that many movements and social scientists continue to call for, are even more unfavourable than they were back then.

2.4 Shattered illusions

This reveals in what sense the current crisis has a novel quality, even if – or especially if – we are equally sceptical of the pessimistic rhetoric of the end of humanity and the hopeful narratives of the many environmental writers and, instead, try to adopt 'an undogmatic and differentiated perspective'. In late-modern society, not only the hope that the many crises may offer opportunities for an SET has become implausible, but many of the assumptions and beliefs that were constitutive of the EEP and that the social movements had mainstreamed since the 1970s are rapidly disintegrating. They suddenly appear outdated, naïve, idealistic and illusory. This shatters established understandings of personal identity and life, and of society and the world at large.

In fact, the entire range of ideals of the eco-emancipatory movements suddenly appear to be an illusion, and, instead, narratives are gaining momentum that legitimize and secure the established order of unsustainability. When in the autumn of 2019 the German 'Fridays for Hubraum' group (Fridays for gas-guzzlers) polemicized against the Fridays for Future movement, this narrative was still a fringe phenomenon and found little social acceptance. A year later, in the run-up to the 2021 German federal elections, in which the issue of safeguarding prosperity was a priority across all party boundaries, the concern that, as the liberal democrats' (FDP) chairman Christian Lindner put it in an interview, the Greens wanted to 'turn our industrialized nation into a fairytale world with cargo bikes' was already finding a much broader echo (*Neue Osnabrücker Zeitung*, 1 September 2021). Another year later, the broad societal criticism of the 'climate terror' of Last Generation activists showed how fundamentally public discourse had changed – although many still thought that the climate activists had a point but were choosing unacceptable means. Those who had already been ambivalent about the project of an SET before, or who were now becoming increasingly cynical about the demand for fundamental societal change, grasped the opportunity – for in every crisis there is an opportunity, after all – to spread supposedly 'more contemporary' and 'realistic' ideas that are urgently needed to defend the status quo.[1] For them, the widespread criticism of Last Generation's protests had something relieving, exonerating, redeeming and liberating about it: at last there was a socially accepted reason to distance oneself from the climate movement and its inconvenient messages. Those trying to hold on to the hopes, beliefs and principles of the EEP, on the other hand, began to recognize that this project is not only being dismantled by its political opponents but, due to its internal contradictions, is becoming increasingly fragile under its own terms.

After Russia's attack on Ukraine and then German Chancellor Scholz's proclamation of a *Zeitenwende* ('new era'), the contestation of the boomer generation's pacifist attitudes was the spearhead of this change in public discourse. Since the peace movement of the

---

[1] According to a survey conducted by the German news magazine *Der Spiegel* in November 2022, a large majority of respondents believed that the climate movement's forms of protest, such as street blockades or defacement of artwork, went too far and should be punished more strictly under criminal law (*Der Spiegel* 46/2022, pp. 32–39; see also 'ZDF-Politbarometer', 3 May 2023).

early 1980s, criticism of NATO and calls for comprehensive disarmament and drastic restrictions on defence spending, the arms industry and arms exports had been just as much part of the EEP as the dimensions of ecologization, emancipation and democratization. This pacifist attitude was first challenged at the time of the Kosovo War (1998/99). Donald Trump later criticized Germany, in particular, for having made itself comfortable under a military umbrella, to whose financing they contributed little, but under whose protection they had developed extensive trade relations with countries that were hostile to the West. In the wake of Russia's attack on Ukraine, this pacifism – similar to Austria's neutrality status – was then declared unacceptable and irresponsible. Armin Nassehi, for example, referring to all those 'who in the 1980s took part in sit-in demonstrations against the NATO Dual-Track Decision and thought the preceding anti-violence training was a security policy', announced: 'Biographically, there is hardly anything that I am more ashamed of than having participated in such blindness in my early 20s' (Nassehi 2022a). What had been a cornerstone of the personal identity and worldview of an entire generation, and regarded as the expression of a deeper understanding of the morally right, was suddenly declared to be 'a delusion' – by no less an authority than one of Germany's leading sociologists.

In the ecological dimension of the EEP, the belief that the ecological issue could be a unifying, collectivizing issue for humanity is a prominent example of a long-held belief turning into an illusion. The movements had always hoped and believed that even a pluralized, differentiated and multicultural world society would – and must – recognize global risks and threats such as climate change as a common concern and collective interest that would in turn forge a global risk community (cf. Chapter 4.4). Yet, in light of right-wing identitarian movements, divisive and polarizing conspiracy theories, and diversity and cancel cultures within late-modern societies; in view of the weakness and indeed disintegration of the EU or the UN; and against the backdrop of new geopolitical tensions, this belief appears entirely illusory. 'Talking about nature doesn't mean signing a peace treaty', wrote Bruno Latour, 'nature doesn't unify – it divides' (Latour & Schultz 2022: 3). At the annual UN climate conferences, for example, the conflict of interests between different countries is becoming ever more visible and irreconcilable. And within societies, too, the project of an SET has become a major issue of polarization and division. While some sections of society see their own solar panels and electric cars as a means of ecological distinction and an expression of ecological commitment, others – and by no means only on the far right – criticize the SET as an anti-social agenda of privileged elites (e.g. Wagenknecht 2022).

This also reveals that the belief in rational and moral collective self-limitation in favour of a 'good life for all' is an illusion. It is bound to fail, if only because the belief in informed, mature and responsible citizens who can organize the good life for all by joining forces in civil society has become fragile as well. While the eco-emancipatory movements since the 1970s firmly believed in the project of truly enlightened, rational, participatory and collectively responsible self-government, which was also intended to organize rationally guided social self-limitation, environmental education is today in a deep crisis. Current freedom, identity and emancipation movements – whether of market-liberal, right-wing populist or anti-Covid provenance – pursue completely different agendas. They are all part of civil society and see themselves as emancipatory, but certainly not in the sense of the EEP.

Similarly, the conviction that more democracy automatically leads to more sustainability is proving untenable. Assuming that civil society and, in particular, they themselves would represent the truly reasonable, the movements had firmly believed that an expansion of opportunities for political participation and an overall democratiza-tion of democracy were the most promising path to a comprehensive sustainability transformation. Today, however, there is a grow-ing suspicion that this only holds true, at best, to a limited extent. Instead, there is much to suggest that political pressure for greater democratic participation has always been a key driver of the fossil fuel growth economy as well as the continued externalization of social and ecological costs (e.g. Shearman & Smith 2007; Mitchell 2011; Malm 2016). This does not mean, of course, that, conversely, the dismantling of democratic rights and institutions would benefit a sustainability transformation. But it is true that democracies *qua* democracies are particularly responsible for the rapid acceleration in the consumption of raw materials and environmental destruction since the 1950s. The emancipatory struggle for more equality, par-ticipation and self-determination is one major cause of the runaway environmental crisis. And in the current vortex of crises, in particular, democracy is becoming the 'glass ceiling' (Hausknost 2020, 2022) of transformative politics and the essential legitimizing instrument for further sustaining the order of unsustainability (Blühdorn 2018, 2020c; see also Chapters 3.3 and 6.4).

The list of these traumatic disillusionments could easily be extended. But the examples provided fully suffice to illustrate the extent to which fundamental beliefs of the EEP have become untenable in late modernity. Instead, it is becoming increasingly obvious that the eco-emancipatory movements have not only been unable to solve the socio-ecological crisis but have themselves even exacerbated it in various respects: the democratic openings they have fought for have distorted political equality and representation in their own favour (e.g. Nachtwey 2018; Schäfer & Zürn 2021; Elsässer et al. 2021). In comparison to their identity-related agenda of self-determination and self-realization, they have always put the agenda of social justice and material redistribution on the back burner, thereby unintentionally encouraging the rise of right-wing populism (e.g. Boltanski & Chiapello 2017; Fraser 2017). Due to their demanding understandings of freedom and self-realization and their socio-structural roots in the educated and higher-income milieus, citizens with a high level of sustainability awareness often have resource-intensive lifestyles and an above-average ecological footprint (e.g. Kleinhückelkotten et al. 2016; Moser & Kleinhückelkotten 2018). Certain segments of the eco-emancipatory movements have, in an 'unholy alliance' (Fraser & Monticelli 2021: 14), made common cause with neoliberalism (e.g. Amlinger & Nachtwey 2025). And as political, journalistic or academic activists, they have contributed to the dangerous narrative that modern societies have fully recognized the seriousness and urgency of the situation, are determined to initiate a structural transformation towards sustainability, and are already on the right track towards its implementation. But just as the myth of the global leadership role and superiority of modern Western societies is collapsing in the late-modern constellation, the myth of the leadership role and superiority of the pioneers of the EEP is collapsing, too.

Thus, late-modern societies are at a critical and unsettling point. Although the sustainability crisis is tightening in all its dimensions, the pacifist, civil society, ecological and grassroots democratic visions of an alternative society appear to be conspicuously exhausted. Late-modern societies are not only experiencing the multidimensional untenability of the existing social order more concretely than ever before. They are also experiencing the untenability of what they previously considered to be the alternative: the eco-emancipatory project. This dual exhaustion is indeed an abyss. And against the backdrop of the promises of self-determination, self-efficacy and self-empowerment that progressive movements had continuously renewed and deeply engrained in mainstream thinking, looking into this abyss is utterly traumatic, indeed.

2.5 Beyond the critical orthodoxies

As yet, sociology does not manage to do justice to this new constellation. Just like the social movement literature, significant parts of environmental and sustainability sociology – as well as social theory – remain caught up in their traditional normativity. They move primarily in the realm of demands, wishes and appeals. Already in the noughties, Ulrich Beck noted that sociology was 'neither equipped nor inclined to fulfil its proper task of situating the current transformation of its research object in the social-historical process and thus to offer a diagnostic perspective on the epochal signature of the new era of modernity' (Beck 2009: 192). This is still – or once again – true today. (Sustainability) sociology remains ill-equipped and unwilling to grasp the special nature of late-modern society and its transformation. The task would be, firstly, to grasp its distinctive features, the specifically late-modern, much more precisely and, secondly, to go beyond theorizing late modernity towards conceptualizing the emerging next society without this endeavour becoming stuck in the transformative normativity that is currently still dominant. For social theory is not about hoping for a better or liberated society but about grasping and explaining the specifically late-modern and the other modernity that is actually emerging beyond such hopes. However, both in their analysis of the present and in their perspectives on the next society, significant parts of the activist literature and critical sociology remain in their established paths. Horrified by the abyss that is opening up in late modernity, they are, adopting a term from Zygmunt Bauman's *Retrotopia*, drawn back to critical sociology's 'tribal fire' (Bauman 2017: 49ff) – in the hope of finding some warmth and reassurance from the remnants of the discipline's traditional values and agendas. This is noticeable even where sociology makes an explicit effort to break out of its traditional normativity.

Andreas Reckwitz, for example, distances himself from the legacy of critical theory: 'Critical analysis, yes', he notes, but 'debunking, no' (Reckwitz 2023: 88).[2] However, when he speaks of the 'disillusioned present' (Reckwitz 2021: 1–13), he primarily refers to the crumbling of the assumption of classical modernization theory that ongoing modernization brings a continuous improvement in living conditions for all sections of society. Reckwitz's diagnosis of the 'end of illusions'

---

[2] This is a more direct translation of the German original. Official translation: 'an attitude that was pro-critical analytics and anti-iconoclastic deconstruction'.

is thus directed at the classic, linear optimism about progress that 'many people in Western countries had harboured since the end of the Cold War in 1989/90', but which has since been 'fundamentally disappointed, or at least relativized'. He rightly notes that the hopes and promises of classical modernization theory 'from today's perspective [. . .] seem rather naïve' and that, instead, 'the genre of *dystopia*' now prevails (ibid.: 2, 5). However, Reckwitz does not grasp the actual trauma and the distinctive quality of the disillusioned present, since the classical, linear optimism of progress had already collapsed much earlier. And today's specifically late-modern disillusionment does not primarily stem from the disappointed promise of classical, industrial modernity, but from the secondary optimism of progress fostered by the participatory and eco-emancipatory revolution. Their protagonists had already broken with the blind trust in linear progress in the 1970s and, following on from Horkheimer and Adorno's analysis of the *dialectic of enlightenment*, aimed to address the 'organized irresponsibility' of the modern 'risk society' (Horkheimer & Adorno 1994 [1944]; Beck 1992).

Today's disillusionment is thus much more serious than what Reckwitz captures. From today's perspective, the illusion does not lie in the belief in *linearity*, but – this is explained in more detail in Chapter 5 – in the belief in *reflexivity*. The (ecological) apocalypse was already feared in the 1970s and during the Cold War. Since then, the biophysical conditions have deteriorated significantly, while at the same time both the demands for self-realization and the expectations regarding the ability to influence and control politics have grossly increased. It is precisely this aggravated imbalance between social expectations and demands, on the one hand, and the experience of biophysical limits and narrow boundaries of the ability to control and shape, on the other, that forms the core of the late-modern constellation and disillusionment.

This said, Reckwitz is right in pointing out that 'the end of illusions' does not necessarily have to 'lead to all-encompassing pessimism'. He correctly notes that 'the absence of illusions can also be a virtue' that opens up the space for a differentiated analysis and sheds light on 'the paradoxes and ambivalences' of late-modern society (Reckwitz 2021: 6). Furthermore, he convincingly portrays societal development as an alternation of waves of 'contingency opening' and 'contingency closing' and the crisis of late modernity as a 'crisis of contingency excess' (Reckwitz 2023: 72ff). And in contrast to many others, Reckwitz no longer sees the malaise of late-modern societies, first and foremost, as a crisis of capitalism. He no longer thinks primarily from the perspective of power, domination, oppression and alienation, but from the perspective of emancipatory boundary-crossing and excessive liberation (cf. Chapter 4).

This is an approach also shared by Carolin Amlinger and Oliver Nachtwey (2025) who no longer explain the pandemic protests, the tide of populism and the wide appeal of conspiracy theories as a lack of education and understanding, but as the result of emancipatory processes and the unfulfilled expectations they had nurtured (e.g. 2025: 126). However, with their portraits of those *drifting*, of the *fallen*, the *twisted*, the *crazy*, the *out-of-touch*, the *aggressive*, the *destructive* and the *regressive*, they renew the familiar bourgeois categories and self-righteousness (ibid., chs. 6–8; see also Amlinger & Nachtwey 2021). Their analysis reproduces the established categories of critique. They examine the 'aggressive energies' that 'increasingly turn destructively against the social order', but they fail to grasp the untenability of this order itself and its metamorphosis into the next society (ibid.: 321, 303). In late modernity, however, taking a step beyond those norms that Amlinger and Nachtwey simply reaffirm would be more than overdue. After all, these norms have long been criticized from a variety of emancipatory perspectives – ecological, feminist and postcolonial; and as I will explain more thoroughly in Chapter 6, they have long since reflexively unhinged themselves, too. And empirically, Europe and the West, which stand for these norms, have forfeited their geo-cultural leadership role.

Another author who seeks to move beyond the critical orthodoxy and, for this reason, has been very present in recent debates in Germany is Philipp Staab. Staab criticizes the sociological mainstream for 'clinging to an outdated normativity' when, instead, it should 'explore the departure from modernity as the distinctive feature of the next society' (Staab 2022: 92). He turns against the 'classical sociologies of freedom' because he believes that, empirically, there is evidence for a 'replacement of the cultural primacy of self-development' and for the 'rejection of a modern concept of emancipation' (ibid.: 39, 27, 25). In late-modern societies, he claims, the 'actual leitmotif' is no longer 'self-development', but rather 'self-preservation' (ibid.: 7). The agenda of emancipation, he suggests, is increasingly replaced by that of 'adaptation', which seeks 'relief' from the heavy burdens that the notion of emancipation implies. This is an important hypothesis which will be explored in more detail later in this book (see Chapters 5 and 6.3). But, ultimately, Staab does not grasp the specifically late-modern, either. In the end, he, too, is still concerned with realizing potentials for freedom that he suspects he will find in the 'relief from the impositions of self-development', in 'the rejection of a modern concept of emancipation', and in the liberation from the syndrome of excessive demands and overload caused by the pressure of late-modern singularization (ibid.: 107, 28, 25). More specifically, Staab believes that the 'adaptive society' will give rise to an 'adaptive way of life that is completely alien to modern progressive thinking', and to an 'adaptation politics' that gives 'priority to the general over the particular' and focuses on 'collective obligation and self-responsible self-management at the expense of competitive self-development' (ibid.: 27, 115, 23). Thus, essentially, Staab's thinking about the adaptive society is still inspired by the prolonged hope of *a good life for all*. Ultimately, Staab, too, is warming himself over the dying embers of sociology's tribal fire. But the empirical evidence for this asserted priority of the general over the particular is thin. In late-modern societies, a *liberation from* the neoliberal, singularized subject 'as an effect of increased subjective reflection' (ibid.: 107) is, at best, a very marginal phenomenon, while the evidence for the progressive *liberation of* the neoliberal, singularized subject from collective obligations is much richer.

In the sociological theory of late modernity, it is, therefore, no longer enough to think of a 'halved' modernity or the 'unfinished project' of modernity with a view to completing it (Beck 1993: 25; Habermas 1980). Rather, the objective must be to grasp a fundamentally different modernity. The suspicion that the earlier beliefs and hopes of progressive, critical, emancipatory politics and sociology may have become illusory, untenable or anachronistic today, invariably runs the risk of being misunderstood and/or appropriated for ideological purposes that are actually alien to it. This makes the sociology of late modernity a dangerous terrain (see Blühdorn 2020c). However, the diagnosis of the untenability of certain assumptions and established beliefs of critical (sustainability) sociology and the EEP in no way implies a call for anti-democratic, anti-egalitarian, anti-ecological or anti-emancipatory values. Rather, it is about recognizing that many of these earlier assumptions and beliefs have proven empirically wrong in late-modern societies – and normatively questionable: not only do they not lead to the promised solution, they sometimes even exacerbate the problem. These beliefs and the political struggle to realize them have quite obviously not led late-modern societies to a socially and ecologically pacified society. Neither as the sole cause, of course, nor consciously and intentionally, have they led to the brink of disaster and to the threshold of a new modernity that leaves the basic values of the previous one behind – or spells them out in an entirely different way. Transformative sustainability research can and must recognize this, even if this fundamentally upsets its critical orthodoxies – and even if it is not immediately clear what could take the place of the shattered illusions. For, in sociology, too, a limit has been reached, and by refusing to face up to the untenability of its own categories and beliefs, critical (sustainability) sociology not only violates the standards it sets for itself. Like those parts of the emancipatory movements that Nancy Fraser and others accuse of 'progressive neoliberalism', it is at risk of slipping into an 'unholy alliance' with the established order (Fraser 2017, 2019; Fraser & Monticelli 2021; see also Blühdorn & Dannemann 2019).

— 3 —

GREAT TRANSFORMATIONS

In line with public discourse, the epochal societal change (*Zeitenwende*) discussed in this book has so far been described as an *abyss*, a *state of emergency*, as the *shattering of illusions*. Moving a step further, I will now approach it somewhat more neutrally via five major transformations, which are primarily discussed in the social science literature. Thus, sociological diagnoses of crisis now shift into the centre of attention which have been offered from a variety of different perspectives – the critique of capitalism, the emphasis on planetary boundaries, the analysis of the autocratic-authoritarian turn, the technological perspective on the digital revolution and artificial intelligence, and the geopolitical or geo-philosophical point of view. The implications of each of these transformations are so comprehensive that for every one of them one might rightly say, as Naomi Klein (2015) put it: *this changes everything!* In the respective literature, each of these diagnoses is usually immediately translated into counter-strategies and demands aiming to safeguard the central norms that the respective diagnoses perceive to be under threat. The focus on the transformations addressed here is selective, of course. There is no intention to provide a complete picture of the profound societal change that is going on. Rather, the aim is (a) to identify specific characteristics of late-modern society; (b) to determine more precisely what is actually untenable, unsustainable and exhausted in late-modern society; (c) to determine what, conversely, can be regarded – even if it violates established norms – as a likely characteristic of the emerging new modernity and the next society; and (d) to identify a common core of these five diagnoses of crisis and major transformations, which in subsequent chapters will then be further investigated from the perspective of social theory.

The term 'great transformation' has recently become popular in the wake of a revival of Karl Polanyi's classic *The Great Transformation* (Polanyi 1957 [1944]). In Polanyi's work, the concept primarily refers to the destructive transformation of early modern society through its progressive marketization and liberal individualism. Polanyi argued that, together, the two were driving the disembedding of the market from its social context and the disintegration of the basic social and biophysical conditions of modern societies. Polanyi was convinced that the idea of a self-regulating market was a 'stark utopia', that the philosophy of liberalism was destructive and that a pure market society 'could not exist for any length of time without annihilating the human and natural substance of society' (Polanyi 1957 [1944]: 3). He described the dynamics of marketization as a 'satanic mill'. The 'inevitable result of the liberal philosophy', he wrote, was first the comprehensive destabilization of society and then the 'victory of fascism', which implied 'freedom's utter frustration' (ibid.: 73, 257). However, Polanyi also developed the thesis that the socially destructive forces of liberal capitalism could mobilize counter-forces that would once again contain the market and the individual's striving for freedom. And if the economy was once again 'embedded in social relations', he hoped, and society was no longer treated merely 'as an adjunct to the market', the 'ruins of the Old World' might give rise to the 'cornerstones of a New'. However, Polanyi was doubtful whether such counter-movements would really be strong enough. He feared that the fierce resistance of liberals to any reform involving 'planning, regulation and control' would ultimately block such attempts and that 'the victory of fascism' would then, indeed, be the 'inevitable result' of liberalism (ibid.: 57, 254, 257).

Polanyi was concerned with the great transformation on the threshold from feudal to industrial society, that is, the early phase of modern, capitalist society. Today, in contrast, we find ourselves in late modernity and, if we follow the diagnoses of neo-Marxist observers, in crisis-ridden *late capitalism* – which, incidentally, leading sociologists had already diagnosed in the early 1970s (cf. e.g. Offe 1972; Habermas 1976). Polanyi had left open the question of where a fully marketized society might find, and how it might mobilize, the resources that could provide the normative yardstick and a political roadmap for the social (and ecological) containment of market liberalism. Today, this question is even more difficult to answer. Notwithstanding, in the wake of the banking and financial crisis from 2008 and of the warnings by the Intergovernmental Panel on Climate Change about the clearly foreseeable consequences of climate change, not only Polanyi's radical criticism of market liberalism developed great appeal, but also his idea of a corrective counter-movement. After all, Polanyi had held out the prospect that 'the passing of the market society could become the beginning of an era of unprecedented freedom', in which freedom could be realized 'not only for the few, but for all'. Furthermore, anticipating the concerns of the new movements sparked by the financial crisis, he explicitly referred to the 'natural substance of society' and warned that industrialism and market liberalism would ultimately lead to the 'inevitable self-destruction of civilisation' and 'extinguish the [human] race', if they were not 'subordinated to the requirements of man's nature' (Polanyi 1957 [1944]: 256, 3, 4, 248).

First, the German Advisory Council on Global Change (WBGU) used Polanyi's term in the German title of its landmark report *World in Transition: A Social Contract for Sustainability* (*Welt im Wandel: Gesellschaftsvertrag für eine Große Transformation*; WBGU 2011). Then the term 'socio-ecological transformation' quickly became standard in the relevant literature (e.g. United Nations 2015; U. Brand 2016; K.W. Brand 2017; Schneidewind 2018; Luks 2019; Aulenbacher et al. 2019; U. Brand et al. 2019). Yet, in comparison to Polanyi's work, the term changed its meaning: the ecological or biophysical aspect had played a rather marginal role for Polanyi, but now it moved to the centre. Also, Polanyi's focus was on the retrospective analysis of the dynamics that led to the social crisis he was discussing, whereas in today's transformation literature, the focus is on the counter-movement that is supposed to lead us out of the late-modern sustainability crisis. Furthermore, the current appropriation of the term ignores the fact that the actors of the EEP see themselves as this counter-movement and as the avant-garde of an SET, but are at the same time heirs of the liberal project that Polanyi holds responsible for the great crisis. And the question of the normative resources that can be mobilized for the counter-movement and an SET, which Polanyi had left unresolved, remains largely unanswered in the current literature, too, although the shift in focus to this counter-movement should actually make this question central. And finally, today's ecosociological appropriation of the concept is also questionable insofar as Polanyi aimed to restore a claim and enforce a norm – freedom and a good life for all – that he fully believed in, while in late modernity exactly this norm is, arguably, being challenged or even abandoned (see Blühdorn 2020d and Chapters 5 and 6).

3.1 Capitalism in crisis?

For these reasons, I want to shift the emphasis back towards those major transformations that can actually be observed in late-modern society, which render an SET in the eco-emancipatory sense increasingly impossible, and which are at the same time – using Polanyi's words – the 'cornerstones of the new world' and the key parameters defining the framework for the truly great transformation that this book is ultimately about. For many observers, the first such key parameter that comes to mind in this context is the crisis and transformation of capitalism. Particularly after the banking and financial crisis of 2008/9, the condition of late-modern societies and their transformation were, once again, widely viewed from this perspective. Since the mid-1980s and especially after 1989, the critique of capitalism and the framing of the sustainability crisis as a consequence of capitalism had receded into the background. The banking and financial crisis, however, triggered a striking renaissance of Marxist crisis theory. In view of the catastrophe of neoliberalism, which had become hegemonic in the 1990s, the old thesis was rehabilitated that 'the heterogeneous grievances – financial, economic, ecological, political, social – that surround us can be traced back to a common root' and that 'our crisis can best be understood [. . .] as a *crisis of capitalism*' (Fraser 2015a: 94). It is obvious, Nancy Fraser noted, that the current multiple crises do not correspond to the 'traditional standard models of capitalist crises', because they encompass 'not only the official economy, including the financial sector, but also non-economic phenomena such as global warming, welfare deficits and the erosion of state power at every level' (ibid.: 95). However, if capitalism is understood not only as an economic system, but also as an 'institutionalized social order' and a 'certain way of life' (Fraser 2015a: 107–109; Jaeggi 2013: 16–20; Fraser & Jaeggi 2018), she suggested, then the malaise of late-modern societies and their social struggles can very well be understood as a crisis of capitalism.

With the financial crisis, Fraser believed, the contradictions and the 'deep-seated crisis tendencies' of this order have now become 'painfully obvious' (Fraser & Monticelli 2021: 8). And as 'reforms that do not address the deep structural causes of these grievances are doomed to failure', there is now a realistic perspective for an SET and a post-capitalist society (Fraser 2015a: 94). In her view, especially those areas of society that are not yet fully commodified, that are not yet fully penetrated by marketization and the commodity logic, are reservoirs for 'alternative normative and ontological grammars', which are 'rich in critical-political possibilities' and could release 'emancipatory potential' for 'new configurations of economy, society, nature and political communities' (ibid.: 107, 110, 114). In times of crisis, it is not just Fraser who believes that 'resources for an anti-capitalist struggle' could be found here, in which the 'most progressive currents' of society would have to unite to form a 'bloc against the system' (ibid.: 112, 94), a 'radical, counter-hegemonic and anti-capitalist alliance' (Fraser & Monticelli 2021; see also Crouch 2004; Tauss 2016; Mason 2016; Mouffe 2023; Brand et al. 2021).

There is no doubt that ideological market liberalism and deregulated international financial capitalism ran into a fundamental crisis in 2008/9. It is also widely documented that the capitalist economic system is incessantly eroding its social and ecological foundations and has for decades produced only modest growth rates in developed industrial societies – which has benefited relatively small sections of society, while others, being the so-called 'losers of modernization', are paying the price for this increasingly expensive low growth. However, all this does not mean that the inherent contradictions of capitalism are now coming to a head in its final crisis, nor that it makes sense to understand the current multiple crisis primarily as a crisis of capitalism. Also, there is nothing to suggest that these multiple crises would offer particularly favourable conditions for the formation and political success of an 'anti-capitalist alliance'.

Already many decades ago, Claus Offe and Jürgen Habermas had believed that capitalism had entered its late phase (Offe 1972; Habermas 1976). Offe had described the Keynesian state as an essential instrument for stabilizing capitalism, which in its postliberal phase, he believed, could only be secured and supported by comprehensive state intervention and control – that is, Keynesian investment policy and welfare state protection. Habermas saw the neoliberal attack on these two political instruments as the trigger for a political legitimation crisis in late capitalism, which was further intensified by the increasing colonization of people's everyday lives by system logics and system imperatives. However, there were other instruments beyond the Keynesian state that could ensure the continued existence of capitalism (cf. e.g. Streeck 2013). And while the neoliberal attack on the welfare state as well as the colonization of the 'lifeworld' by the logics of the economic-administrative system did cause a political crisis of legitimacy, this did not lead to the collapse of capitalism. Rather, so-called 'late capitalism' proved to be surprisingly adaptable, resilient and durable. It was able to use the emancipatory agendas of the NSM since the late 1960s to forge a 'new spirit of capitalism' (Boltanski & Chiapello 2017) and metamorphose into a new form: creative knowledge capitalism. Similarly, capitalism was, and remains, able to use the ecological, technological and cultural conditions of late modernity for a further adaptation that renews it once again, strengthens it and makes it more resilient. Climate change and the decarbonization project have long since become a driving force for the development of innovative technologies and for the opening up of new markets. The same applies to the digital revolution, in the course of which gigantic data collections are becoming an essential resource for a renewed capitalism (cf. e.g. Zuboff 2018).

The crisis of globalized financial capitalism, therefore, by no means heralds the end of capitalism. While the end of *democratic* capitalism has indeed been in sight for some time, capitalism itself survives well without democracy and human rights (cf. e.g. Crouch 2004; Streeck 2014); indeed, under the logic of 'capitalist realism', it no longer needs legitimacy, especially not democratic legitimacy (Fisher 2009). China, which is striving for global dominance, provides unmistakable evidence. In Germany, trade policy towards the People's Republic and energy procurement policy towards Russia, Qatar and other authoritarian states illustrate that economic interests and securing prosperity, ultimately, tend to take precedence over democracy and human rights. A final crisis of capitalism, on the other hand, is just as little in sight as a politically promising alternative to capitalism, be it as an economic system, an 'institutionalized social order' or as 'a way of life'. In fact, even Nancy Fraser concedes that, as yet, 'despite the widely felt reality of an acute system crisis, intense suffering and pervasive malaise do not become a practical force of social transformation' (Fraser 2015b: 186f).

It is therefore hardly surprising that the renaissance, which the theory of the crisis of capitalism experienced after the banking and financial crisis of 2008/9, has already faded once again. The main problem with this theory is that it draws on norms that no longer have the power in late-modern society that the critics of capitalism and the champions of a post-capitalist society ascribe to them. 'The fundamental or comprehensive critique of capitalist modernity', Carolin Amlinger and Oliver Nachtwey write, 'can barely be heard these days – and if it does make itself heard, it essentially lacks any prospect of ever being considered or implemented' (Amlinger & Nachtwey 2025: 255). Contrary to all hopes for an 'anti-capitalist alliance', there is no widespread experience of alienation and no societal longing for a transformation of capitalism in late-modern societies that is sufficiently strong and politically organized. Despite the proliferation of increasingly violent social conflicts, the kind of legitimation crisis once predicted by Habermas has not materialized. And although there is much talk about 'pioneers of change' and their 'prefigurative politics' (cf. e.g. Monticelli 2021; Fians 2022) already rehearsing what eventually will be extended to a good life for all, there is no sufficiently integrative and attractive vision of a better societal alternative. The proponents of crisis theory not only under-estimated the adaptability of capitalism, but also that of citizens and of the limits of what is socially perceived as acceptable, reasonable and controllable. Yet from as early as the 1960s, Herbert Marcuse had pointed out that, in view of the amenities of capitalist consumer society, 'the very notion of alienation', which is so important for the concept of the legitimation crisis, is becoming 'questionable'. The 'consciousness of servitude', he noted, on which 'all liberation' neces-sarily depends, is becoming less and less common and, thus, 'critical theory is left without the rationale for transcending' the established form of society (Marcuse 1964: 11, 9, xliv).

This early reminder of the centrality and adaptability of social norms is important here because the proponents of Marxian crisis theory disregard too easily that any critique of capitalism is, ulti-mately, always normative. This is true even if they claim not to apply any external normative criteria to capitalism, but to focus on its inter-nal contradictions only, and to expose its built-in tendency towards self-destabilization and self-destruction. For, 'if capitalism seems set to fail as a social and economic system', Rahel Jaeggi correctly points out, 'this failure is always linked to the fact that we *do not want to live* in this particular way – and not that we *cannot* live this way' (Jaeggi 2013: 7). 'The crisis', Habermas, too, had already emphasized in the early 1970s, 'cannot be separated from the viewpoint of the one who is undergoing it' (Habermas 1976: 1). Accordingly, the observation that capitalism is destroying its own – ecological, social, political – foundations does not necessarily mean that its collapse is imminent but, first and foremost, that it will have ecological, social and political consequences that violate established ideals and norms of ecological, social and political acceptability. That is a crucial dif-ference! Whether and for how long capitalism can then continue to exist in conditions that, when measured against these norms, appear as ecologically, socially and politically unsustainable, that are con-sidered socially undesirable, is a completely different matter. 'If we are of the opinion', Jaeggi elaborates, that capitalist 'society *does not work*, it is [. . .] precisely because we think it *does not work well*, i.e.

it *should* not work in this way'. So, the point is not actually that this society and capitalism really do not work, but that the ways in which they work contradict certain norms and expectations. 'We consider certain ways of functioning – for example, an economic dynamic at the expense of the future or at the expense of the excluded – to be *wrong*', Jaeggi notes. A society 'behind bars does not correspond to our idea of what society is or should be' (Jaeggi 2013: 7). However, this does not mean that a society behind bars – or behind fortified border fences – is not possible, nor that common ideas of what society is or should be are unchangeable. If necessary – and this is, in fact, a quite normal social practice – they can be adapted according to prevailing value preferences and social priorities.

All this suggests that it is not capitalism that is in crisis today and threatening to collapse – though it is perhaps undergoing another adjustment crisis. Rather, in late-modern society, the system of norms on which Marxian crisis theory and the visions of a post-capitalist society are based is losing its power. Hence, a crisis of legitimacy in Habermas's sense is not to be expected. At least, not one that would jeopardize the continued existence of capitalism. Instead, in late modernity, the self-description and self-image of modern societies as liberal, democratic, inclusive, ecological 'open societies' are being readjusted. Only on the basis of these modernist norms and self-descriptions can the perceived crisis of capitalism be understood as a crisis at all – and these norms are the core of emancipatory visions of a better society. Capitalism, on the other hand, can continue to exist beyond the disintegration of this modernist value system – as long as ways and means are found to politically manage and psychologically withstand the socio-ecological norm violations that capitalism continues to generate.

So, there is no doubt that capitalism and its logic are largely responsible for the current state of modern society and its multiple untenability. However, in order to better understand the late-modern condition and transformation, sociology must go beyond the traditional narratives of capitalism's systemic crisis and post-capitalist society. For, although the current multiple crises and untenability can be explained – at least in part – by the logic of capitalism, for the time being they do not concern capitalism itself but, above all, the norms on the basis of which capitalism has so far been described as crisis-ridden and which underlie the ideas of a post-capitalist society. If we attribute the multidimensional sustainability crisis primarily to the destructive logic of capitalism, we fail to grasp what is special about late-modern societies. And if we think of the current crisis primarily as the transitional stage between the escalating untenability of the existing order and the liberated, socially and ecologically pacified post-capitalist society, we adopt a rather restricted perspective.

3.2 Planetary boundaries and the Anthropocene

From an environmental perspective, the key terms currently used to describe and discuss the peculiarity of late modernity and its untenability are the Anthropocene as the name for a new geological age and the concept of planetary boundaries, which has already been mentioned repeatedly. The term Anthropocene has found its way into many debates since the beginning of the new century (Crutzen & Stoermer 2000; Crutzen 2002; Crutzen & Steffen 2003). It means that humans have become a determining force in the history of the Earth. From the perspective of natural and Earth system science, the term takes up what was already widely discussed in the humanities and social sciences in the 1980s and 1990s as the 'end of nature', the complete socialization of nature and, thus, the loss of supposedly objective, extra-societal reference points and fundamentalist norms (cf. e.g. Merchant 1980; Beck 1986; Luhmann 1986a; McKibben 1990; Böhme 1992). The concept of planetary boundaries became prominent a few years later. It updates what has been discussed since the early 1970s as the limits to growth and refers to parameters such as global land use, global (fresh) water resources, available phosphorus and nitrogen reserves, biodiversity and, in particular, the man-made warming of the Earth's atmosphere. The attempt to determine planetary boundaries in these areas, which must not be exceeded, aims to identify tipping or trigger points, the transgression of which sets in motion destructive dynamics that can no longer be controlled and could ultimately even endanger the survival of humanity (cf. e.g. Rockström et al. 2009a, 2009b; Steffen et al. 2015; Rockström et al. 2021; Brand et al. 2021; Blühdorn 2022a).

Both terms imply an entirely new perspective from which so-called ecological or environmental problems, questions and solutions are conceived. Crucially, they both radically question the traditional dichotomy between humans and nature, society and the environment, social systems and ecological systems. The more recent adoption of the term 'environment', in contrast to the older concept of 'nature', no longer refers to something radically different and independent, but to something related to society. Yet, the Anthropocene fully dissolves this dualism. As Ulrich Beck put it almost forty years ago, the global 'triumphant procession of the industrial system causes the boundaries between nature and society to become blurred'. Accordingly, he continued at the time, 'the destructions of nature can no longer be shifted off onto the *environment*, but as they are universalized by industry, they become social, political, economic and cultural contradictions inherent in the system' (Beck 1992: 154). In the new geological age, a distinction is no longer made between social systems and ecosystems; instead, the Earth system is viewed as a whole in which social and ecological systems are integrated (Schellnhuber 1999). The terms 'Anthropocene' and 'planetary boundaries' therefore describe a fundamental transformation of socio-ecological relations. There is no longer an 'environment' that is external to society, from which raw materials could be imported into the system and into which waste materials could be exported. Everything is an 'inner world', and what were previously described as environmental hazards are now 'inner world hazards' (Beck 1988: 173).

Against this backdrop, conventional terms such as 'nature conservation' or 'environmental policy' no longer make sense, for, so-called environmental policy no longer has its own object and sphere of influence. In fact, it no longer has its own institutions that are distinct from the institutions of social, economic or foreign and security policy. The concept of sustainability policy – which, depending on the underlying understanding of sustainability, also had economic, social, political and cultural dimensions – was much more comprehensive than the older concept of environmental policy or even nature conservation. But in the Anthropocene the ecological dimensions can no longer be separated from other dimensions of politics, at all. Rather than the protection of and responsibility for the extra-societal world, the core issue is now the safeguarding of the preconditions of life (or survival) on the planet. Food security, rising sea levels, biodiversity and migration dynamics – these are all global concerns of a global domestic policy that can no longer be organized nationally and can no longer be managed by the traditional institutions of climate and environmental policy.

On the one hand, reaching and crossing planetary boundaries and the new geological age of the Anthropocene represent a considerable danger and threat. At the same time, however, for many observers, both concepts and the specificity of the constellation they attempt to capture also hold hope and promise. For, in a sense, the planetary boundaries and the catastrophic consequences of transgressing them are a new opportunity to diagnose objective problems, that is, problems that are independent of changing social perceptions and norms, from which truly categorical imperatives for action can be derived. The scientific definition of 'non-negotiable planetary conditions that humanity needs to respect' promises concrete instructions for action and objective imperatives of ecological limitation (Rockström et al. 2009b, no page number). And reaching or exceeding tipping points beyond which human action will no longer be able to 'reverse, steer, or substantially slow' the destructive dynamics of 'strong, intrinsic, biogeophysical feedbacks' implies that 'widespread, rapid, and fundamental' countermeasures must be taken immediately (Steffen et al. 2018: 6). The great appeal of the concept of planetary boundaries lies, therefore, in this combination of concrete instructions for action or limitation and absolute urgency. The attempt by Earth system science to define a 'safe operating space for humanity' within such boundaries could provide exactly what ecological movements have been urgently lacking (Rockström et al. 2009a, 2009b, 2021). It renews earlier attempts to derive from ecological issues what Marxist social criticism had always sought but found increasingly difficult to offer: compelling reference norms, imperatives and guidelines for a fundamental social transformation.

However, the hope that the concept of planetary boundaries could provide a significant impetus for an SET is questionable insofar as the supposedly non-negotiable boundaries actually always have a normative core. As with the functional critique of capitalism, in the case of planetary boundaries, too, we may not want to live in a society and world that exceeds these boundaries because this contradicts established norms and expectations, but this does not mean that we could not live in such a world. The frequent reference to the (un)inhabitability of the planet is therefore misleading. We are back here to the problem known from Marxist crisis theory: if planetary boundaries are exceeded, there is certainly no longer a good life for all, since devastating catastrophes, great suffering and the increasing loss of the ability to control and steer are among the unavoidable consequences. These are the central characteristics of the Anthropocene, and there is ample empirical evidence of such catastrophes, suffering and loss of control. But this says nothing about society's ability to accept and cope with these consequences, and accordingly nothing about the durability and sustainability of the practices and arrangements that cause them.

What is untenable beyond these planetary boundaries is, therefore, not necessarily the established practices and arrangements that movements and scientists describe as unsustainable, but first and foremost the standards used to assess them. However, as noted above, these are flexible, and accordingly, the tenability of the unsustainable is essentially a question of adaptation and resilience. Adaptation and resilience have, in fact, long since become the primary goal in sustainability research; and they are the priority project of late-modern sustainability policy. Neither researchers nor policymakers talk explicitly about adapting social norms and expectations, of course, regarding de-problematizing increasing inequality, ecological destruction or social exclusion. However, this does not mean that there is not considerable potential for this, the realization of which is, in fact, a core component of any resilience and adaptation policy (see Chapters 7.3 and 7.4). The hope that determining, reaching and exceeding planetary boundaries could provide a significant impetus, a normative guideline and a concrete roadmap for an SET is, therefore, misguided.

Regarding the new geological era, the Anthropocene, the situation is similar. This term is also associated with hopes. Just like the concept of planetary boundaries, the arrival of the Anthropocene is widely expected to have a mobilizing and enabling effect. For, in the Anthropocene, the familiar questions of: *How do we want to live in the future? In what world do we want to live in the future?* are more important than ever. When there is no longer an outside or counterpart of society from which categorical imperatives may emanate, the so-called ecological question becomes a radically social question. Everything becomes negotiable then, and everything must be negotiated. While for the EEP, the question: *How do we want to live in the future?* was still a largely rhetorical question, as noted in Chapter 1.2, which was never really open, in the Anthropocene this has changed fundamentally. For the EEP, the only possible moral, reasonable and responsible answer to this question emerged automatically from the modernist, normative foundations on which it was based. In the Anthropocene, however, all normative certainty (see Chapter 1.1, Table 1 and Chapter 5) – and at the same time also the EEP's confidence in its ability to act, its firm trust in the maturity, reason and responsibility of civil society – has dissolved. In the Anthropocene, the question: *How and in what world do we want to live?* is no longer normatively pre-decided in any respect, but is instead radically open in all directions. However, while the necessity of integrated *Earth system management* and coordinated *Earth system governance* (Biermann 2014) is becoming ever more pressing, the modernist assumptions and prerequisites underpinning these concepts have evaporated. These include, firstly. that a problem is first clearly identified and corresponding policy goals are determined, then suitable policy instruments are selected, and finally suitable actors and institutions implement them in a coordinated and consistent manner until the goal is achieved.

So, on the one hand, the Anthropocene is an age of unprecedented necessity and possibilities: everything is negotiable and can be shaped, and this comprehensive shaping is no longer an option, but a requirement. At the same time, however, it is also the age of hopeless overload and inbuilt failure, because all necessary prerequisites for the success of comprehensive management are missing. This failure – if there are still criteria in the new age to categorize it as such – has its cause in the core and essence of the Anthropocene itself. For the end of the dualism of nature and society means, as highlighted before, that ecological questions fully metamorphose into social questions, and there is no longer a reliable normative reference point for answering them that is not socially shaped and therefore contingent. 'Without nature', wrote climate activist and author Bill McKibben with horror back in the early 1990s, 'there is nothing but ourselves' (McKibben 1990: 54). But only the Anthropocene fully reveals what this pure self-referentiality means: nature and ecology, which after the death of God and the end of transcendental reason were supposed to act as a kind of normative substitute anchor, leave a yawning void (see also Chapters 4.4 and 5.1).

Hence, the Anthropocene means the radical centralization of social values and subjective preferences, as there is no longer any externalizing objectification. This amounts to a hyper-centring of the human that goes far beyond any anthropocentrism in eco-political thinking so far. Unsurprisingly, therefore, eco-modernist ideas of science- and technology-based Earth system governance are once again gaining considerable momentum in the Anthropocene – in the Promethean dream of the 'good Anthropocene' (cf. e.g. Neyrat 2019). At the same time, however, the Anthropocene itself leads beyond this subject- and human-centred thinking – just as Luhmann's theory of social systems had already considered the classic subject- and autonomy-centred thinking of sociology to be misguided. For, in the integrated socio-ecological system that emerges with the dissolution of the traditional dualism, the human being is an integrated player and no longer has an elevated position, in particular no control position. In line with the old ecological critique of Promethean arrogance and the old demand that humans must integrate themselves into nature and comply with its laws, the literature on the Anthropocene is, therefore, also renewing the demand for a radically different understanding of subjectivity, autonomy and emancipation (cf. e.g. Latour 2017, 2018; Dobson 2022; Pellizzoni 2022).

Thus, at the planetary boundaries and in the global domestic politics of the Anthropocene, the need for management, limitation, regulation, disaster management – that is, for Earth system governance – is greater than ever, at least from the traditional modernist perspective. However, as the preconditions for this project are not met (or are rapidly disintegrating), related efforts remain limited to tentative experimentation as a mode of coping with a condition of *ecological ungovernability*. Because the complexity of the circumstances is too high and the volatility of the situation too great, because the perceptions of the problems and priorities are too diverse and there are no institutions for a coordinated, long-term and effective global domestic policy, the project of Earth system governance has little prospect of success. The hope that a 'safe operating space for humanity' can be determined and maintained by specifying planetary boundaries is unfounded. Instead, late-modern societies operate in a notoriously and chronically unsafe operating space. Instead of Earth system management, they are limited to continuous experimentation with ever new attempts to adapt and become as resilient as possible (cf. e.g. Bulkeley 2023; also Chapter 7.3).

So, just as it is wrong to expect planetary boundaries to provide a significant impetus for the EEP and the SET, the same also applies to the Anthropocene. It is, therefore, hardly surprising that the transgression of planetary boundaries and the arrival of the Anthropocene have so far remained primarily the subject of scientific discourse and have had no concrete impact at the policy level (cf. e.g. Biermann 2021; Bulkeley 2023). Nevertheless, the eco-political perspective on late-modern society, that is, its observation through the lens of planetary boundaries and the Anthropocene, makes a truly great transformation visible: the distinguishing feature of late modernity lies in the disintegration of modernist dualism and all the foundations of eco-modernist thinking that are based on this dualism. On the one hand, the emergence of the integrated system radicalizes the ecological 'principle of responsibility' insofar as humans are now a force shaping the history of the Earth (Jonas 1984). On the other hand, it also abolishes it and replaces it with a radicalized form of Ulrich Beck's 'organized irresponsibility'. By undermining the preconditions of modernist politics and destroying the belief in the ability to shape and control, the Anthropocene once again exposes human beings to unpredictable and uncontrollable conditions. Although the catastrophes of the Anthropocene are no longer natural disasters, but man-made, people have no control over them, neither in their role as the cause of these disasters nor as their victims.

The vast majority of people are largely defenceless and helpless in the face of them.

The Anthropocene thus brings back the complete insecurity of the state of nature that was thought to have been overcome. Although human lifeworlds are now completely artificial and designed, radical insecurity, vulnerability and exposure to the mercy of the uncontrollable are back. They no longer come from outside, from nature, but from within, from organized irresponsibility – which is an even more unbearable prospect from a modernist perspective. In this new state of nature, what modernist thinking had so far called 'civilization' and 'Western values', and what had been the goal of the European Enlightenment, has become untenable. Beyond the hopes for an SET and Earth system governance, the Anthropocene brings ecological ungovernability and the most favourable conditions for the rule and law of the strongest (see also Chapter 1.4). For the vast majority, however, life may well, as Hobbes put it in *Leviathan*, become poor, nasty, brutish, and short again. As in the case of crisis capitalism, the ecological and Earth system science view of late modernity, too, shows that it is not the established order of unsustainability that is untenable but, above all, the assumptions and norms that underpinned the project of the SET.

3.3 The autocratic-authoritarian turn

From a political perspective, the peculiarity, the crisis, the untenability and the great transformation of late-modern societies present themselves as the crisis of democracy and the 'autocratic-authoritarian turn' (e.g. Lührmann & Lindberg 2019; Schäfer & Zürn 2021; Blühdorn 2022a). What conservatives had feared in the 1970s and blamed on the emancipatory movements, which they criticized as hedonistic, unbridled and irresponsible (cf. e.g. King 1975; Crozier et al. 1975), has now fully materialized: perhaps the greatest political achievement of modern societies, liberal democracy, is in decline. Late-modern societies are becoming increasingly difficult to control politically, especially democratically. Their crises, conflicts and disasters – and not just ecological ones – are indeed increasingly 'ungovernable'. Although the conservatives at the time fell considerably short in their explanations of the 'ungovernability' they feared, the fact is that today the political ability to steer and control, the ability to plan and shape, is increasingly being lost. The state is less and less able to meet the high expectations of citizens, especially in the face of crises and disasters. The sustainability crisis, climate change, the migration problem, the Covid pandemic and the war in Ukraine illustrate a fundamental and structural 'overload' of the state (cf. Chapter 2.3; also Nassehi 2021). Political institutions are unceasingly losing public trust, and this applies in particular to the institutions and procedures of democracy.

The crisis of democracy has many causes. It is often attributed, above all, to the dominance of the logic of capitalism (competition, inequality, capital accumulation) over the logic of democracy (equality, inclusion, redistribution). This imbalance has become ever greater with globalization, in particular, which has rendered it much easier for international corporations to evade political control and, conversely, set the pace for politics. At the same time, globalization has weakened the power of national democratic institutions, without an adequate replacement being created at transnational level. Wendy Brown, for example, writes that 'globalization and the curtailment of the sovereign power of nation states' are 'decisive factors in the current de-democratization of the West'. With globalization, democracy is losing 'a necessary political form and containment', and with the curtailment of nation state sovereignty, states are giving up the 'claim to embody popular sovereignty and thus to carry out the will of the people'. Thus, 'democracy separated from a delimited sovereign territory', Brown argues, becomes 'politically meaningless' (Brown 2012: 60f; see also Jörke 2019).

Relatedly, the democratic crisis is also often seen as a crisis of representation: as globalized market liberalism has radically increased social inequality, ever larger sections of society no longer feel represented by political institutions (cf. e.g. Nachtwey 2018; Manow 2020; Amlinger & Nachtwey 2025). Armin Schäfer and Michael Zürn speak of a 'dual estrangement' that distances the actual political processes further and further from the democratic ideal and the citizens further and further from democratic institutions (Schäfer & Zürn 2021: 20). At the same time, the continuous expansion of formalized participation opportunities brought an asymmetrical gain in influence for social classes with strong educational and articulation skills. And the fact that, in terms of their socio-structural background, parliamentarians predominantly come from a rather narrow and in many respects privileged spectrum of society again reinforces the asymmetrical responsiveness of liberal democracies (cf. e.g. Elsässer et al. 2021).

Furthermore, the decline of democracy is also widely explained by the rise of right-wing populism and the 'aggressive' and 'destructive' energies of 'regressive rebels', who are described by many as the greatest threat to democracy (e.g. Schäfer & Zürn 2021; Amlinger & Nachtwey 2025: 220–247). Another major cause is the recent structural change in the public sphere as a result of the spread of social media and the digital revolution (cf. e.g. Habermas 2021). Social media in particular are held responsible for the fact that the public sphere and public discourse are breaking down into ever smaller arenas in which communication is primarily identity-reinforcing and self-confirming, that is, oriented towards the in-group, but much less pluralistic and oriented towards recognizing, let alone understanding, alternative positions. Another key factor in the crisis and transformation of democracy is the change in prevailing social understandings of subjectivity, self-determination and a good life. Ideals of the complex and flexible personality, of dynamic and fleeting identity, are just as problematic in relation to democracy, as understandings of freedom and self-determination that cannot be generalized (e.g. Blühdorn 2013, 2020d, 2022a; see also Chapter 6.4). And last but not least, the decline of democracy is also seen as a crisis of acceleration and as a consequence of the ongoing differentiation and increase in complexity (e.g. Bauman 1999, 2000; Rosa 2015; Reckwitz & Rosa 2023; Nassehi 2021).

These different explanations are not alternatives to each other, but rather complement and reinforce each other. Taken together, they mean that very diverse social groups develop a profoundly ambivalent relationship to democracy, each for their own specific reasons (cf. e.g. Blühdorn 2018, 2020c). However, the hypothesis of an *emancipatory* de-democratization, in particular – which is discussed in greater detail in Chapter 6.4 – receives relatively little attention. Yet, in terms of democratic politics, it is exactly this that is, arguably, the specifically late-modern feature of the current constellation and of the great transformation towards the next society. From this perspective, the distinctive quality of late modernity actually lies in the fact that democracy, which, despite its roots in ancient Greece, was a specifically modern invention and an ideal that is closely linked to the Enlightenment idea of the autonomous subject, is simply no longer tenable in and beyond late modernity – and not just because the empirical prerequisites are no longer fulfilled, but also in normative terms. Indirectly, of course, this has long been recognized. This can be seen, for example, in the new mistrust of green parties towards the previously favoured idea of grassroots democracy, or in the climate movement's demands on the state to take leadership. The neoliberal attempts to deliberately depoliticize (and therefore also de-democratize) public administration may be seen as evidence of this, too; likewise, the tendency to no longer interpret so-called experimental politics primarily as a promising strategy for a socio-ecological sustainability transformation, but – at least also – as a response to the crisis of modernist politics and the problem of ecological ungovernability (e.g. Bulkeley 2023; Blühdorn 2023; Haderer 2023; see also Chapter 7.3).

However, in most of the relevant literature, more or less detailed diagnoses of the crisis of democracy are immediately followed by suggestions for how democracy might be stabilized, defended or restored. The idea that under the conditions of late modernity such a restoration and defence of democracy might not only be empirically hopeless, but perhaps not even normatively desirable, is rarely explored (cf. e.g. Brennan 2016; van Reybrouck 2016). But in fact, in late-modern societies – even if the vociferous criticism of democratic deficits and the manifold demands for genuine democracy seem to suggest otherwise – the claim to democratic self-determination is often willingly abandoned and ceded, not least because of the burdens, obligations and responsibilities that necessarily accompany democratic self-government. The unceasing calls for commitment, engagement and responsibility and the associated moral pressure are widely perceived as excessive and as democratic overload (Blühdorn 2013: 143ff; Friedrichs 2022; Staab 2022; see also Chapters 6.3 and 6.4). For most people, the management of the increasingly complex and precarious arrangements of their everyday life takes up all available resources, and they simply do not have the time, the energy, nor often the required skills to help ensure that, at the societal level, the conditions are right for a good life for all.

While the emancipatory movements had been determined to try out and practise new forms of collective, democratic self-government, today, in the face of multiple crises and 'in the ruins of the liberal world' (Wakefield 2018, 2021), the defensive retreat into the private sphere has become the norm. Political leadership and binding decisions, which can no longer be achieved democratically at the required speed and with the desired reliability, are expected from the state and from science (Haderer 2023). In the late-modern condition, 'neither further democratization nor the emancipatory transformation of the established order', writes Philipp Staab, are still 'the focus of political concerns'. Instead, the 'longing for technocratic depoliticization' and the 'successive normalization of social risks' prevail. A 'protective technocracy', he believes, is the 'envisaged goal of the social contract' (Staab 2022: 30–31). This diagnosis may be overly generalizing, but this autocratic-authoritarian longing can actually be observed in different variations among climate and sustainability activists, market liberals and right-wing populists.

For the critical social sciences and emancipatory movements, these increasing doubts about democracy, this voluntary surrender and relinquishment of democratic claims and competencies, represent a fundamental problem. The normative critique of democracy is not new, of course – just as the notion of the autonomous subject has often been challenged from an ecological perspective. Initially, the critique of democracy was primarily directed at liberal, representative democracy, but then also at direct and deliberative democracy. However, this always tended to be a critique in the name of the free, self-determined subject, that is, a critique that itself referred back to this norm. Yet the historical contingency of this norm itself is an idea that critical sociology finds difficult to deal with, and so is the societal de-problematization of the loss of democracy and of the autocratic-authoritarian turn. Critical sociologists speak of the *aporias* of freedom and examine how, in late modernity, citizens rebel against democratic institutions *in the name of* self-determination and self-realization (cf. e.g. Manow 2020; Blühdorn 2020c, 2020e; Amlinger & Nachtwey 2025). But, retaining the normative perspective of modernity, they then, time and again, propose new initiatives of democratization and consider the formation of new alliances of democratic actors as a promising strategy. Just as Nancy Fraser dreams of a 'counter-hegemonic bloc' or Chantal Mouffe of a 'left-wing populism' and a 'green democratic revolution', Carolin Amlinger and Oliver Nachtwey, for example, hope for an 'insurgent democracy' that 'renews democracy' turning it 'into a true democracy' (Crouch 2004; Fraser 2019, 2022; Schäfer & Zürn 2021: 195–222; Amlinger & Nachtwey 2025: 262f; Mouffe 2023).

However, the question of which guiding norms the democratization of democracy could actually follow remains unanswered. After all, it was not least the earlier attempts to democratize democracy, which for their part have increasingly distorted political representation, which have driven the differentiation and ungovernability of late-modern societies ever further, and which are the bone of contention for the 'regressive rebels' today. Democratization movements themselves – and in this respect the conservatives of the 1970s were right – have played a significant role in the late-modern crisis of democracy and politics (see in more detail in Chapter 6.4). The question would therefore be how to ensure that further democratization efforts do not exacerbate the now familiar side effects. Moreover, new democratization initiatives are never guided by absolute, supposedly unchangeable criteria of 'true' democracy, but always by those ideas and understandings of freedom, self-determination and a good life that are dominant in a given society at a given point in time. And in late-modern societies, there is little reason to assume that this could lead to more equality, justice, ecology, human rights, etc.

This does not mean, of course, that demands for democratization have subsided or that such demands are fundamentally unjustified, futile and counterproductive. Especially in small, limited and concrete contexts, this is clearly not the case. But just as the critics of capitalism and post-capitalist, post-growth movements make a range of rather questionable assumptions regarding the spread and effectiveness of experiences of alienation and about hopes for liberation, and just as the belief in the transformative power of planetary boundaries and the Anthropocene is based on untenable assumptions, this applies here, too: the hope for a democratization of democracy presupposes that in late-modern societies the necessary framework conditions for this project are in place, along with the necessary viable and promising guiding norms. Unfortunately, neither is the case. Conversely, as regards the autocratic-authoritarian turn, that is, the mainstreaming of post-democratic and post-political forms of governance, the social de-problematization of post-democracy is in fact well advanced. In view of the autocratic desire and the libertarian authoritarianism which are widespread in late-modern societies, framing the ongoing transformation of late-modern democracies as a crisis is increasingly dubious. As in the cases of the critique of capitalism and the ecological perspective on late modernity, the democratic-political perspective, too, suggests: the distinguishing feature of late modernity is that the modernist norms on the basis of which democratic deficits were previously diagnosed and democratization projects formulated are disintegrating. In terms of democratic politics, it is precisely the untenability of traditional norms, diagnoses of deficits and hopes for transformation, that is the great transformation of late modernity. The specifically late-modern characteristic is that democratic claims are readily abandoned and relinquished and autocratic-authoritarian forms of governance are accepted as necessary and even actively demanded. Accordingly, it can be assumed that the next society will not only continue to be capitalist and unsustainable in terms of ecological standards, but also autocratic and authoritarian – not only because this is imposed from above by anti-democratic elites, but also because there is a democratic exhaustion and fatigue, a perception of democratic dysfunctionality, from below.

3.4 Digitalization and artificial intelligence

In technological terms, the great transformation of late-modern societies and its distinguishing feature is the digital revolution. It started with the spread of computer technology in personal and home computers from the late 1980s and the gradual switch to electronic data processing in business and public administration. When the 1990s saw the spread of the then new information and communication technologies – mobile phones, the Internet, email and the first social networks – the digital revolution was initially associated with great emancipatory hopes. These innovations were seen as offering great opportunities for widening and deepening democratic participation. Digital media were supposed to improve social integration, promote social networking across social, geographical and political boundaries, and strengthen the capacity of emancipatory movements for political organization. At that stage, digitalization was not yet a revolution. It was to be a tool, an instrument for the more effective realization of the modernist values, norms and goals that had been updated once again in the EEP of the early 1980s.

To some extent at least, these hopes have actually come true. Today, however, this transformation is also perceived by some as threatening and crisis-ridden. The main fears associated with it are the loss of individual autonomy, the threat to democracy and the scenario of total digital surveillance (cf. e.g. Hofstetter 2014, 2016; Zuboff 2018; Augstein 2017). In terms of democracy, the digital revolution has indeed facilitated activist networking. At the same time, however, it is destroying social cohesion and presenting a challenge to the political culture of late-modern societies. People are finding it easier to network, but digitalization also reinforces acceleration and pushes distraction beyond a level that is conducive and tolerable for democracy. In particular, it leads to the disintegration of a shared social reality and public sphere (cf. e.g. Mounk 2018; Habermas 2021; Dörre 2021). Virtual realities are emerging and virtual communities arise that do not consist of individuals but of curated social media profiles. In the digital world, the more or less successful communication and integration of multidimensional individuals is being replaced by the confrontation and conflict of much less complex and, above all, non-sentient profiles. This has an effect on the analogue world. In political discourse, protest, rebellion and aggression prevail over deliberative negotiation and constructive collaborative action. Digitalization radicalizes what had long been apparent as the 'individualization' and then the 'singularization' of modern societies (cf. e.g. Beck & Beck-Gernsheim 1994; Reckwitz 2020): the decomposition of collective actors and identities into individualized subjects, which, in turn, then differentiate themselves into multiple, fragmented, fluid identities with little internal consistency and stability. In terms of realpolitik, the digitally duplicated society with its fragmented, virtualized and dynamized realities and inhabitants is becoming increasingly difficult to govern.

With regard to the modernist ideal of autonomy, concerns about the digital revolution relate, in particular, to the expansion of the comprehensive infrastructure for collecting data in practically all areas of life and everyday activities, to its processing by algorithms that the involuntary data donors do not understand, and to the use of the data for purposes that are unknown to them and over which they have no control. Big data transforms the analogue world into an infinite mass of information that is detached from its respective contexts and can be recombined by algorithms and used for any purpose. A digital parallel world – or a multitude of such parallel worlds – is being created, controlled by algorithmic intelligence, which is becoming independent of the analogue world, gaining autonomy and increasingly imposing its rules on it.

In fact, digital parallel worlds, algorithm-supported decision-making processes and artificial intelligence have already become a central and indispensable part of the infrastructure of late-modern societies. They play a key role in practically all areas of the economy, politics, administration and public and private life, and it is barely possible any longer to imagine life without them. However, the fear of panoptic surveillance, algorithmic heteronomy and artificial intelligence rarely translates into the demand to suspend the digital revolution. This is because the notions of efficiency, freedom, self-determination and a good life cultivated in late-modern societies are inextricably linked to and dependent on digital technologies. Although the high vulnerability of digital systems is increasingly becoming a fundamental threat to late-modern societies, the digital revolution is being promoted as a priority project by practically all political actors. Even green parties see it as a positive contribution to addressing urgent societal problems. Perhaps the only remaining way in which autonomy, the right to shape and the ability to control our lives, can be articulated and experienced in late modernity is the proactive campaign for their digital abolition. It leads 'almost inevitably to an ontological reconfiguration' of late-modern societies, 'in which human subjects become objects' of observation, management and control by artificial intelligence (Block & Dickel 2020: 112).

To counter this threat, some activists are calling for strict regulation to protect democracy and the autonomy of citizens – understood, above all, as their privacy – and to make algorithms and the use of personal data transparent. Based on the argument that learning machines are ultimately only technologies that are not normatively pre-programmed and per se hostile to autonomy or democracy, but always open in their development, design and application, these critics invest hopes in the politicization and critical containment of the digital revolution (cf. e.g. Hofmann 2022). The distribution of information, knowledge, data access and so on, which is currently highly unequal, could be made transparent, they suggest – it could be restructured and democratized overall through political control and regulation. In this way, the benefits of digitalization could be reconciled with the defence of human rights, individual autonomy and democratic self-determination. A variety of organizations and networks are, therefore, seeking to develop ethical criteria for the development and use of these technologies. The scope and the possibilities for the democracy- and autonomy-friendly design and use of algorithmic systems, they point out, is considerable, and they hope to realize this potential. Accordingly, they aim to develop guidelines and seals of approval to differentiate between *good* and *bad* digitalization and good artificial intelligence and AI that should be rejected (cf. e.g. Djeffal 2018; European Commission 2022).

Such efforts for a *good* digitalization and AI are directly comparable to the well-known discussion about *good* and *bad* economic growth, the distinction between market instruments that *promote* sustainability and those that *harm* it, or the hopes for a *good* Anthropocene. Yet, in all of these areas, the fight for political oversight, greater transparency, accountability, democratic openness and links to ethical and ecological standards has had only limited success. These efforts have never led to a structural correction and reversal of the logic and order of unsustainability. Accordingly, the hope for democratic control of the digital revolution and artificial intelligence seems to have little foundation. Not only is the development and control of AI highly centralized in the hands of very few tech giants maintaining close links with autocratic leaders, but any democratization of its design and management would not follow any categorical guidelines, but only the prevailing, strongly context-dependent norms of the demos (however defined).

In fact, when the threat to democracy and the threat to autonomy are used as normative points of reference to criticize digitalization (cf. e.g. Crouch 2015; Hofstetter 2014; Welzer 2017; Zuboff 2018), the close connection between emancipatory values and agendas, on the one hand, and the digital revolution, on the other, tends to be ignored. The extent to which prevailing ideas of a self-determined, good and fulfilling life are based on the conveniences brought by the digital revolution – which are, therefore, essentially non-negotiable – is commonly neglected. Similarly, little consideration is given to the fact that in late-modern societies, the claim to freedom and self-determination is emphasized everywhere, but that the complexity of life and the constant need to take difficult decisions have long since turned into a paralysing overload, in the management of which digital technologies play a central role and are perceived as an emancipatory gain. And the critique that algorithms and artificial intelligence only reproduce the extant and reinforce the social status quo, but can never imagine something fundamentally new, alternative and better, neglects that in late modernity, the natural intelligence of citizens can, obviously, no longer imagine a social future or alternative to the existing order, either – and that to most people such visions would hardly be attractive, especially if they wanted to suspend or reverse the digital revolution.

Furthermore, the hopes and narratives of political control and containment of digitalization also fail to recognize the categorical leap of the digital revolution from the modernist project of participation, inclusion and involvement of people understood as autonomous subjects to their total capture, translation and dissolution into binary-coded data. In other words, the narrative of political control overlooks or denies what is actually revolutionary about the digital revolution. For, in digital society, individuals understood as autonomous subjects, to whom the modernist tradition attributes reason, morality and an inviolable dignity, are no longer the relevant point of reference. Instead, artificial intelligence controls, manages and utilizes data sets that supposedly depict people and their communities, but are, in fact, radically detached from them and categorically different. In so far as the digital revolution not only transfers autonomy from the human, moral, rational subject to self-learning machines, but also that machine-generated data sets, rather than humans, are becoming the point of reference for interactions that, in turn, are controlled by algorithms, digitalization is a revolution, indeed. Just like the Anthropocene, this revolution completely undermines the basic principles, fundamental values and self-understanding of European modernity. While modernity aimed for the 'inclusion of the entire population in political, legal, economic, educational and cultural processes', Dirk Baecker points out, 'the project of digitalization is the transformation of analogue processes into discretely countable, binary-coded, statistically evaluable, machine-calculable processes' (Baecker 2018: 9). The digitalized society, therefore, revolves less and less around people – and certainly not around autonomous subjects which have always just been a regulative ideal, of course. In the digitalized society, their participation and inclusion are being replaced by the most complete possible translation of citizens and their lives into statistically recordable and administratively and economically exploitable data sets. Participation and involvement are 'no longer a question of individual decision, but of exhaustive recording' (ibid.).

Against this backdrop, the idea that the digital revolution, that is, the reconfiguration and reinterpretation of the modernist, analogue world of autonomous subjects as a new world of digital data and artificial intelligence, might be politically controlled, effectively regulated or even stopped is not very convincing. It is based on an amalgam and confusion of two categorically different logics or grammars and two incompatible worlds. The same applies here as with climate change: if there was ever a possibility and a window of opportunity for the modernist containment of the digital revolution, then it has long since closed. Even critics of digitalization have to admit: 'It is not clear how to imagine the development and use of machine learning for the benefit of all beyond manipulative algorithms and decision automation' (Hofmann 2022: 9). In fact, the very idea of a good AI society 'that acknowledges the great importance of these technologies but realizes the choices they offer in such a way that the challenges they present can be dealt with democratically' seems illusory (ibid.). Just like the idea of the good Anthropocene, it is a contradiction in terms. Both ideas are attempts to implant the logic of analogous modernity of autonomous subjects ('good' in the sense of modernist values and ideals) into a new modernity that functions according to a fundamentally different logic. Attempts at politicization and democratic control will, therefore, probably do just as little to slow down the digital revolution as they do to put the breaks on the further unfolding of the Anthropocene. Much more likely, late-modern society and its citizens will come to terms with these profound revolutions by adapting their modernist norms, self-understandings and expectations.

The digital revolution is not taking place by itself, of course, but – like neoliberal globalization in its day – is being deliberately pursued as a political project. This suggests that particular actors have power and are in control. However, its operators are themselves driven, and their project not only cannot be stopped, but it can only be controlled and governed to a very limited extent. More than anything, it can be only accelerated. It has long since progressed so far, and digitalization, datafication and algorithmization have already become such an essential part of everyday life, the prevailing understandings of freedom and self-determination and the completely non-negotiable normality, that serious politicization and questioning can no longer be expected. Digital technologies and artificial intelligence make an indispensable contribution to overcoming the disorientating diversity of options that emancipatory movements themselves have helped to create. Artificial intelligence cuts a path through the thicket of late-modern complexity for the individual as well as social decision makers; it makes late modernity liveable and bearable in the first place. It fills the void that was torn open and remained open after emancipatory movements had cleared away the power structures and beliefs of tradition but failed to replace them with new imperatives of socio-ecological reason and morality.

Against the backdrop of individual and collective overload, loss of control and ungovernability, at a point when emancipatory movements themselves are losing their normative orientation and political self-confidence, autonomy and sovereignty are now being transferred to algorithms and artificial intelligence. These are perceived ever less as a threat, but rather as salvation, an enabling condition and indispensable infrastructure. At the same time, they are becoming a new mode of generating legitimacy, as trust in the citizens' ability to take decisions and in a self-governing civil society is crumbling. Artificial intelligence facilitates a new variant of 'evidence-based' decision-making, administration and governance. And if the 'singularization' of late-modern individuals, identities and lifestyles is a consequence and achievement of the emancipatory revolution (cf. Reckwitz 2017), then it is precisely this development, that is, emancipation itself, that makes the digital infrastructure necessary – not only to articulate and develop this singularity, but also to recapture it and make it governable. Accordingly, emancipatory values are of little use as a normative basis for criticizing and regulating the digital revolution.

In fact, in view of the promised improvements and cost savings in areas such as healthcare, crime prevention or public administration, it is becoming increasingly difficult to justify the abandonment of datafication, algorithmization and 'demos-scraping' (Ulbricht 2020). In all these areas, and many others, it would be irrational and completely irresponsible not to draw on the skills and recommendations of algorithms when making individual and collective decisions and not to be guided by them. As a data- and, thus, evidence-based technology, AI is more powerful and more legitimate than any democratic negotiation and decision. After all, what use is a democratic decision if it is not made in time, if it is not sustainable, or if it is rejected as unacceptable by major parts of society? 'The hope of being able to avoid fatally wrong decisions with the help of algorithms', writes Jeanette Hofmann, 'may indeed prove to be a temptation that is difficult to resist' (Hofmann 2022: 10). The situation is no different, for example, with learning, fully communicative chatbots: they have long become superior to people in terms of the knowledge they draw on, their speed and very often also their articulation skills. Since the market launch of OpenAI's software ChatGPT, at the latest, it has become irrational, inefficient and irresponsible not to use such programmes when dealing with regular tasks – from the very mundane to the highly scientific. 'It is, therefore, to be expected' that 'algorithmic processes will become increasingly normalized in the course of their use' (ibid.: 9). However, the inevitable 'price for a general recognition of algorithmic judgements' is the parallel 'fading of autonomy as a democratic norm' and as an 'indispensable basic prerequisite for democratic coexistence' (ibid.: 10).

So, the digital transformation of late-modern societies shows even more clearly than the great transformations discussed before to what extent the 'total loss of the autonomous subject' is not only anticipated and passively accepted, but normatively affirmed and demanded, because 'the idea of the autonomous subject appears' in late modernity to be 'quite practically anachronistic' (Block & Dickel 2020: 114). In a sense, the digital revolution completes the abandonment of this ideal as modernity's central norm. The system-theoretical analysis of modern society had already banished the idea of the autonomous subject from the centre of society into the environment of its various function systems (cf. Luhmann 1995). Ideological market liberalism then wanted to replace the autonomous subject with the self-regulating market; and theories of 'liquid modernity', 'second-order emancipation' or 'singularization' suggested that the emancipatory logic itself points beyond the traditional ideal of the autonomous subject (cf. e.g. Bauman 2003; Blühdorn 2013; Reckwitz 2017; see also Chapter 6.3). The digital revolution takes this another step further and puts artificial intelligence in its place. In the sense that it signals the demise of the phase of modernity that centred on the bourgeois ideal of the autonomous subject, the triumphant advance of artificial intelligence may be regarded as the cultural counterpart to the demise of humanity feared by the climate movement. While those who warn of the uncontrollable catastrophes of climate change and the Anthropocene fear the biophysical end of humanity, the digital revolution signifies the *cultural-historical* end of humanity, that is, of civilization, which was hoped to incrementally realize the supposedly universal values and ideals that form the normative core of European-Western modernity. Interestingly, these comprehensive transformation processes are 'increasingly popular research questions in the social sciences', Jeanette Hofmann notes, 'but they do not actually receive any attention in political action' (Hofmann 2022: 9).

3.5 China and the new geopolitical conflict

Finally, a fifth great transformation of late modernity is China's rise as a new global superpower and the new geopolitical East–West conflict associated with it. After the centre of the modern world, the centre of power and the front line of progress had first shifted from Europe to America, and the New World looked back to Old Europe, they are now shifting – contrary to the assumption that the end of history would lie in the globalization of European-Western values and liberal democracy – to Asia and in particular to authoritarian China. China's President Xi Jinping explicitly aims for global leadership in economic, technological and military terms. To this end, China offers its own vision of an integrated global society, the implementation of which it is driving forward in a targeted and strategic manner – for example with the 'New Silk Road' project announced in 2013. Initially, the crisis narrative launched by Western countries, particularly the USA, framed the rise of China as the loss of the global leadership role of the so-called 'free world' and the new competition between liberal, democratic systems and their authoritarian, autocratic challengers. However, going far beyond questions of political organization, the creeping reorganization of the global balance of power affects the Western value system and European-Western modernity as a whole, which are not only radically challenged or explicitly rejected by China, but also by Russia and many other states – and, increasingly, from within Western countries themselves. This narrative of systemic competition between the authoritarian People's Republic and the free, democratic world took up the old rhetoric of the Cold War and at the same time updated the even older narrative of the 'fall of the West' (Spengler 1991 [1922]). It suggests that the various manifestations of the new modernity described in the previous sections may well be an Asian, a Chinese modernity.

The rise of China and the geopolitical shift in power result, inter alia, from the fact that the Western economy's dependence on the People's Republic as a manufacturer of inexpensive products for Western mass consumption and as a sales market for Western products has grown very rapidly in recent years. Secondly, China is a key global investor in critical infrastructure, among other things. Thirdly, the country is highly developed, particularly in the field of digital technologies, without being restricted by issues such as data protection. Fourth, the People's Republic is forging geopolitical alliances and dependencies wherever the West and the industrialized nations have pursued (post)colonial exploitation interests but neglected the development interests of the respective countries. In public debate about China's rise, issues such as the violation of the human rights of the Uyghurs interned in re-education camps and the digital social credit system, which has been developed at an accelerated pace since 2020, figure prominently, as do China's practice of extensive product piracy and industrial espionage, the violent suppression of the democracy movements in Hong Kong and China's threat to Taiwan's independence. Furthermore, the People's Republic is criticized for having the largest, and still growing, coal consumption and the highest CO_2 emissions. And of course, there is the total claim to power of President Xi Jinping, whose term in office has no formal limit and who is also General Secretary of the Communist Party and Chairman of the Central Military Commission. And since the war in Ukraine, the strategic alliance between China and Russia has become yet another issue of concern.

Thus, the fear of China's rise combines a wide range of aspects also relevant in the crises addressed above: the overwhelming power of capital which the system of state capitalism strengthens even further, the autocratic-authoritarian turn, the spectre of total digital surveillance, concerns about freedom and human rights, fears of global warming and the threat to the West's self-perception of economic, political and moral superiority – that is, of a radical loss of status compared to its previous service provider. However, this narrative of the systemic competition and China's threat to the West is easily recognized as an ideological mobilization narrative that primarily aims to reconfirm the West's claim to moral superiority and global leadership. In particular, it entirely ignores the multilayered crisis and unsustainability of the Western system itself. A critical look at this narrative sheds light on the ways in which late-modern societies discursively process and cope with their own crisis and untenability. It further develops some aspects that have already been touched upon above.

What is particularly significant about this narrative is that it largely shifts the threat to freedom, democracy and so-called Western values to the outside world and bundles them into a single or primary opponent. This makes it possible, indeed, to a certain extent necessary, to disregard the complex and difficult to deal with internal contradictions and dynamics of self-destabilization, so as to fully focus attention on the struggle against the external enemy. This distracts from the fact that the very values which are supposed to be defended have themselves proven to be fundamentally problematic – and untenable. In this constellation of profound uncertainty, the narrative of system competition offers new normative orientation and reassurance:

- Capitalism itself – its ecological, social and democratic unsustainability – is now no longer the problem but, above all, state capitalism in China.
- The Western inability for ecological self-limitation and post-growth policies recedes into the background, while emphasis is placed on the growth orientation, technology fixation, coal consumption and centralism of the 'ecological civilization' project propagated by the Chinese leadership (cf. e.g. Liu et al. 2018; Kuhn 2019; Tyfield 2021; Tyfield & Rodríguez 2022).
- The autocratic-authoritarian turn in the home countries of liberal democracy now seems secondary to the threat to democracy posed by China.
- The disregard for basic values and universal human rights – for example in migration policy or in the procurement of raw materials and consumer goods – in favour of maintaining prosperity and increasing wealth in Western countries disappears behind the human rights violations in the People's Republic.
- The digital revolution no longer appears to be a problem per se, but the primary problem with it is the digital surveillance project in authoritarian China.

This externalization of the threat not only ignores the long tradition of both conservative and emancipatory reflection on the self-destabilization and self-destruction of Western societies, but also the fact that autocratic-authoritarianism is by no means fundamentally alien to Western societies themselves. And the further the autocratic turn advances in the supposedly free and open West, too, the more obvious it becomes that the conflict with China is only superficially about a competition between political systems, but rather between different variants of capitalism.

At the same time, it is becoming ever clearer that it is not external pressure that makes Western societies abandon the fundamental values for which they used to claim categorical and universal validity, but rather free choice and the determination to secure and defend their own prosperity. They voluntarily divest themselves of these values – or redefine them on an ongoing basis – in the interest of their understandings of freedom, self-determination and a good life. In fact, Western societies have always had an ambivalent relationship to their fundamental values and rights. De facto, these rights and values have always been exclusive, that is, neither categorical nor universal. And it is not only material prosperity in industrialized nations that is directly dependent on poverty in other countries. The democratic, political, social and ecological rights granted to some have always implied the denial of these same rights to others (cf. e.g. Lessenich 2019a, 2019b). For example, since the 1980s, ecological modernization and improved environmental quality in the wealthy countries of the Global North has been largely based on the relocation of pollution-intensive industries to countries with lower environmental and social standards. This remains the case with the current transition in Western countries to supposedly clean, renewable energies, which is associated with a considerable demand for raw materials and devastating environmental damage, particularly in the Global South (cf. e.g. Jasansky et al. 2023). And the neo-colonial recruitment and concomitant brain drain of well-qualified people from countries in the Global South, too, is apparently unproblematic for the wealthy countries of the Global North.

The Western commitment to universal rights and values has therefore always been ambiguous, and in late modernity, at the planetary boundaries, which are also the boundaries of externalization, corresponding self-commitments are becoming more of a burden than ever. Hence, it is not only in international politics that Western states are retreating from the fight for universal human rights, freedom and democracy, but within Western communities such as the EU, too – Brexit is just one prominent example – they willingly abandon their commitment to alleged fundamental social and ecological values when this seems beneficial. It is not only in the USA that so-called isolationists are gaining ground. Accordingly, the feared demise of the West is neither imposed from outside, nor can it really be described as a crisis, for it is taking place in the interest of securing freedom and prosperity – at least for some. And depending on the underlying understanding of emancipation, it may even be said to have emancipatory potential (see Chapter 6.3).

More than anything, the portrayal of the geopolitical transformation as a competition between freedom and democracy on the one hand and authoritarianism and dictatorship on the other is – or was – therefore, a narrative cultivated to stabilize the shaky order of unsustainability and generate legitimation for its further continuation. As a purely defensive narrative, it does little to shed light on the actual untenability and transformation of late-modern societies. However, its critical investigation illuminates a mechanism that enables or even forces the perpetuation of sustained unsustainability. Talk of competition between freedom and authoritarianism, democracy and dictatorship, implies a moral obligation to side with freedom and democracy, and thus against China and Russia. There may well be good reasons for doing so, but it would surely be wrong to believe that the autocratic-authoritarian turn in Western countries originates from the authoritarian threat by China or Russia. And, conversely, it would be equally wrong to assume that to increase support now for the project of the 'free West' will be beneficial for freedom and democracy.

3.6 Interim results: The metamorphosis of modernity

The five crises of late modernity discussed above and identified from different perspectives have a common core: ultimately, they all diagnose violations of the central norm of European-Western modernity, the idea of the *autonomous subject*. And the demands for transformation associated with the respective diagnoses are always aimed at defending or restoring precisely this norm. But in late modernity it transpires:

- What is untenable is not capitalism, but the normative narrative of its crisis and collapse and of the liberated post-capitalist society.
- Crossing planetary boundaries does not mean the downfall of humanity but the full and irreversible implementation of a geological turning point; and this, in turn, the Anthropocene, means the disintegration of the worldview and way of thinking on which the diagnoses of the ecological crisis and the ecological-emancipatory project of an SET have always been based.
- The post-democratic and autocratic-authoritarian turn is not a relapse or loss per se; rather, democracy, in late modernity, is

increasingly perceived as dysfunctional and lacking legitimacy. To many, alternative methods of decision-making and governance appear superior and desirable.

– The digital revolution and artificial intelligence are perceived less and less as a fundamental threat, but rather as an indispensable prerequisite and infrastructure for a good life, self-development and public administration.

– The disintegration of European-Western self-descriptions and the loss of the West's global leadership role are not due to an external threat (China), but rather result ever more visibly from the implementation of the internal logic of European-Western modernity itself.

Thus, in the discussion of the five major transformations that have been addressed, a sixth has incrementally become visible, a cultural one, and this is ultimately the decisive one. The crises highlighted here initially appear to be a 'multiple' crisis, and this is how they are widely discussed in the relevant literature (cf. e.g. Brand 2009; Demirović et al. 2011). But they are actually indicators or facets of one single crisis. For, in all these dimensions, the crisis is, at heart, about the violation of the one anchor norm of European modernity. It is correct to assume that the multiple crisis is a 'systemic crisis'. Yet, contrary to the common assumption, the system that is falling apart is not capitalism (neither as an economic system nor as a social order in a broader sense), but the value system of European-Western modernity. The empirical-factual side of the transformations highlighted here remains unaffected by this, of course. But these empirical facts are perceived less and less as problematic, as a crisis, because the norms underpinning such an assessment have less and less power. And accordingly, their violation is also mobilizing fewer counter- and defence-movements. Or to be more precise: there is no lack of protests and social movements, because contrary to the thesis of post-politics (e.g. Wilson & Swyngedouw 2014), late modernity is a phase of hyper-politicization (cf. Blühdorn & Deflorian 2021; Jäger 2023). Yet counter-movements in the tradition of the EEP are incessantly losing strength.

Thus, the examination of the various transformations of late modernity – the main dimensions and results are tentatively captured in Table 2 – leads to a much more comprehensive understanding of both the untenability and the really great transformation that late-modern societies are currently undergoing. Ultimately, the entire value system of European-Western modernity and the social institutions and

Table 2. Great transformations in late modernity

Perspective	Crisis perception	Required/ hoped-for transfor- mation	Factual transfor- mation	Factual untenability	De-problem- atization
Economic	collapse of capitalism	post-capitalism; liberated post-growth society	adaptation of capitalism	reference norms of the traditional critique of capitalism	capitalism without democracy and human rights
Ecological; Earth system science	collapse of biophysical systems; danger to the habitability of the planet and the survival of the human species	SET; Earth system governance; collective self-limitation	society of sustained unsustaina-bility; ecological ungoverna-bility; new state of nature	dualisms of modernity; eco-political imperatives; principle of responsibility	end of Nature; violation of the modernist standards of the EEP
Political	threat to (liberal) democracy	defending and strengthening (democratiza-tion) of democracy	autocratic-authoritarian turn	political freedom; democratic self-determination	autocratic-illiberal post-democracy
Technological	end of autonomy; authoritarian surveillance society	reclaim autonomy; digitalization in line with autonomy and democracy	algorithm-controlled, panoptic society	autonomous subject	autonomy of the machine; rule of systemic imperatives
Geopolitical; geo-cultural	decline of the West	defence of Western values and the open society	shift in the international power order	European Enlightenment; Western leadership role	inequality, exclusion; de-civilization, barbarism

arrangements which are based on these values are becoming untenable. Like Polanyi's *Great Transformation*, the great transformation that this sets in motion appears to be normatively undesirable. Yet it is unfolding independently of the questions whether it is desired and its significance understood. This new world, the emerging next society and other modernity, is not, as Polanyi, the eco-emancipatory movements and critical sociology had hoped, a world of 'unprecedented freedom for all' (Polanyi 1957 [1944]: 256), including nature, but a world beyond European-Western core values and beyond traditional notions of ecological integrity. It emerges from the ruins of liberal thought and life, of democracy, of the 'open society', the 'free world' and of the eco-emancipatory SET (see Wakefield 2018; Blühdorn 2023). This great transformation really 'changes everything'.

As yet, significant parts of the sustainability literature continue to revolve around the normative goals and horizons of meaning that in the course of this transformation have become anachronistic. They are stuck in the traditional ideas of critique, progressiveness and transformation. Hence:

- Anyone who continues to talk about the end of capitalism and a post-capitalist society in late modernity is neglecting the fact that the fundamental prerequisites for both are missing.
- Those who call for collective responsibility and democratic self-limitation in the face of increasing instability and the collapse of biophysical systems overlook the fact that, on the one hand, the Anthropocene radicalizes this responsibility but, on the other, radically dissolves the foundations of this way of thinking.
- Those who lament the end of democracy and the autocratic-authoritarian turn in a traditionally critical manner are refusing to recognize that autonomy, democracy and civic maturity have long since become an unbearable burden and that late-modern citizens long for relieving simplicity, orientation, leadership and authority.
- Anyone who sees digitalization and artificial intelligence primarily as a threat to autonomy and democracy and calls for the political regulation of AI is ignoring the fact that both are resolutely advocated and promoted as a project of relief and liberation.
- Those who perceive the rise of China and the so-called 'decline of the West' as an external threat are ignoring the fact that the so-called 'free world' itself is softening and abandoning its universalist values and its claim to moral leadership in the interests of its current understanding of freedom and self-determination.
- And when critical sociology and transformative sustainability research cling to modernist notions of autonomy, political efficacy and controlled transformation, they only confirm to what extent the social sciences, too, are determined to sustain what has long become unsustainable.

Nevertheless, the actual transformation does not, and this is crucial, lead to dystopia. Instead, as the considerations above suggest, it carries late-modern societies – although the term 'late-modern' actually suggests otherwise – into a new modernity that leaves the unfulfilled promises and ideals of the Enlightenment behind, 'without this entailing dystopian scenarios' (Block & Dickel 2020: 118; see also Chapter 7.3). For, along with the traditional ideas of a normatively desirable transformation, the traditional ideas of the dystopia to be avoided become untenable, too. The future, which necessarily appears dystopian from the perspective of subject-centred modernity, loses its horror. Of course, there are grievances about the ongoing transition that are articulated in many different ways. A prominent example of this is the syndrome of 'offended freedom' diagnosed by Carolin Amlinger and Oliver Nachtwey among corona deniers and the critics of the so-called 'deep state' (see Amlinger & Nachtwey 2025) – which, incidentally, is by no means limited to only these particular social groups. Indeed, late-modern societies are characterized by a contradictory coexistence of (a) phenomena that can be traced back to the disappointment of modernist promises of self-determination and self-realization, and (b) the conscious abandonment of the ideal of the autonomous subject, which not only de-problematizes this abandonment, but even demands it normatively and expects emancipatory benefits from it. This simultaneity is a phenomenon characteristic of the transitional phase (see Chapter 7). For, late modernity has not yet completed the farewell to the autonomous subject, nor the mourning process related to it.

The attempt to grasp and theorize this great transformation is not the same, of course, as approving of it normatively and propagating the abandonment of Western values. Nor is it a question of claiming that the actual transformation, the metamorphosis into a different modernity, is not actually a major disaster and that people will soon become accustomed to it. These are matters of individual judgement. The point here is, instead, to understand more thoroughly what I described in Chapter 2 as the specific situation and dilemma of late-modern societies, that is, as the double untenability of the established societal order, on the one hand, and the EEP, on the other. Closer consideration of the factual transformations and of the prospects of the transformations demanded from the perspectives of the diverse crisis diagnoses has helped to further illuminate this constellation and the dilemma of double untenability. The significance of the pandemic and the war in Ukraine, which can hardly be overestimated, is now also much clearer: they have shifted the untenability of the established order right into the spotlight, and at the same time they have highlighted the lack of alternatives and the non-negotiability of so-called 'normality', that is, of the order of unsustainability. This order is being defended 'whatever it takes'. When the then head of the European Central Bank, Mario Draghi, issued this motto in the euro crisis that followed the banking and financial crisis of 2008/9, he was referring to financial costs. This was also the case when Olaf Scholz adopted this formula during the Covid pandemic to underscore his determination to get 'back to normality' as swiftly as possible. Yet, the cost of defending 'normality' is not only financial, but in late modernity, the defence of this normality is essentially paid for by the suspension of the values that underpin the EEP and European-Western modernity as a whole. Ultimately, this is precisely the great, the greatest transformation. It is just this uncompromising defence of so-called normality that accelerates the development of the 'next society' and the new modernity. Both emerge not through the managed transformation to a desired alternative, but as a side effect of the resolute defence of the status quo – as well as through the implementation of emancipatory logic itself. They come, as Ulrich Beck put it in the mid-1980s, 'on the tip-toes of normality' (Beck 1992: 11).

REFLEXIVE MODERNIZATION

Since the crisis and transformation which confront affluent societies of the Global North must, ultimately, be understood as a crisis and transformation of Western modernity as a whole, the abyss, the emergency, described in the preceding chapters will now be conceptualized in terms of social theory and, more specifically, modernization theory. The considerations in the previous chapter have shown that, in the phase that I refer to as late modernity, the idea of the autonomous subject, in particular, loses its power. In fact, this late modernity can only be described as such because, and only to the extent that, this basic and anchor norm of previous modernity fades. However, this does not mean that modernity as a whole is coming to an end. Such an assertion would be nonsensical, as there are no signs that other dynamics characteristic of modernity, such as rationalization, differentiation, technologization or acceleration, have come to a standstill (on the dimensions of modernization cf. e.g. van der Loo & van Reijen 1992; Degele & Dries 2005 or Rosa et al. 2007). It only comes to an end insofar as this central norm – in the understanding that the NSM and the EEP had once again updated and strengthened – is losing significance, and Western societies are, therefore, as Ulrich Beck put it in the German subtitle of *Risikogesellschaft*, 'on the way to a different modernity' (Beck 1986).

Drawing on Ulrich Beck's theory of 'reflexive' modernity and modernization, I will now further explore the motor and logic of this transformation from the outgoing to the newly emerging phase of modernity. This also will bring the eco-emancipatory project and its alleged unsustainability back into focus, which in the previous chapter remained in the background. In fact, the focus is now, very specifically, on the connection between the unsustainability of modernity and that of the EEP. The phase of modernity that is currently fading, I will argue, can be paralleled with what I call the EEP – and both are fading at the same time. This outgoing phase of the modernist project was characterized by precisely those values – autonomy, ecology, equality, democracy, inclusion – that had become hegemonic in Western societies with the so-called silent revolution since the turn of the 1970s (Inglehart 1977). It was the phase of modernity that was determined, more than ever, by the ideal of the autonomous subject, which had always formed the core of the Kantian liberal Enlightenment project, but which, for significant parts of society, had remained far removed from the reality of life, until it was fully democratized with the silent revolution of the 1970s, and became the political objective for society as a whole. Insofar as this norm and the values it implied were also constitutive for the EEP, this project may be understood as the substantive concretization, as the political programme, of this phase of modernity; and its fading in late modernity then also means that of the EEP. Yet, just as modernity as a whole does not come to an end, the ecological question does not become entirely irrelevant, either: in the new phase of modernity it is reformulated and renegotiated under fundamentally changed normative conditions (cf. Chapter 6).

So, building on Ulrich Beck's periodization of different phases of modernity, the EEP is now presented as the substantive programme of Beck's 'second modernity' and framed as an attempt to 'modernize modernity'. Following on from there, the double untenability of today's late modernity and the EEP is later conceptualized as a consequence and a process of 'reflexive modernization' (cf. Chapter 5). This term sheds light not only on the emergence of the EEP but also on its disintegration and the emergence of a new modernity. Prior to that, however, it must be clarified why it makes sense at all to frame and explain the double untenability in terms of modernization theory. After all, the 'grand narratives' in general, and modernization theory in particular, had clearly fallen into disrepute. Also, a bit more needs to be said about why the double untenability should be explained with recourse to Ulrich Beck's variant of modernization theory and not with recourse to other, more recent approaches, which also appear more empirically plausible and more consistent, conceptually (e.g. Nachtwey 2018; Amlinger & Nachtwey 2025; Reckwitz 2021; Rosa 2015; Reckwitz & Rosa 2023).

4.1 The return of modernization theory

In the 1980s, Jean-François Lyotard proclaimed the 'end of the grand narratives', especially the narrative of modernity (Lyotard 1984, 1988). The project of modernity, which he understood, taking the perspective of cultural theory, as the belief in one single universal reason and in the possibility to explain the world by means of one all-encompassing scientific rationality, had failed, Lyotard argued, and was being replaced in 'the postmodern condition' by a multitude of equally valid perspectives on the world, each of which followed its own rationality (cf. e.g. Welsch 1987). In view of the plurality, complexity and dynamics of change in postmodern societies, their international interaction and multilayered global political relationships, sociologists have since spoken out against the grand, overarching theories of society and development. Society no longer seems readily definable, less and less distinguishable from nature or the non-social (cf. Chapter 3.2), and different societies can hardly be demarcated from one another. Instead of grand theories, empirical social research and small-scale theories, many have argued, are more likely to do justice to the reality of contemporary societies, both in terms of describing them and explaining their often contradictory dynamics of change.

This new scepticism towards sociological theory formation relates, in particular, to the forms of modernization theory that declared certain ideals to be universally valid, which had emerged from specifically European traditions of thought, and assumed that all societies worldwide – in linear manner, irreversibly, deterministically – would follow a more or less uniform development path to the realization of these ideals. From this perspective, the industrialized countries were regarded as having moved already further along this path, while others, especially the 'developing countries' of the so-called 'Third World', were still lagging behind. Modernization theory considered the spread of secular-rational norms, the development of liberal individualism, science, technology, free-market capitalism, efficient administration, the rule of law and parliamentary democracy to be the indicators of civilizational progress (cf. e.g. Lipset 1959, 1960; Parsons 1971; Zapf 1975, 1991; Inglehart 1997; Inglehart & Welzel 2005). Measured against these interrelated criteria, non-Western societies were considered to be non-modern or pre-modern, backward and less civilized. Critics, however, insisted that neither the central values of European philosophy and the Enlightenment nor the belief in linear progress should be regarded as a universal yardstick of progress and civilization, that there were many possible paths of societal development and that the development of each society depended to a large extent on its geographical and cultural characteristics and, very importantly, also on global political power, dependency and exploitation relationships. Accordingly, this particular form of modernization theory was portrayed as an ideological instrument to justify Western fantasies of superiority, interventionist-colonial policies of development and the transfer of Western institutions into non-Western contexts (cf. e.g. Eisenstadt 2000; Chakrabarty 2002; Knöbl 2007, 2013; do Mar Castro Varela & Dhawan 2020).

More recently, however, more ambitious and larger-scale social theories and, in particular, approaches based on modernization theory have become more popular again. Authors such as Zygmunt Bauman, Oliver Nachtwey, Andreas Reckwitz, Hartmut Rosa and others, who all think explicitly in terms of modernization theory – albeit no longer in the traditional sense described above – are finding considerable public resonance. Bauman speaks of 'liquid modernity', in which structures that were once presented as stable and consistent dissolve at an accelerating pace (Bauman 2000). Nachtwey diagnoses 'regressive modernization' (Nachtwey 2018: 59–101), which falls back behind standards that had already been achieved, and in which 'principles of modernity often continue to exist only as an empty husk' (Nachtwey 2018: 99; see also Butterwegge 1999). Reckwitz refers to the present as 'late modernity', in which, he believes, the pressure to 'singularize' and 'curate' one's own identity and life becomes unbearable for many people. As regards the demarcation of different phases of modernity, Nachtwey uses the criteria of equality and inclusion to distinguish between a 'social' and a 'regressive' modernity (Nachtwey 2018; Amlinger & Nachtwey 2025). Adopting a more encompassing historical perspective, Reckwitz distinguishes between 'bourgeois', 'industrial' and 'late' modernity (Reckwitz 2021, 2023: 59–79). And Rosa, who focuses on the pace of societal innovation as the key criterion, differentiates between 'early', 'high' and 'late' modernity (Rosa 2015, 2023).

This new tide of larger-scale social theories and, in particular, modernization-theoretical approaches is to be welcomed, for, without theoretical approaches with a broader scope, it is hard to see the links and interrelationships between seemingly disconnected social phenomena, and to understand longer-term developments such as the decline of liberal democracy or the emergence of new political actors. Also, comprehensive social theories are, in fact, particularly important in just those conditions – high complexity, dynamization, contradictions, international interdependence, etc. – that supposedly make them impossible and unhelpful. For it is precisely in these conditions that there is a great need for explanations of the opaque and seemingly mysterious, for assistance in trying to make sense of everyday life, and for orientation and perspectives into the future. And this applies even more, when significant parts of society have firmly internalized emancipatory values like intellectual independence, critical judgement, democratic self-determination and control over one's own life. Under such conditions, culturalist approaches are particularly important, since they pay special attention to the value orientations, ambitions and fears of citizens. But if sociology does not face up to this need and limits itself to exploring and explaining only smaller-scale issues, leaving the large and more incomprehensible ones 'in God's hands', as it were, this is not only unduly convenient, but by refusing to offer more comprehensive theories, this kind of sociology also plays into the hands of those offering 'grand narratives' outside the realm of the social sciences – for example, in the form of conspiracy myths.

In contrast to the older modernization theories, the more recent approaches have largely abandoned the idea of linear progress for the better, as well as the idea of a more or less uniform development path for all societies worldwide, on the basis of which Western industrial societies can be portrayed as pioneers, others as their followers and still others as laggards. At the same time, terms like 'regressive modernization', 'retrotopia' or 'the great regression' signal that the perspective of Western modernist norms in many respects still prevails (Nachtwey 2018; Bauman 2017; Geiselberger 2017). However, current analyses of the further development of societies that already see themselves as 'advanced modern' are often no longer guided by visions of a better, future society in which these ideals will be even more fully realized. This applies to Amlinger and Nachtwey's analysis of 'offended freedom' as well as to Armin Nassehi (2021), Stephan Lessenich (2022), and to Reckwitz or Rosa. Reckwitz explicitly replaces societal progress for the better with a 'dialectic without a telos' between forces or phases of 'opening' contingency and 'closing' contingency (Reckwitz 2023: 41–45). As if by chance, this dialectic leads to the superiority of the bourgeois middle class – which Reckwitz, thus, naturalizes to a certain extent. This kind of sociological theorizing essentially provides an apologia for the status quo. It remains affirmative and accepts the loss of transformative utopias. Perhaps it is precisely this that is the key to its popularity:

The 'proactive attitude toward progress', Reckwitz notes, 'has clearly been replaced by a defensive orientation toward prevention, resilience and the minimalization of loss' (ibid.: 69).

However, the fact that dialectics is without a telos does not mean that it has come to a standstill; and the loss of political utopias does not mean that the status quo of late-modern societies can be sustained, if only for the medium term. Hence, social theory needs to clarify: where does the dialectic lead? Neither Nachtwey nor Reckwitz dare to venture into the 'transcendental homelessness' (Lukács), the normative void of a modernity that not only has to cope without the security and orientation of religion, but also without that of the Enlightenment, that is, the emancipatory narratives of the 'collective exodus from self-incurred immaturity', and without the traditional beliefs of critical theory. In particular, their approaches ignore that these modernist values might be abandoned in an 'emancipatory' manner, so that the world emerging beyond them is perhaps no longer perceived as dystopian. And they take far too little account of the fact that the modernist, progressive, emancipatory ideals – freedom, self-determination, democracy, and so on – have no essentialist meaning, but are 'essentially contested concepts' (Gallie 1956) which are constantly being concretized anew for the respective temporal, community and contextual conditions (cf. Chapter 6). Nachtwey's reference to modernist norms being maintained 'only as empty husks', too, implies the ongoing belief in a supposedly original and true content and, thus, in a supposedly fixed normative yardstick for what society and the world ought to be like. Therefore, the specifically late-modern situation, in which the beliefs and arrangements of civil society's project of self-government have become just as untenable as had the beliefs and arrangements of classical modernization theory before it, demands an expansion of social and modernization theory beyond such approaches. And if the specifically late-modern is precisely the untenability of the EEP, then an updating and expansion of modernization theory is required that shifts the dimensions of precisely this project into the centre of attention.

4.2 Why Ulrich Beck?

Ulrich Beck's work is promising in this respect. He first developed his theory in his books *Risk Society* (1992), *Gegengifte* (1988), which has not been translated into English, and *The Reinvention of Politics* (1997). He later elaborated it further in *World at Risk* (2009) and the posthumously published book *Metamorphosis of the World* (2016). Beck undertakes a radical critique of traditional modernization theory, but at the same time remains firmly committed to it in essential respects. Beck's work has often been criticized as essayistic, feuilletonistic and as 'sociological fantasy' (Römer et al. 2020). His genre, many have argued, is the analysis of the present (*Zeitdiagnose*) rather than sociology proper (cf. e.g. Dimbath 2020; Nassehi 2020). Also, his time was clearly in the nineties. His concept of the second, reflexive modernity has not become established as a description of contemporary Western societies. As Oliver Römer notes, one might actually 'ask today where exactly the lasting impact' of Beck's work 'could lie for the discipline (of sociology)' (Römer et al. 2020: 9). But today, the genre of *Zeitdiagnose* is no longer disreputable. The books by Reckwitz, Rosa, Nachtwey and Nassehi are also aimed at a broad audience far beyond academia and have indeed become bestsellers. In the age of acceleration, 'liquid modernity', the search for orientation and conspiracy myths, the diagnosis of the times has an important function. And well beyond the fact that in the face of Covid-19, global warming and new military conflicts, the concept of the 'risk society' has certainly gained rather than lost in relevance, there are also numerous other reasons today for referring back to the writings of Ulrich Beck:

– Similar to the theorem under discussion here – that of double untenability – Beck saw a direct connection between the crisis of a certain phase of modernity and what I conceptualize here as the EEP. The phase of modernity which he referred to was, of course, not the same as the one we are concerned with today.
– Beck rejected scenarios of the end of the world (cf. Chapter 1) and was, instead, interested in 'what arose at the time before the unseeing eyes of the time' (Beck 2009: 219). He tried 'to recognize the signs of new world beginnings' (ibid.) and 'to move the future which is just beginning to take shape into view against the still predominant past' (Beck 1992: 9). Exactly this is, arguably, the key task in late modernity – at the abyss – whereby, today, the 'still predominant past' is precisely what Beck then saw as 'the future which is just beginning to take shape', which he sought 'to move into view' – and which the writings of Nachtwey or Reckwitz, for example, do not capture at all.
– With his concept of the 'age of side-effects', Beck addressed precisely the loss of control, of the open future and of the perspective of progress, which is even more relevant in today's late modernity

than it was in his own time. For Beck, the NSM and the EEP turned this loss, once again, into a new departure and a new creative optimism. The malaise of late modernity, in turn, only becomes understandable in its causes and its full scope, if it is seen against the background of precisely this new departure – for which Beck provided a comprehensive theory.

– Beck updated early critical theory, which had a significant influence on the emerging environmental movement (cf. Blühdorn 2000). He shared critical sociology's dual commitment to social analysis, on the one hand, and the transformation of society, on the other. He held on to critical sociology's central norm, the autonomous subject, but turned away from the traditional critique of domination and alienation and, instead of the logic of oppression, explored the logic of liberation as the main driver of social development and crisis. His theory thus rejects the cultural-critical pessimism and hopelessness of Horkheimer and Adorno and, rather than focusing exclusively on the logic of capitalism, provides important impulses for exploring the inner contradictions of the EEP as the cause of the current malaise, that is, the double unsustainability of late modernity.

– Beck's concepts of 'victory-crisis', 'success-failure', 'automotiveness' and 'metamorphosis' (of modernity) are especially helpful for explaining the double untenability of late-modern society and the EEP as an unavoidable dialectical consequence of their own inner logic. With these concepts, Beck moved away from the narrative that the liberation from capitalism would be the solution and back to Horkheimer and Adorno's hypothesis in *Dialectic of Enlightenment*, that the problem – insolubly – lies in the project of Enlightenment itself (cf. Chapter 6.3).

– For Beck, individualization and the ecological side effects of industrial modernity were two equally constitutive aspects of the risk society. This facilitates an understanding of the EEP as a specific combination of societal value preferences that emerged in the wake of the 'silent revolution' and biophysical changes perceived from the perspective of these norms (cf. Chapter 1.1). Beck's approach, very early on, acknowledged the direct and inseparable connection between biophysical phenomena and subjective value orientations – and did so much more explicitly than is still the case in much of the literature today.

– At the same time, Beck did not understand the emergence of new values of self-determination and self-realization as linear progress. In contrast to Inglehart, for example, who drew false conclusions from the change in social value preferences regarding the democratization and ecologization of modern societies, Beck saw the liberation from traditional predeterminations as both a blessing and a curse. He anticipated the self-overburdening of the NSM and the EEP, which on the one hand aimed for self-determination freed from all pre-modern and traditional strictures, but on the other hand were unable to cope with this self-imposed commitment. Beck thus laid the foundations for the theorem of 'second-order emancipation' (see Blühdorn 2012 and Chapter 6.3). Gerhard Schulze, Zygmunt Bauman, Richard Sennett, Andreas Reckwitz and many others have taken up the theme of individualization and its double-edged nature, but unlike Beck, they never linked it to the theme of ecology and the other dimensions of the EEP.

- With his multidimensional understanding of 'reflexivity', Beck developed a concept that is ideally suited to explain not only the formation and the agenda of the EEP, but also its crisis and untenability. Similarly, Beck's 'reinvention of politics' can be applied not only to the formation phase of the EEP and its agenda, but also to the repoliticization of the – at one stage almost hegemonic – consensus on the necessity and urgency of a major SET. Beck's own thinking was double-tracked and inherently contradictory. His writings articulate an inconsistency that has always been inherent to the EEP, too, but which its proponents, from their activist perspective, were – and still are – themselves unable to reflect on.
- And finally, as early as the 1990s, Beck spoke of an 'uprising against the 1970s and 1980s' (as cited in Chapter 1), of the counter-revolt, pent up 'against the individualization, feminization and ecologization of everyday life', which aimed to restore the 'priorities of orthodox industrial society' (Beck & Beck-Gernsheim 1994: 33f). He thus anticipated the postliberal repoliticization that the EEP is subject to, today.

Hence, there are very good reasons to return to Beck in order to reconstruct the EEP and analyse the double untenability of late modernity (cf. Staab 2022). Today, however, Beck must be read 'against the grain', so to speak, that is, by subtracting the political hope that guided him. In late modernity, Beck is not primarily interesting because of these hopes – they have obviously not been fulfilled – but because of his analysis of the logic and dynamics that led to the emergence of 'second modernity' and the EEP, and because this analysis also very clearly outlines why second modernity and the EEP are experiencing a victory-crisis today, out of which a third modernity is emerging.

4.3 Second modernity

Beck described industrial, Fordist, nation state modernity as 'first modernity'. It was characterized, he said, by a belief in linear progress, constant economic growth, continuous improvement in living conditions, the development of science and technology as well as ongoing rationalization and efficiency improvements in business and administration. All of this promised a steady increase in individual and collective creative power and control, increasing predictability and control over destiny. However, in its quest to shape the world, to make it controllable and predictable, Beck argued, first modernity also produced side effects that called into question the benefits of progress. He did not believe that this double-edged character of modernization was new. Rousseau, Marx, Horkheimer and Adorno, Polanyi and many others had already critically examined the side effects of modernity and modernization. But what was new about the side effects to which Beck referred, and what in his view justified the talk of a new age, was, firstly, the ecological effects of industrial modernity, which had a completely new quality both in terms of their geographical and their temporal scope, and secondly, the subjective, cultural side, namely in the way in which these ecological effects in the biophysical world were subjectively perceived and socially evaluated.

In the course of first modernity, new self-understandings and a new individual and collective self-confidence had gradually evolved: the ideals of the Enlightenment, which attribute free will, the right to self-determination, inviolable dignity and universal human rights to human beings as rational and moral subjects, increasingly determined the actual self-perception and expectations of citizens. Norms and self-images that had previously been reserved for a small elite began to have a broader impact on society. Industrial, Fordist modernity initially left very little room for this. People remained firmly embedded in collective structures, expectations, traditions, social constraints and highly standardized (mass) product markets. But the more the demand for independent thinking, an independent opinion, self-determination, an independent personality and an autonomously chosen life developed, the more the traditional structures and constraints were perceived as unbearably restrictive, Beck noted, as 'a conspiracy to conform' (Beck 2001: 4). This required, firstly, liberation from the predetermined social structures and norms of industrial modernity and, secondly, the shaping of one's own life, the practical implementation of the claim to self-determination and self-realization. For this project, there was no longer a predetermined script but, to an ever-larger extent, people now could choose and shape their own personality and life.

For Beck, the development of these new understandings of subjectivity and the self and the ecological side effects of industrialization were two equally important results of first modernity and modernization in the traditional sense. And it is precisely their interplay that is essential for his concept of the *risk society*. The ecological side effects of industrial modernity appeared to be particularly threatening and problematic when seen from the perspective of these new self-understandings, the new demands and expectations with regard to self-determination and self-design: the freedom to self-model that had only just been won by overcoming established social constraints and ties was immediately threatened by the burden of the ecological and social legacies of industrial modernity, by the need to manage and cope with them. And the heteronomy caused by these legacies was diametrically opposed to the claim to an open future, an open horizon for the project of free self-realization and a self-determined life that had only just evolved. So, when Beck described the risk society as the 'age of side-effects', as the age in which the side effects of industrial modernity become dominant, he did not just refer to the changes in the biophysical environment. For him, the change in social patterns of perception and the cultural standards by which the reality of the lifeworld is measured were an equally essential part of this.

However, the cultural side of first modernity was not only relevant insofar as new understandings of subjectivity and new expectations of self-determination asserted themselves here, which politicized social conditions, but also insofar as the emancipation from traditional values and the release from traditional social bonds brought with it new uncertainties. While tradition and the established structures of industrial society had demanded adaptation, acceptance, subordination to established norms and the fulfilment of duties from the individual, Beck wrote, the progress of modernization implied that a general 'compulsion to break with norms' developed (Beck 2001: 3). In the more recent literature, the pressure for self-organization and self-responsibility is often described as a phenomenon of the neoliberalism of the 1990s. However, neoliberalism did not first create this pressure and the burden that comes with it, but only further expanded it into market- and competition-oriented self-optimization and turned it into a negative mass experience. But as Beck had rightly emphasized, this compulsion and the corresponding burden went hand in hand with the process of individualization, that is, the liberation from the structures and ties of traditional modernity. And the more the binding force of traditional structures and norms loosened, the more the compulsion for social conformity that had prevailed in first modernity was replaced by the social compulsion for independence and originality. Beck therefore described individualization as a 'paradoxical social structure' (Beck 2001). It is a 'social dynamic that is not based on a free decision by individuals', but rather people 'are condemned to individualization'. It means the compulsion 'to produce, shape and stage not only one's own biography, but also one's connections and networks' (Beck & Beck-Gernsheim 1994: 14). 'Everyone is now referred back to themselves and has to make sense of the advantages and disadvantages of being who they are' or want to be (Beck 2001: 4). However, this task – without a script – is almost impossible to accomplish; it necessarily means an unmanageable burden, because there is no certainty regarding the norms that people might rely on in their search for identity, self-development and self-realization, in trying to determine their 'authentic' Self and the means by which they might realize it.

For Beck, this problem was not only related to the individual subject but also has a societal dimension. The question arises as to how society, which is drifting apart centrifugally in the wake of individualization, can still be integrated. What, Beck asked, will replace the previous traditions and authorities as a unifying force? Can 'highly individualized societies still be integrated at all' (Beck & Beck-Gernsheim 1994: 33)? What can social cohesion still be based on if individual identity and a self-determined life are freed from religious ties and all traditions and are based '*only* in themselves'? 'Does the age of *self-determination* abolish the socio-structural prerequisites of collectively binding decisions and state-political action?' The new understandings of subjectivity, self-determination and self-realization thus transformed not only the project of each individual's own life, but also that of social coexistence and political organization 'voluntarily or involuntarily into an experimental constellation with an open outcome' (Beck 2001: 5–6). In this respect, the downsides and side effects of liberation from the traditional structures and constraints of industrial modernity were a constitutive element of Beck's notion of the risk society.

It was precisely this uncertainty and the signs of dissolution and disorientation that in the early 1980s motivated the diagnosis of 'postmodernism'. For a broad audience of the educated middle class, Samuel Beckett's plays became an expression of the vague feeling that modernity was bankrupt and finished. 'Something is coming to an end, something is running its course', one of the protagonists says vaguely and threateningly in *Endgame*. In Beckett's best-known play, *Waiting for Godot*, Vladimir and Estragon wait in a cleared landscape under an almost bare tree for someone who remains unknown, who might not even exist at all, and whose arrival, if it ever comes about, might either mean salvation or catastrophe. The protagonists in *Endgame* live in a claustrophobic shelter that they cannot leave, surrounded by a devastated world. They are crippled, bully each other and cower in garbage bins whose lids they can only lift a crack. Modernity and its promises had come to an end, for them, and with it all meaning and orientation. Beck, however, resolutely opposed the term and what he called the 'fatalistic thinking' of postmodernism. Inspired by the spirit of optimism and the creative will of the NSM, he spoke instead of a 'reinvention of politics' and 'the political' and of a second modernity that would take modernity which had so far remained 'halved' or 'truncated' to its full completion.

He paralleled the transition from first to second modernity with that from pre-modernity to first modernity: 'The *tradition* of industrial society itself' now took the place of 'pre-modernity'. 'Just as the forms of living and working in feudal agrarian society were dissolved at the turn of the nineteenth century', Beck wrote, 'the same thing is happening today to those of developed industrial society: social classes and stratification, the nuclear family with the embedded standard biographies of men and women, the standardization of labor, and so on' (Beck 1992: 153). With the transition from first to second modernity, Beck noted, 'a nineteenth century myth is demystified', namely 'the legend that industrial society is a modern society in its plan of work and life'. For, in the risk society, it became apparent 'that the project of modernity', which had initially gained historical reality in the form of industrial society, had remained *'truncated institutionally* in that form' (ibid.). The social institutions, Beck wanted to say, corresponded only partially to the ideals of modernity and ultimately hindered their full realization. And precisely because 'in industrial society we have, as yet, been dealing with a halved modernity' (Beck 1993: 25) and a 'semi-modern society' (1997: 32f), second modernity was not a 'post-modernity' for him, but a new, different modernity that tackles the second half of the, as yet, unfinished project. This, Beck noted, 'is the meaning of the expression *reflexive modernization*: we are not living in a *post*-modern world but in a *hyper*-modern world' (Beck 2009: 55), which seeks to address the negative side effects of industrial modernity and, at the same time, to fully realize those central norms of modernity that only towards the end of first modernity had become firmly established throughout society.

What is crucial – and instructive for the analysis of today's late modernity – is that Beck did not understand second modernity as the consequence of the failure of first modernity, but rather as a consequence of its success. For, without first modernity, neither the new standards of perception of ecological and social crises would have developed on a broad scale, nor the NSM, that is, the subject and key actor of the politicization and transformation of industrial modernity and its institutions. It is 'modernization itself that shifts the coordinates of modernization', Beck explained, and this 'happens unreflectedly, unintentionally, unseen' but with a major societal impact. 'Modernization – *undermines* modernization', Beck said in the German original of *The Reinvention of Politics* (Beck 1993: 31). First modernity itself creates the basis for a critical rebellion and reflexive modernization; and the transition to second modernity takes place 'compulsively in the course of the independent dynamics of modernization according to the pattern of latent side-effects' (ibid.: 36). For Beck, the risk society and second modernity were, therefore, '*not an option* that could be chosen or rejected in the course of political debates'. Both emerge 'in the course of uncontrolled processes of modernization which are blind to their consequences and deaf to all threats' (ibid.). They come 'not in the form of an open but a *silent* revolution, as a consequence of *everyone's* change in consciousness' on the 'tip-toes of normality' and cannot be avoided (Beck 1992: 78, 11).

Critiques of modernity and modernization had been around for a long time, of course. But firstly, they had remained limited to relatively small niches and were, therefore, not as broadly effective as the reflexive modernization in Beck's second modernity. Secondly, the critique of modernity had often been anti-modernist, anti-egalitarian, anti-democratic, conservative and reactionary. Although a progressive critique of modernization had emerged in the labour movement and the critique of capitalism, it had remained class-specific, was not directed against the productivism of the industrial system and, as a critique that focused primarily on issues of distribution rather than limitation, did not have a strong ecological dimension. It was only with the emergence and social anchoring of the new eco-emancipatory norms and the ecological and social side effects of first modernity that a progressive critique of modernization gained a much broader societal basis. And in just this respect, the crisis of modernity diagnosed by Beck was indeed a 'victory-crisis'. For him, nature and ecology played a dual role in that, firstly, in second modernity the ecological side effects that first modernity had caused were to be remedied and, secondly, ecological imperatives were to become a functional substitute for the moral imperatives that could no longer be derived from religion, tradition or a supposedly transcendental reason (cf. e.g. Böhme 1992).

4.4 Ecologization, democratization, cosmopolitan society

For Beck, second modernization thus meant a 'modernization of modernity' in accordance with precisely those emancipatory norms, those understandings of subjectivity, freedom and self-determination, that the 'silent revolution' around the turn of the 1970s had firmly established as universalist values and social aspirations. In line with the newly diagnosed deficits of first modernity, the substantive agenda of second modernity for Beck included above all (a) the ecological restructuring of industrial society, which was a prerequisite for the realization of the new ideas of subjectivity as well as for the intrinsic value attributed to nature by parts of the movements, (b) the full democratization of politics and society, which were still perceived as very incompletely democratic, and (c) the development of a cosmopolitan world society, which was a necessary prerequisite both for solving ecological problems and with a view to realizing universalist norms of freedom and self-determination.

With regard to the ecological restructuring of industrial society, Beck's expectations and hopes – as well as what I refer to as the EEP – must first be clearly distinguished from what since the mid-1980s has been known as 'ecological modernization' and has remained the dominant paradigm of environmental, sustainability and climate policy ever since (cf. Chapters 5.1 and 6.2). This distinction is important because the literature sometimes distinguishes between 'industrial' and 'ecological' modernization, as if they were different phases of modernity (cf. e.g. Spaargaren & Mol 1992). Both speak of ecology and both are about modernization. But what Beck had in mind was much more comprehensive than the project of 'ecological modernization' (cf. also e.g. von Prittwitz 1993; Jänicke 2007). The crucial difference is that for Beck – as well as in what I call the EEP – the emancipatory dimension is absolutely central, because emancipatory norms determine how ecological phenomena are perceived and how the 'ecological question' is framed. Emancipatory norms are therefore at the very heart of both the definition of ecological problems and the formulation of proposed solutions. For 'behind all the objectifications', Beck rightly emphasized, 'sooner or later the question of *acceptance* arises and with it anew the old new question: *how do we wish to live*? What is the human quality of humankind, the natural quality of nature which is to be preserved?' And if in public debate reference is made to the ecological catastrophe, Beck noted, this is ultimately, more than anything, 'an objectivized, pointed, radicalized expression that this development is *not wanted*' (Beck 1992: 28; cf. Chapters 3.1 and 3.2). It is precisely this subject perspective that makes ecologization, as Beck understood it, a dimension of the second modernity, which explicitly aimed to rebuild industrial society in accordance with the new subject norms that had become hegemonic in the course of the silent revolution.

In contrast, in 'ecological modernization' in the technocratic sense that prevails today, the subjective and emancipatory dimension does not figure at all – or only very indirectly. Instead, this ecological modernization fully corresponds in spirit to Beck's first modernity. For here it is assumed in the conventional modernist sense that ecological problems exist 'objectively' and can be scientifically determined. The question from which perspective and on the basis of which norms they are perceived as problematic is not asked or addressed. Instead, in the spirit of traditional modernism, it is assumed that science, technology and efficient management can clearly identify these problems and then solve them. Ecological modernization in this understanding therefore relies entirely on the certainties and instruments of traditional modernity and perpetuates its logic and grammar. In contrast, Beck's hopes – and the EEP – were aimed precisely at replacing this traditional understanding. They reacted to the dissolution of traditional certainties and, in the name of the new emancipatory norms, endeavoured to change the grammar and logic of modernity in such a way that modernity, which had hitherto remained 'halved' or 'truncated', would now actually become fully modern.

Beck believed that in the risk society the conditions were particularly good for this. 'The constellation for criticism', he noted, 'even for radical criticism[,] has never been so favourable' (Beck 1993: 53). In view of the ecological and social side effects of modernization, he believed, society is becoming seriously 'self-critical' (Beck 1993: 54). While (ecological) social criticism had previously come primarily from intellectual elites and avant-garde niche movements, in the risk society it comes from all parts of society and from people's everyday experience of, and concern about, the new risks. Hence, Beck diagnosed a 'democratization of critique' (ibid.) and hoped that humanity's common interest in survival would now become a catalyst for a truly transformative politicization of society as a whole. For, the 'destruction of nature', he suggested, is a 'morality beyond morality' that enables 'a social critique beyond social critique' (Beck 1988: 93). By this he meant that the ecological crisis provides standards, criteria and imperatives that in comparison to the norms of earlier social criticism could unleash much more power. The ecological threat offers the opportunity for a *'remoralization* of all areas of social action', Beck believed, and 'a sense of morality that permeates the whole of society down to its capillaries' (Beck 1993: 17, 28).

With this kind of thinking, Beck actually threatens to undermine his own distinction between the ecological restructuring of industrial society as a project of second modernity, which is characterized by radical uncertainty, and ecological modernization in the sense of first modernity, that is, according to supposedly objective, scientific diagnoses of problems and solution strategies. On the one hand, he described it as the 'fixed star' of the risk epoch 'that the normative system of rationality, with its authority and power of enforcement, abolishes its own foundations' (ibid.: 43). Yet, on the other hand, this did not prevent him from placing great integrative and transformative hope in the overall social experience of ecological risks and disasters: 'The risk of climate change' triggers 'a revaluation of values' from 'postmodern cultural relativism to a historical new fixed star by which to mobilize solidarities and actions' (Beck 2016: 43f). Beck saw the emergence of a 'society of guilty conscience' (Beck 1993: 23) and assumed that this guilty conscience would continue to grow as awareness of the ecological threat in society increased. Because 'the apocalypse knows no constraints', he believed – or at least hoped – the climate crisis would spur 'the co-production of risk perceptions and normative horizons'. The 'global risk of climate change', he noted, represents something like a 'compulsive collective memory' and conscience (Beck 2016: 35, 36). Hence, 'it only seems as if the post-traditional world is disintegrating into anomic individualities'. For, 'in the challenges of self-induced endangerment, it also possesses an inexhaustible source of re-moralization and motivation'. The ecological crisis is creating 'a cultural Red Cross consciousness', Beck said in the style of activist movements: 'Action is imperative, immediately, everywhere, by everyone and under all circumstances' (Beck 1998: 156, 158).

As regards the project of democratization, Beck's core concepts are the 'reinvention of politics' and the new 'subpolitics'. With both terms, he was aiming at the new self-confidence of citizens, which had grown stronger with the silent revolution, and to their new claim to political maturity and self-determination. In view of the side effects of modernity to date, Beck noted, people no longer trusted the existing political institutions to solve the problems at hand and were no longer prepared to leave responsibility to the established elites. Given their democratic deficits and the limitations of the nation state, citizens see both, that is, the institutions and the elites, Beck argued, as a significant part of the problem. They stand for the system of 'organized irresponsibility'. However, to the same extent that the 'three pillars of security', that is, the state, science and the economy, which supported first modernity, were crumbling and 'failing to provide security', the 'self-conscious citizens' would become 'their legal heirs' (Beck 2009: 45f). In 'semi-modern' societies, Beck argued, citizens could not yet really decide for themselves. Democratic institutions were representative at best, but not democratic in the sense of genuine citizen sovereignty. Technology developed rapidly, but its development primarily followed the interests of the economy and could not be determined by the citizens themselves. The economy, in turn, served the interests of capital owners, but not those of citizens and the common good. Accordingly, 'the reinvention of politics' was, firstly, about the participatory democratization of liberal, representative democracy, secondly about the reorientation of the previously dominant liberal individualism towards the interests of the community and the well-being of society at large, and thirdly about the development of a global civil society, as only new forms of political organization beyond the modern nation state are suitable for dealing with the specific problems of the globalized risk society.

Only this reinvention of politics, Beck believed, could create 'institutions that enable an ecological renewal of modernity and make technology collectively agreeable'. It could make the ideal of the autonomous subject and the values it implies the benchmark for politics, administration, the economy, technology and every other area of society. Only then, Beck argued, 'we, the citizens, can really consider anew: How do we want to live – with or without technology or with which technology, and how?' (Beck 1993: 25).

In practice, Beck saw the reinvention of politics as taking place in the new experimental 'subpolitics', that is, the diverse movements and civil society initiatives which politicized and self-confident citizens had started since the 1970s. 'The term subpolitics', he explained, 'denotes the decoupling of politics and government'; it refers to the fact that 'politics is also possible beyond the representative institutions of nation-states'. Beck spoke of a 'new political constellation': 'As the awareness of risks spreads', he believed, 'the foundations, coordinates and ready-made coalitions are thrown into turmoil' (Beck 2009: 95, 100). Subpolitics, he wrote, is repoliticizing all areas and issues in society: 'All fields of action – the economy and science, private life and the family and politics – face a decisive turning point: they need new justification, they must be renegotiated and rebalanced' (ibid.: 94). In this exercise, the crucial questions are: 'How is (political) design possible?' 'How is intelligent self-limitation possible? How are forms of production, life and politics possible that overcome the suicidal nature of industrial modernity', so that 'the transformation from a national self-destructive economy to a global and democratic world civilization succeeds'? (Beck 1993: 65, 64)

Beck already saw 'indicators of a global self-organization of non-state politics that has the potential to mobilize all areas of society'. He believed that 'in the playful merging of opposites into trans-cultural global resistance, cosmopolitan society feels its direct power' (Beck 2009: 95, 100). Well before the new climate movement and Fridays for Future, he spoke of a 'global consensus on climate protection which is now within reach' that would create ideal conditions for global subpolitics. He discerned 'the initial contours of a global citizenship' (ibid.: 102, 94): A 'new constellation of a global subpolitics is emerging'. Hence, he explicitly rejected 'the widespread talk of the end of politics and democracy or of the demise of all values' (ibid.: 94, 100). Just as his concept of second modernity challenged the diagnosis of postmodernism, his notions of the 'reinvention of politics' and 'subpolitics' were explicitly directed against the diagnosis of post-politics and post-democracy. As a pioneer of alternative forms of politics, life and society, Beck believed, subpolitics organized what in social movement research, too, many described as a 'departure to a different society' and as 'democracy from below' (Brand et al. 1983; Roth 1994).

Beck's third central dimension of reflexive modernization has already been mentioned several times: the overcoming of the nation state of the 'semi-modern' age. Beck was convinced that the risk society would inevitably and automatically evolve beyond the nation state into a cosmopolitan world society, because the ideas of autonomy and subjectivity that had become hegemonic in the silent revolution were universal values, and the problems of the first modernity could not be solved by the nation state. Beck believed that the problems of the risk society not only have an integrative effect within societies and act as an antidote to the centrifugal forces of individualizing liberation from traditional constraints, but that they also pave the way for a globally inclusive society. In the 'post-religious and post-national world', the 'idea of human rights, as the internalized basis and identity of one's own life', is a 'source of immanent transcendence and self-limitation of individualization', he noted, which can establish a 'cosmopolitan society' (Beck 2001: 6). Beck hoped that the pressing questions of the future might further a 'projective integration' (Beck & Beck-Gernsheim 1994: 35). It is a 'bitter and tragic irony', he wrote, a 'cunning of history', that the risk society mobilizes its own antidote and nation state modernity creates its own corrective: the 'cosmopolitan moment' (Beck 2009: 55ff); a 'planetary sense of pain', he envisioned, 'shocks and unites the hyper-individualized world risk society' (ibid.: 70).

Accordingly, Beck diagnosed the transition from 'normative' to 'descriptive' cosmopolitanism and from 'cosmopolitan idealism' to 'cosmopolitan realism' (Beck 2009: 187f; 2016: 10). By this he meant that in second modernity, every aspect of life, whether citizens want or realize it or not, is shaped by, and embedded in, transnational and global structures. 'Everyday life is becoming cosmopolitan' (Beck 2009: 15). And in view of their international and global effects, catastrophes 'for-others' inevitably turn into catastrophes 'for-us' (Beck 2016: 122). The 'perceived globality of the dangers produced by civilization itself' triggers 'the revitalization of national politics and the development of cooperative international institutions', Beck wrote. It promotes the development of 'a global and direct subpolitics', which can relativize and circumvent the coordinates and coalitions of national politics and forge 'worldwide *alliances of mutually exclusive convictions*' (Beck 2009: 81f; emphasis in original). Beck firmly believed in the possibility of 'a wholesale reinvention of the basic institutions of modern national society' (ibid.: 49). Both within and between societies, he wrote, the perception of global crises acts as 'a kind of *glue* for diversity'. Global risks contain '*in nuce* an answer to the question of how new kinds of *risk communities*' could emerge in the 'cacophony of the globalized world', 'based neither on descent nor on spatial presence', but rather on a 'compulsory cosmopolitanism' (ibid.: 188).

4.5 A providential gift

Thus, in Beck's eyes, ecological re-moralization, the reinvention of politics and the cosmopolitan moment add up to a transformative dynamic, to a self-propelling modernization triggered by the risk constellation, which transforms the previously truncated modernity into a new, a second modernity, in which social institutions will fully correspond to the ideals of modernity. In contrast to the activist movements, Beck was not interested in the side effects of industrial modernity per se but saw them primarily as a catalyst for its crisis and for its metamorphosis into a new modernity, which in comparison to the first, industrial modernity promised to represent a clear advance in ecological and democratic terms as well as in terms of the world society. Beck's interest was primarily in social and modernization theory: 'Against the still predominant past', as quoted above, he wanted 'to move the future which is just beginning to take shape into view' (Beck 1992: 9).

Overall, Beck was convinced that the new risk situation presented modern society with a 'Herculean task', but also with an urgently needed new horizon of meaning (Beck 1998: 157). He saw the ecological crisis as an opportunity to restore a clear sense of direction to the society that Beckett portrayed in his plays: a society that after the collapse of the grand narratives seems to have lost its bearings, orientation and perspective. The ecological question, Beck argued, is a kind of 'providential gift for the universal self-reformation' of the 'postmodern, jaded, saturated, meaningless, and fatalistic *pâté de foie gras* culture' (Beck 1997: 159f) because it creates 'new certitudes' and 'rigidities' beyond religion and transcendental reason, which finally 'put an end to permanent doubt and self-doubt' (ibid.: 90). Against the scenarios and fears of the *ecocalypse* that were widespread in the 1980s, Beck insisted: 'Far from intensifying and confirming the general pointlessness of modernity, environmental dangers create a *substantive semantic horizon of avoidance, prevention and helping*'. This 'moral climate and milieu', he believed, 'intensifies with the size of the threat' (Beck 1997: 159) and has the power to 'awake' post-modern society from its 'lethargy and pessimism' (Beck 1998: 160).

So, Beck firmly believed in a 'rebirth of modernity', which would remedy the fundamental shortcomings and deficits of the modern age so far (Beck 2017: 155). In his model, the ideal of the autonomous subject which had been a regulative ideal ever since the Enlightenment but had gained much more political force at the transition to second modernity, remained the normative yardstick for further modernization. Rather than becoming lost in scenarios of cultural pessimism and decline or in postmodern cultural criticism, Beck insisted: 'solutions and redemption were always fashioned out of the discarded certainties of the previous age'. The risk society and the crisis of modernity he did not see as the 'end of the world', but merely as the demise of 'the world certainties of the first modernity' (Beck 2009: 218; cf. Chapter 1). And he saw a new modernity emerging out of its ruins – much more concretely than Polanyi, for example, who had recognized only 'the cornerstones' of a new world (cf. Chapter 3). Out of the crisis of industrial modernity, Beck thus forged a new 'grand narrative': that of second modernity.

— 5 —

DECONSTRUCTING THE 'LEGEND'

From today's perspective, Beck's hopes – especially in the somewhat reductionist simplicity in which they have been presented here so far – appear 'overly optimistic' (Staab 2022: 16). However, with regard to the great political optimism of the seventies and early eighties, the great disillusionment and disenchantment of today's late modernity and the metamorphosis of this late modernity into an entirely different kind of modernity, Beck's theoretical approach is particularly illuminating. It depicts quite precisely the hopes, values, convictions, self-perceptions and the spirit of political departure that were typical of the NSM and constitutive of the EEP, and whose disintegration and disappointment are, in turn, the distinguishing feature of late modernity today. Beck saw the NSM as pioneering forces, as the political subject of a fundamental societal transformation, and thus mirrored the hopes and expectations that were very present not only in the activist movements but also in the academic literature of the time (cf. e.g. Rucht 1994) – and to some extent still are to this day. But even though his work documents the beliefs and core elements of the NSM and the EEP very precisely, Beck saw himself primarily as a social theorist, not as a chronicler of the NSM or an activist movement researcher. And as a sociologist, he also articulated what the actors of the movements and the EEP could not or did not want to see or say – because that would have been politically counterproductive – and what they often still do not say to this day. In his role as a sociologist, Beck repeatedly emphasized that whatever he expected from second modernity were, at best, hopes and possibilities, but by no means certainties. From his perspective as a social theorist, he always provided a subtext in which he explained why his own hopes, and those of the movements and activist literature he described, would

129

perhaps – or even probably – not be fulfilled, and that the EEP would therefore quite possibly never achieve the goals it had set itself.

In this respect, Beck occupied an intermediate position between the sociological analysis of 'what is' and the activist literature, which is primarily committed to political mobilization for what 'ought to be'. The genre of *Zeitdiagnose* and Beck's role as a public intellectual allowed him a considerable degree of ambivalence and inconsistency, which fellow sociologists have often criticized him for. But it is precisely this barely concealed inconsistency, Beck's struggle with his own hopes, his uncertainty, that is instructive. From today's perspective, the point in reading Beck is not that one might learn from him how and why an SET can get off the ground and succeed, but (a) that he portrays the values, hopes, perceptions, diagnoses and beliefs that were or are constitutive for the EEP, (b) that he reflects – without this being his main focus and interest – on why the SET can ultimately hardly succeed, and (c) that, with the tension between the hoped-for and its failure, Beck's work reveals precisely what is specifically late-modern, today, and the special character of the late-modern 'abyss' – namely the collapse of the narrative of reflexive modernization and the EEP.

While the previous chapter referred to Beck in order to create a social- and modernization-theoretical framework for the interpretation of the crisis of modernity and the EEP (double untenability), the aim now is to draw on Beck's theory of reflexive modernization for a purpose for which it was never actually intended. Firstly, Beck was referring to a different crisis of modernity than the current one, and secondly, he focused on the emergence of the EEP and of the SET narrative, while the focus here is on their untenability and disintegration. Accordingly, what was reconstructed in the previous chapter – Beck's narrative of the second modernity and the hope for a civil society-organized departure into a socio-ecologically transformed society – is now deconstructed from a late-modern point of view. For this purpose, I will zoom in on the subtext, through which Beck always sceptically regarded his own hopes. I will begin by calling to mind Beck's often-repeated warnings that in contrast to the crisis of first modernity, which unfolds inevitably and unstoppably, its resolution in second modernity is, ultimately, no more than a hope, an aspirational project. Seeking to explain why this optimistic hope and project did, in fact, remain unfulfilled, I will then turn to Beck's multilayered concept of 'reflexivity'. From there, the focus will shift to the internal contradictions of the EEP which obstructed its full realization and at the same time – unintentionally, unnoticed, unconsciously and as a side effect – promoted the emergence of something new that the NSM had neither intended nor ever considered possible or even desirable. Overall then, this chapter is an attempt to go beyond Beck – to use, appreciate, expand and update his theory in a way that, in line with the agenda of this book, makes a contribution to the theory of late modernity and helps to explain the unsustainability, disintegration and repoliticization of the EEP.

5.1 No automatism

The threat of disasters, Beck wrote, 'opens our eyes and raises our hopes'. Although it might seem paradoxical, he noted, the threat also provides 'encouragement' (Beck 2016: 43). For, 'the moment of existential threat' unintentionally opens up 'the (mis-)fortune of a possible new beginning'; 'the shock of danger' is a call 'for a new beginning' (Beck 2009: 49). The EEP was precisely this project of a new beginning. Like Beck, the activists of the EEP always believed in the 'enlightening function of global risk' and in the 'cosmopolitan moment of world risk society'. It was a 'cunning of history' (ibid.: 55ff), Beck wrote, that the threats and uncertainties of the present would *bring people to their senses* and thus secure emancipatory progress. To this day, movements that regard 'planetary boundaries' as categorical imperatives and demand 'listen to the science!' cling to this hope. But Beck always harboured doubts. He explicitly emphasized that there are no simple solutions and that 'the positive side-effects of negative side-effects' do not 'automatically create a better world' (Beck 2016: 47): 'There is no automatic transition from the desecuritization of classical industrial society to the critical reflection on this self-destruction and self-transformation' (Beck 1993: 15). Beck did hope that 'the second modernity into which we have long since slipped' would be a political modernity, that is, 'a modernity that, among other things, triggers a reinvention of politics'. Yet, the 'analytical core' of his theory, he emphasized unambiguously, 'states in a completely amoral and hope-free way: reflexive modernization generates fundamental shocks which, as counter-modernity, *can either be* used as grist to the mill of nationalism and neo-fascism (namely if, when certainties dissolve, the majority calls for and reaches out for new-old rigidities) *or*, in the other extreme, to reformulate the goals and foundations of Western industrial societies' (ibid.: 14 and 16f; emphases in original).

From today's perspective, it is obvious that instead of the optimistic hopes, the flip side that Beck always had in the back of his mind has come true: climate protection and the SET have not become issues of consensus or humanity at large but a major trigger of social division and political hatred. A risk community has not emerged, neither within nor between societies. An ecological restructuring of industrial society has taken place to a limited extent, at best, and only in the sense of an ecological modernization that reinforces rather than changes the basic logic and grammar of first modernity. Beck was clearly right in saying that the issue of climate change and the ecological restructuring of society strongly moralize, politicize and polarize the public. But contrary to his expectations, the 'refusal to do ecological service' has become an option, indeed, and a fairly popular one, too. Also, in late-modern societies, an ecological-political 'defence consensus' has indeed emerged (Beck 1995: 186), but it does not defend the EEP and the idea of an SET, but primarily the prosperity achieved and the established order of unsustainability (see Chapters 1 and 2; also Blühdorn 2020b). In fact, in view of the new moralization and polarization as well as the diversity of incompatible values and interests in society, a state of eco-political self-paralysis and ungovernability has long since established itself (see Chapters 3.2 and 6.2).

Beck had regarded all this as a realistic scenario. He was certain 'that the ecological question forms a fantastic moral *milieu*' (emphasis added). However, he left open in which direction this moralization would take effect, and he also saw that 'in practice' moral value systems were eroding 'seemingly without replacement' (Beck 1993: 28, 27). Beck even feared that we might be 'situated at the beginning of a historical process of habituation', in which the newly acquired eco-political norms and 'standards disappear' again 'as a result of their violation' (Beck 1992: 83; cf. also the central thesis of Chapter 3.6). At one point, he explicitly described the calls for an ecological restructuring of industrial society as 'empty political formulas and ambitions', thus admitting that, ultimately, there are no categorical ecological imperatives that provide guidelines for the EEP (Beck 1993: 19). Hence, the *'historical opportunity* of an ecological morality' never meant for him that an ecologization of modern society was certain – or even particularly likely (Beck 1993: 29, emphasis added).

The reinvention of politics, which was supposed to secure democratic self-determination and a good life for all, has not taken place in the hoped-for form, either. Instead, the break from tradition, the liberation from the structures of industrial modernity, the severance from social ties, has left a void that, contrary to Beck's hopes, could not be filled with either civic maturity or ecological reason and collective responsibility. A mature, inclusive civil society has not emerged and, in particular, has not developed a shared consciousness as a political actor and collective bearer of eco-social responsibility. Instead, disorientation, 'alternative facts' and conspiracy myths flourish in late modernity. The reinvention of politics did not lead to the empowerment of citizens vis-à-vis the elites, but rather to the further expansion of the (political) privileges of an already privileged middle class. It did not lead to the hoped-for democratization of democracy, but to a further distortion of political representation (cf. e.g. Manow 2020; Schäfer & Zürn 2021; Elsässer et al. 2021; see also Chapter 6.4). The NSM and their new, experimental politics were, ultimately, not the pioneers of an SET, but often only of inner-city gentrification and social distinction (cf. e.g. Helbrecht 1996; Wiest & Hill 2004; Holm 2010). And eventually, their value orientations, lifestyles and activism became the trigger for massive counter-movements of anti-ecological, anti-diversity and anti-wokeness rebellion. Philipp Staab, for example, rightly diagnoses a 'historical disappointment with the lack of effectiveness of sub-political forms' of addressing social problems in late modernity (Staab 2022: 178). This disappointment, in turn, causes repoliticizations in quite diverse parts of society. Thus, Beck's reinvention of politics is repeating itself. However, today it is no longer – or not only – the established social institutions that are radically called into question, but also the beliefs, achievements and agendas of the EEP.

This, too, Beck had foreseen as a possibility: just as he had identified that the ecological re-moralization of society would not necessarily result in an ecological restructuring of industrial society, he had also made clear that the new subpolitics would not automatically lead to a better democracy. With the reinvention of politics, he noted, 'undoubtedly no age of hope, no paradise is opening up', but in this respect, too, 'disasters of a completely new dimension' are looming: 'ecodictatorship, violence, fundamentalism'. The reinvention of politics, Beck wrote, can put even established democracies 'into a tilt that accelerates destruction' (Beck 1993: 65, 64). The civilizational side effects of modernity to date have political side effects, he warned, that 'threaten the continued existence of the democratic political system' (Beck 1992: 80). 'With the increase of hazards *totally new types of challenges to democracy* arise in the risk society', he wrote: the risk society 'harbors a tendency towards a *legitimate totalitarianism of hazard prevention*' (ibid., emphases in original). Therefore, the reinvention of politics could mean either 'neo-fascism *or* ecological democracy; eco-dictatorship, violence, fundamentalism *or* a further development of democracy and enlightenment' (Beck 1993: 64, emphasis in original). And indeed, late-modern societies provide ample evidence for tendencies towards '*legitimate* totalitarianism' as well as for new nationalisms and neo-fascism.

And finally, cosmopolitan fraternization and the formation of a global world risk community have also remained an unfulfilled hope. Beck repeatedly emphasized that global risks, crises and threats might act as 'motors of a growing awareness of globality' (Beck 2009: 183). In practice, however, neither a cosmopolitan state nor a cosmopolitan civil society have emerged. Rather, in late modernity, the fragmentation of civil society as well as the disintegration of the so-called international community and its institutions is rife. It had always been a contradiction that Beck, on the one hand, highlighted the dissolution of collective identities and established social structures – as Gerhard Schulze, Zygmunt Bauman, Andreas Reckwitz and others later continued to argue – but on the other hand believed that the shared experience of risk could and would establish a global risk community. There is no doubt that individualization has created new needs for community and identity, in late modernity. However, these are not satisfied in a global risk community, but rather in neo-communities and communicative bubbles that cultivate specific narratives of meaning without having to address the complexity of real people, lifeworlds and societal conditions. In comparison, the idea of forging and identifying with the cosmopolitan community was far too demanding, abstract and overwhelming. However, with regard to this vision, too, Beck had seen the signs of a new risk-induced cosmopolitanism only as an '*in nuce*' response (Beck 2009: 188) to the threat of the disintegration of the modern risk society, not as a fully fledged perspective for solving the problem.

Thus, reflective modernization and the EEP have not delivered what Beck had hoped for. Rather, second modernity produced traumas of 'offended freedom' in very different parts of society. They arise from the glaring contradiction between the highly developed demands for self-determination and self-realization and the factual experience of increasingly narrow boundaries of autonomy and self-efficacy. In fact, the horizon of what individuals can still shape and control has contracted considerably. As Stephanie Wakefield put it, late-modern societies find themselves in the ruins of the 'exhausted and imploding era of humanism', at the 'end of liberal life' and in the 'wreckage of the old fantasies of the good life' (Wakefield 2018: 4, 7). Politically, this constellation is increasingly explosive and ungovernable – precisely because of the highly developed emancipatory demands and expectations. It is diametrically opposed to Beck's scenarios of hope. However, Beck's analysis is, ultimately, much less 'overly optimistic' than it initially appears. After all, he explicitly saw the ambivalence of reflexive modernization but – counter to his own scepticism – consciously opted for the positive side: 'action is possible and full of opportunity'! He described this choice of perspective as 'magnificently naive'. But he justified it by saying that he was simply 'tired of pessimism'; 'rehashing the general doom and gloom', he said, seemed 'unappealing' to him (ibid.: 33).

Today, however, the situation has been reversed. In the 'wreckage of the old fantasies of the good life for all', late-modern citizens cling to ubiquitous narratives of hope, to the renewed promises of self-efficacy and control, which various actors throw out to them like lifebuoys (cf. Chapter 7). However, in view of the rather limited room for manoeuvre, these narratives appear increasingly less plausible and are regarded as increasingly irksome. Accordingly, there is something like a late-modern 'optimism fatigue', against the backdrop of which – rewording Beck – *rehashing the general white- or greenwashing seems unappealing*. However, this reversal in no way contradicts Beck's theory, since he always had the possibility of an undesirable outcome in the back of his mind. And this is precisely why Beck's theory is so revealing for the analysis of today's turning point, the abyss, the late-modern untenability.

5.2 Reflexivity and destabilization

So why was it that the hopes for a second modernity and those of the EEP did not come true? With his concept of reflexive modernization, Beck himself provided an explanation that not only goes far beyond the usual explanations offered, for example, by the critique of capitalism or Luhmann's systems theory, but that also makes a significant contribution to understanding the late-modern abyss, the double untenability and the current metamorphosis of the society of unsustainability into a new, very different modernity. In this context, the multidimensionality of the term 'reflexive' is particularly important. At least three understandings are alluded to in Beck's work:

- reflexive in the sense of *as a reflex*, that is, uncontrolled, unconscious, automatic, unavoidable;
- reflexive in the sense of *reflected*, that is, considered, controlled, self-critical, rational;

- reflexive in the sense of *turning against itself*, that is, self-destabilizing, self-undermining, self-destructive.

These diverse understandings are not readily compatible with each other. But they are equally constitutive for Beck's concept of reflexive modernization; and they are very instructive for understanding the crisis and unsustainability of the EEP. Just as the concept of second modernity focused on the completion of the previously 'halved' or 'truncated' modernity, this also applies to the concept of reflexive modernization: Beck explicitly described it as a path to a world that is 'more modern' than its predecessor (Beck 2007: 108). This was to be a prudent, coordinated, reason-guided path that would address the unexpected side effects of the first modernity and fully realize its ideals. Yet, 'understood empirically and analytically', Beck emphasized, reflexivity does not mean '*reflection*, but *self-confrontation*' (Beck 1993: 36). The term is aimed, first and foremost, he pointed out, at 'the independent, unintentional and unseen, so to speak, reflex-like transition from the industrial to the risk society', which leads to the self-confrontation of society 'with risk-societal consequences', 'which can no longer be adequately dealt with and processed in the system of industrial society'. Thus, industrial modernity slips uncontrollably, 'so to speak, reflex-like', into the risk society, Beck suggested, but is then supposed to find its way out or beyond it, to overcome the self-generated dangers that are 'gaining predominance' in the risk society (ibid.: 37) through prudence and reflection.

In order to be able to diagnose such dangers and such a predominance in a politically relevant way, and to translate corresponding diagnoses into transformative strategies for action, there must, of course, be supra-individually recognized standards of evaluation and objectives. Reflexivity understood in this way, therefore, presupposes that corresponding standards either remain unaffected by the modernization that otherwise calls everything into question, or that new ones are created in this process. Supplementing his comments on the 'remoralizing' power of the new risks, Beck emphasized that in reflexive modernization and the reinvention of politics, the 'basic principles' and the great 'achievements of European modernity' – parliamentary democracy, the rule of law, human rights, individual freedom – are 'not up for discussion', but only 'the way they are implemented in the moulds of industrial society' (Beck 1993: 17). Thus, these so-called basic principles are, it seems, exempt from the modernizing questioning. However, this is hardly plausible, because reflexive modernization – in the third understanding of reflexivity – affects these standards, too: firstly, in that it challenges and destroys all existing norms and, secondly, in that it places newly emerging norms under constant critical fire, which hardly allows them to solidify and establish their legitimacy. And it is precisely in this way that reflexive modernization makes the consensual diagnosis of 'self-generated dangers that are now gaining predominance' and the development of related strategies for counter-action increasingly difficult.

Of course, Beck himself knew that the idea of supposedly non-negotiable basic principles of modernity is based on a rather restrictive and hardly tenable understanding of reflexive modernization. 'Reflexive modernization', he said, 'contains both elements: reflexive self-endangerment of the foundations of industrial society through successful, danger-blind further modernization, on the one hand, *and* the awareness of, the reflection on this relationship', on the other (Beck 1993: 56; emphasis in original). And it is 'the combination of reflex and reflection', he claimed, 'that can open up fatalistic industrial modernity to self-criticism and self-transformation, as long as the catastrophe does not occur'. Together, reflex and reflection were supposed to lead the way to a 'self-critical modernity' (ibid.: 57, 56).

Thus, on the one hand, Beck's concept of reflexive modernization suggests that modernity, which has so far remained semi-modern, can be brought to completion in a second attempt. On the other hand, however, the ongoing 'reflexive, danger-blind further modernization' in second modernity means that the 'basic principles' of modernity that have not yet been touched get eroded, too, and modernization becomes completely uncertain. This implies – in the same way that Beck claimed for first modernization – the self-endangerment of the foundations of second modernity.

Here, Beck's concept of reflexivity points us to an essential reason – not the only one, of course – why the hopes of the EEP (and those of Beck himself) have remained unfulfilled. Still, it would be wrong to say that the EEP has failed. For it is not, as the critique of domination and capitalism suggests, suppressed and marginalized by a logic that is alien and opposed to it, but the EEP and second modernity undermine themselves in the wake of their own implementation. In this sense, they fall into a 'crisis of victory', just as first modernity did before: reflexive modernization is, on the one hand, the modernization of the still pre-modern, the foundations of semi-modernity that have not yet been called into question and plunged into radical uncertainty. In this respect, it implies the uncontrollable, reflexive, self-destructive erosion of its own indispensable foundations. On the other hand, reflexive modernization is also intended to mobilize the norms – the 'basic principles' – of modernity in order to criticize and bring to completion the modernity that has so far remained halved. Yet, this simultaneous decomposition and activation of the same norms is an impossibility. Reflexive modernization and second modernity can, therefore, not possibly achieve the correction and completion of first modernity. This hope has been misguided from the outset – and it gives rise to the spectre of 'counter-modernization'. Beck himself recognized the 'conflict between counter-modernization on the one hand and the renewal and radicalization of modernity on the other' (Beck 1993: 17). Counter-modernization, he said, means taking resort to manufactured certainties as a reaction to the excessive demands placed on people by their liberation from established constraints. The radicalization of modernity, he suggested, means radicalized liberation – which, however, necessarily reinforces the already existing disorientation and excessive demands because it also undermines the remaining 'basic principles'. Beck was unable to resolve this dilemma, and being 'tired of pessimism', he opted for the appeal of 'renewal and radicalization'.

Particularly with regard to the ecological issue, Beck elaborated quite thoroughly on this destabilizing, self-destructive contradiction between the activation of supposedly reliable basic principles and their modernizing (subjectivizing) questioning. On the one hand, he counted on ecological dangers as a non-negotiable, extra-societal point of normative reference – 'morality beyond morality', 'social critique beyond social critique' (cf. Chapter 4.4). On the other hand, however, he clearly saw that such extra-societal norms and standards do not actually exist, that all supposedly categorical ecological imperatives are ultimately social imperatives and that ecological protest, above all, points to the violation of social norms, not to objective, scientific urgencies and necessities of survival (Beck 1988: 79). If ecology movements hoped to use nature 'as a yardstick against its destruction', he said, they fall victim to a 'naturalistic misunderstanding' (Beck 1988: 62–95) and may be accused of 'forgetting the social' (ibid.: 68). And reflexive modernization itself steadily erodes all supposedly objective norms and thus further weakens its own prospects of success. At the same time, cultural norms and the cultural willingness to perceive are becoming ever more important. Especially since the silent revolution and in the risk society, as Beck rightly emphasized, these norms decide *which destruction is accepted and which is not*, how the acceptance of the unacceptable arises and maintains itself against the background of the self-evident' (Beck 1988: 76; original emphasis).

Accordingly, the prerequisites for industrial society becoming 'an industrial society with a bad conscience, that understands and accuses itself as a risk society' and is then actually capable of a targeted ecological transformation, are not – and ever less – fulfilled (Beck 1998: 160). Ecological self-criticism and the ecological transformation of industrial society can hardly succeed because there are no politically reliable reference norms, either for diagnosing the problem or for effective counter-strategies. Against the odds, Beck still hoped that the topic of ecology could mobilize a social consensus for transformation. As a sociologist, however, he saw and articulated the contradictory and untenable nature of his own activist hope. Still, this inconsistency is not a weakness in Beck's thinking, but rather a strength. Beck made visible and problematized what the NSM and the EEP cannot concede and reflect on, but which is, nevertheless, a very important reason why they never achieved their goal – and instead promoted developments that radically contradict their own intentions. This, one might say, is self-undermining, self-destructive and self-paralysing reflexivity 'at work'.

5.3 The ecological paradox

Beck's theory of the reflexive modernization of a modernity that has so far been halved thus turns out to be *a halved theory of reflexive modernity*. From this perspective, the reason that the EEP and the agenda of the NSM, that is, the SET, could not be implemented as hoped (also by Beck) is that in the course of reflexive modernization, the already weak normative foundations of the EEP were and are being hollowed ever further. Although it seeks to fully enforce the norms of modernity, reflexive modernization simultaneously continues to critically question everything that has not yet been called into question – including these norms themselves – and demands rational justifications – which, however, it is unable to provide. This is a cycle of self-destabilization and self-destruction. This internal contradiction, this tension between the attempt to critically question the norms of modernity and at the same time to invoke them as non-negotiable basic principles for further modernization, points to further contradictions inherent in the architecture of the EEP, which also contribute to its destabilization and ultimate unsustainability.

At the forefront of this is the contradiction between the liberating, emancipatory objective of reflexive modernity and the EEP and its agenda of compliance and subordination: on the one hand, the EEP and second modernity want to break free from established constraints, from all external determination, from everything that is supposedly unchangeably divine, natural and traditional, so as to make room for the authentic self-determination of the autonomous subject. At the same time, however, they also want to enforce subordination to overriding necessities of nature, ecological imperatives and ecological reason in favour of the autonomy, integrity, dignity and intrinsic value of nature and in order to secure the biophysical framework conditions for their own self-determination and self-realization (good life for all). The EEP thus simultaneously demanded liberation from everything that claimed to be natural and unchangeable and subordination to categorical ecological necessities.

Furthermore, on the emancipatory side of this tension, within the project of self-determination, there is the tension between the autonomy of the individual subject and that of the collective subject. For in addition to collective self-determination and self-government in accordance with ecological reason, political maturity and ecological citizenship, the EEP and the project of second modernity included the fulfilment of the promise of individual self-determination, personality, particularity, authenticity and diversity, which had not been fulfilled in first, industrial, Fordist, mass modernity. This was the romantic-individualistic dimension of the promise of autonomy – the realization of an authentic individual identity, which was not easily reconcilable with the rationalistic-collective dimension, that is, the acceptance of guidance by collective reason, maturity and responsibility (cf. Chapter 6.3). This tension became particularly acute in the course of the silent revolution, which strongly emphasized the romantic-individualistic, expressive, identity-related dimension over the subordination to any higher authority. In this respect, too, the EEP and second modernity were always inherently contradictory.

Thirdly, the NSM and the EEP always aimed at the acceptance of categorical ecological imperatives, ecological maturity, ecological reason, stable, rationally based principles, long-term commitment and collective responsibility, but at the same time also at flexibility, innovation, originality, emotion, the diversity of alternative rationalities, inconsistency, spontaneity and so on. Further contradictions could be added here, for example, the one between the demand for democratic self-determination of citizens and the demand for subordination to non-negotiable ecological necessities. What these contradictions all have in common – Table 3 summarizes some of them – is that they imply a double commitment to conflicting values or goals. And these are not weaknesses of the EEP which might easily be ironed out, but

Table 3. Inherent contradictions of the EEP

The eco-emancipatory paradox	
radical criticism of modernity	defence and continuation of modernity
reverence, amazement towards nature	claim to control, design and management
setting boundaries/limits and subordination to nature for the sake of the autonomy/integrity of nature	crossing boundaries/limitations and liberation from the natural for the sake of the autonomy of the subject
categorical ecological imperatives (duty)	radical self-determination (freedom)
objectivity, biophysical facts	subjectivity, norms of perception
boundaries, limitation, subordination on behalf of the general	liberation, transgressing boundaries in the name of individual singularity
self-determination of the collective subject	self-determination of the individual subject
autonomy as self-determination in accordance with an overriding reason	autonomy as self-realization in accordance with individual uniqueness
democratization as empowerment of the civil society of responsible citizens	democratization as empowerment of heterogeneous individual agendas
equality, justice, full inclusion, universal values and rights	distinctiveness, individuality, diversity, authentic self-realization
long-term perspective, stability, reliability, adherence to principles, commitment to rules, responsibility	spontaneity, openness, independence, flexibility, alternative rationalities

contradictions that are inherent in its DNA, constitutive of the EEP, and cannot be resolved. They destabilize the EEP in that, in each case, the implementation of one commitment erodes the basis for the implementation of the other. These internal contradictions – which will be pursued further in Chapter 6 – add up to an eco-emancipatory paradox.

In this paradox, the tension does not simply lie between the eco-logical and the emancipatory dimensions of the EEP, that is, between the project of ecological limitation and subordination to ecological necessities and the agenda of transgressing established boundaries and liberation in the name of the autonomy of the subject. But there is also a contradiction within each of the two sides: emancipatory efforts aim simultaneously at the emancipation of the individual and the collective subject – that is, they demand liberation from as well as subordination to the general. And ecological efforts focus, on the one hand, on biophysical conditions and nature as the non-societal counterpart (supposedly objective problems and imperatives), but – insofar as every concept of nature and the natural to be protected is a social construction – they also deal with highly diverse and malleable social norms.

Thus, the EEP has always been an inherently inconsistent and conflict-laden project. Its values and objectives, sketched in the introductory chapter as its constitutive elements (see Chapter 1.1, Table 1), can be arranged in pairs of opposites, and by struggling for one value of each pair, the EEP undermines the fulfilment of the other. This inevitably leads – Beck would have said 'by itself' and as a 'side-effect' – to the self-destabilization of the EEP and ultimately to its disintegration. The EEP could ever only appear as a consistent and convincing project because it was implicitly based on (pre-modern) foundations and assumptions – such as the belief in objective environmental problems, categorical eco-imperatives or a reason common to all human beings – which initially bridged and concealed the manifold contradictions. However, it was precisely these pre-modern foundations and assumptions that were continuously eroded in the course of reflexive modernization. And the more fragile they became, the more visible the contradictions became, which appear entirely irreconcilable, today. At the same time, it also became ever more visible that the EEP had always been supported, first and foremost, by some – more privileged – sections of society, which were or are well equipped with various forms of capital (education, social networks, articulation power, economic capital, etc.) and, accordingly, had a strong interest in creating the free spaces they needed to actually realize the potential inherent in their capital. What was understood and presented as a project for humanity at large, and as the realization of universal rights, thus, became increasingly recognizable as the project of a bourgeois-liberal elite. And this is precisely why in late modernity, in which the narrative of universal rights and the good life for all is becoming increasingly untenable, the EEP is becoming a crystallization point for massive social polarization and conflicts.

Regardless of whether we notice or like it (or not), today, these contradictions are forcing late-modern societies, which now command an unprecedented level of ecological information and awareness, once again, 'on the tip-toes of normality', onto the path to a different modernity. Late modernity reconfirms Beck's thesis that the implementation of modern society's own logic, that 'uncontrolled processes of modernization which are blind to their consequences and deaf to all threats' (Beck 1993: 36) are driving the 'side-effects metamorphosis of modern society' (Beck 2016: 48). This is traumatic insofar as, according to this interpretation, firstly, the EEP is not blocked and thwarted by capitalism, but undermines itself. Secondly, the disintegration of the EEP reveals a great self-misperception and hubris of those who like to perceive themselves as modern society's enlightened, mature, progressive and responsible avant-gardes. They denied their self-interest, failed to recognize the dependence of their project on non-renewable social resources, overlooked the inevitable side effects of their agenda of reflexive modernization and never came to grips with the contradictions of the EEP, which, essentially, had always been obvious.

5.4 Metamorphosis to third modernity

Second, reflexive modernity, Beck had hoped with the pioneers of the EEP, was to bring citizens, society and humanity as a whole to their senses and take them, borrowing Kant's words, 'out of their self-incurred immaturity'. Partial successes were achieved as long as, and to the extent that, it was socially possible to agree on what was to count as 'reasonable' and what 'maturity' meant. However, reflexive modernization increasingly eroded precisely this ability to deliberate and agree. Back in the early 1990s, Beck said that 'the model of Western modernity – the *occidental* mixture of capitalism, democracy, the rule of law and national [. . .] sovereignty' had 'slipped into a crisis of victory', had become 'outdated' and now had to be 'renegotiated and redesigned' (Beck 1993: 17; emphasis in original). Today, this is more applicable than ever (cf. Chapter 3.6). But while Beck still assumed that the 'sacred norms of human existence and civilization' (Beck 2016: 117f) and the great 'achievements of European modernity' (Beck 1993: 17) were not themselves up for discussion, things are now fundamentally different. This is the crucial decisive difference between the new modernity that Beck was talking about and the one on whose threshold late-modern societies currently stand. For, today, even the achievements of European and Western modernity that were previously not up for discussion – the autonomy of the subject, democracy, liberalism, the universal validity of human rights, the rule of law, etc. – have become highly uncertain, as have the alternative structures and institutions that were newly created in the wake of the reinvention of politics in order to implement eco-emancipatory values.

Just as Beck's first modernity – in its search for certainty and security – transformed itself unintentionally and reflexively into the risk society and then into second modernity, this second modernity is now transforming itself, unintentionally and reflexively, searching for ecological and social sustainability, into a third modernity. At the transition to second modernity, Beck said that the 'basic institutions' and 'the actors of the first modernity' were 'undermined by the growing awareness that they are ineffective, indeed that their measures are counterproductive' (Beck 2009: 55). Today, the project of second modernity and thus the EEP are coming up against the same limits: its values and institutions are now themselves undermined by the growing awareness of their ineffectiveness and the counterproductivity of their measures (cf. the concepts of 'second-order emancipation' in Chapter 6.3 and 'democratic dysfunctionality' in Chapter 6.4). And just as Beck once described second modernity as 'a kind of involuntary release from the forms of self-incurred tutelage [immaturity] characteristic of industrial society' (Beck 2009: 218), one might say today: late-modern societies are once again experiencing a kind of liberation from self-incurred forms of an earlier immaturity. Of course, one might find it difficult to understand the beliefs and obligations of the EEP as self-incurred forms of immaturity. Factually, however, the beliefs and demands of the EEP are ever more widely perceived as illusions and unreasonable demands that should be thrown overboard – albeit perhaps with hesitation – in defence of 'our freedom, our values and our lifestyle' (cf. Chapter 6.3). And just as Beck had warned at the interface to second modernity not to confuse the end of the world certainties of first modernity with the end of the world itself (Beck 2009: 217ff), the abandonment of what today ever more people see as 'eco-emancipatory ballast' and 'woke ideology' does not mean the end of the world, either, but is first and foremost that of the world certainties of second modernity and the EEP (cf. also Chapter 1).

While in second modernity 'the *application* of certain basic principles of modernity' undermined 'the historical foundations of the institutions of industrial society', today the *abandonment* or fundamental

144

redefinition of these basic principles undermines the historical foundations of the institutions of second modernity (Beck 2009: 216, emphasis added). Just as second modernity dissolved the 'tradition', 'the forms of life and work' of 'developed industrial society' (Beck 1992: 153), today, the tradition and institutions of post-industrial society, that is, of second modernity and the EEP, are being radically questioned and dissolved. While second modernity 'demystified' the 'legend' that industrial society had already been 'a *modern* society' (ibid.), today, on the threshold of a third modernity, the legend is being demystified that reflexive modernization and the EEP can take 'semi-modernity' to its completion, that they can finally realize the essence of modernity and a truly modern society, that the ecological threat, the reinvention of politics and the cosmopolitan moment can bring about a socially and ecologically pacified (world) society, and that ecological reason and maturity can reconcile the inner contradictions of the EEP and resolve the eco-emancipatory paradox.

Thus, late modernity means another 'self-disenchantment of modernity' (Beck 2009: 213f), this time that of second modernity. The abandonment of eco-emancipatory values has often been described as a step backwards (e.g. Nachtwey 2018; Geiselberger 2017). Regressive or reactionary elites, Shoshana Zuboff writes, want to 'reverse emancipation and lock us back into the limited prospects of our childhood' (Zuboff 2018: 63). Referring to the digital revolution, she explicitly speaks of a 'third modernity' (Zuboff 2019: 46ff). Undoubtedly, reactionary elites do pursue such interests; yet, this perspective – and this notion of third modernity – ignores what has been thoroughly traced here, reading Beck 'against the grain', namely, that in the course of reflexive modernization, the modernist belief in the collective ability to shape and control, guided by universal reason and responsibility, may also lose its persuasive force, and that 'progressive' understandings of egalitarian, democratic, ecological and inclusive emancipation are not only suppressed and obstructed by elites, but may also be renounced and voluntarily abandoned in an emancipatory effort. In this case, putting it in Beck's words, it is once again 'the growing awareness of the ineffectiveness, even counterproductivity' of its beliefs, agendas and institutions, that is driving the decline of the outgoing phase of modernity. The crisis of the EEP and late modernity then appears as another 'crisis of victory'.

5.5 Interim results II: Three phases of modernity

Beck's model thus proves to be extremely useful in several respects. Firstly, with the concept of second modernity, it brings into focus precisely what I refer to here as the EEP and what undoubtedly plays a constitutive role for today's late modernity. Secondly, with this concept Beck not only captures the great momentum and the spirit of optimism of the NSM and the EEP, but also their renewed emphasis on the modernist central norm, the autonomous subject, which challenged the moods of postmodernism at the time. Both aspects are essential for understanding today's late modernity, because the distinguishing feature of the present lies precisely in the disappointment of this optimism and the disintegration of this central norm. Third, Beck's model offers very good approaches to explaining the disenchantment and untenability of reflexive modernity and the EEP. In particular, by focusing on the *self*-destabilization and *self*-destruction of both, Beck makes a crucial contribution to understanding the traumatic nature of late modernity. Fourth, if one follows his own logic a little more consistently than Beck himself allowed himself to do, Beck's model can be extended very instructively to include a third modernity. This, in turn, makes it possible to view today's late modernity as an interim phase that may be investigated from the perspective of both second modernity that preceded it and third modernity that supersedes it. And finally, Beck advises sociology, so as not to become 'blind and naïve concerning political realities' (2009: 219), not to confuse the collapse of its own beliefs and certainties, which is undoubtedly traumatic, with the end of the world, and to focus, instead, on the future that is already emerging today. This future, he insisted, must be understood as the dialectic outcome of an earlier agenda of emancipation and modernization that has now become old-fashioned and obsolete.

By way of a further interim summary, we may thus conclude: today's crisis-ridden late modernity can be understood as the collapse of the highly optimistic 'legend' of second modernity and its substantive programme, the EEP. These had emerged from the silent revolution in the latter part of the first modernity; in today's late modernity, however, they are being replaced by a third modernity that appears traumatic – but only when viewed from the perspective of the older spirit of optimism. Table 4 provides an overview of this three-stage process.

Table 4. Three modernities and two transitions

First modernity		Second modernity		Third modernity
Fordist industrial society		Post-industrial society, risk society		Society of unsustainability
abolition of pre-modern certainties; claim to autonomy and self-determination	silent revolution	abolition of the false certainties of first modernity; renewal/ reformulation of the claim to autonomy and self-determination	late modernity	abolition of the outdated beliefs and certainties of second modernity/the EEP

Industrial modernity firmly believed in the linear progress of science and technology as well as in the political power and responsibility of the centralized nation state. Science, technology and politics would continuously increase the predictability and security of social life and steadily increase social prosperity. In this condition of security, more sophisticated understandings of subjectivity evolved, slowly at first, then as a silent revolution, which made central the Enlightenment promise of freedom and self-determination and the benchmark for assessing lifeworld experiences and societal reality – including the social and ecological side effects of industrial modernity, which had become increasingly visible since the 1960s. Measured against these changed norms and expectations, the institutions and achievements of industrial society suddenly appeared to be inefficient and deficient. The society that perceived itself as modern turned out to be semi-modern, at best, and a risk society.

Second modernity was based on the growing awareness 'that the narrative of the controllability of the world has become fictional' (Beck 2016: 49). Nevertheless, it held to the firm belief that rational reflection on the shortcomings of first modernity, the creation of better institutions and the democratic empowerment of responsible citizens could overcome the shortcomings of first modernity. The EEP can be understood as the substantive programme of second moder-nity. Both renewed, reaffirmed and radicalized the Enlightenment idea of the autonomous subject and its claim to self-determination, maturity and the ability to shape the future. They aimed to eliminate the social and ecological side effects, to gain democratic control over the shaping and development of society and to fulfil the unfulfilled promises of modernity. The great beacons of hope of this project, the pioneers of change, those at the vanguard of SET, were the NSM and their 'experimental politics'. It was hoped that they would usher in a new society, and the movements themselves believed that they could actually initiate the transformation.

Contrary to the somewhat unspecific use of this term in much of the literature, 'late modernity' is the late phase of precisely this second modernity. At the same time, it is the late phase of modernity understood as the Kantian project of the mature, self-determined, autonomous subject, which the NSM and the EEP had once again renewed and placed centre stage. It is precisely against the backdrop of this renewal that the feeling of deep disillusionment that characterizes late modernity emerges. The narrative of the dawn of 'another world' and an 'alternative society' becomes a fiction; late-modern society stands on the eco-emancipatory precipice. Although the EEP has undoubtedly achieved much, it has not achieved its primary transformative goals. Instead, a far-reaching loss of control is becoming apparent in late modernity. The ability to shape policy is collapsing. This no longer only applies to traditional politics and its institutions, but also to the NSM's 'new politics'. Movements such as Occupy Wall Street, #MeToo, Fridays for Future or Black Lives Matter were a short-lived renaissance of the practices and narratives of new politics in late modernity – a 'reinvention of the reinvention of politics', so to speak. But none of this was forward-looking or had transformative power in the sense of the EEP. Rather, late-modern societies are characterized by a highly politicized political vacuum. Their crises and conflicts – pandemics, overexploitation of resources, social inequality and polarization, care and nursing emergencies, global warming, digitalization, migration, violent conflicts, etc. – are becoming increasingly ungovernable.

In third modernity, the project of rational, collective control and governance in favour of a good life for all within ecological limits and perpetual peace in a cosmopolitan society becomes a complete fiction. Instead, the society of unsustainability is defended by all means – exclusion and marginalization, in particular. The Kantian project of the collective emergence from self-incurred immaturity, in turn, and the belief in the rational world of free subjects appear to be illusionary, an unbearable burden and – with its ecological imperatives, democratic impositions and social obligations – an unacceptable restriction of updated ideas of freedom and self-realization. Just as the metamorphosis from linear to reflexive modernity had done before, the metamorphosis from second to third modernity unfolds by itself – as an unintended side effect of reflexive modernization.

Whereas first and second modernity were a project of inclusion, equality, universal rights, self-determination and cosmopolitanism, third modernity is dominated by an agenda – in different ideological variations – of closure, surveillance, inequality, polarization and exclusion. In the face of high social complexity and international interconnection, clearly recognizable planetary boundaries and increasingly demanding societal ideas of a good, fulfilled and self-determined life, fundamental doubts about the beliefs of second modernity and its new politics are developing in very different parts of society. In this respect, third modernity can be understood as a counter-movement to its predecessor. However, it is not anti-modern, but rather a counter-modernity, a further development that defends the principles of modernity, but fundamentally reinterprets them. Third modernity is therefore simultaneously emancipatory and traumatic; it is about emancipation from the traditional idea of the autonomous subject – in the name of freedom and self-determination.

Ulrich Beck has been accused of basing his concept of second modernity on an overly simplistic notion of first modernity. This accusation could be extended to the relationship between second and third modernity presented here. It has also been noted that the radical change that Beck saw between his first and second modernity did not really take place, and that Beck selectively 'hypostasizes existing trends and treats it as an epochal break' (Nachtwey 2018: 62). This raises the question whether it is really justifiable to speak of yet another new modernity just a few decades on. However, the three-stage model outlined here is particularly helpful in understanding the emergence, agenda and unsustainability of the EEP and thus creating a background for understanding the late-modern present. Also, in relation to the period Beck described, namely the 1970s and 1980s, the talk of an epochal change or a new modernity is most certainly justified in the sense that the change in values in the 1970s, the NSM's reinvention of politics and their great departure towards a socially and ecologically restructured society are undisputed in the relevant literature. And those who, rather than appreciating this 'participatory revolution' (Kaase 1982, 1984) of the eco-emancipatory movements, are all too quick to focus on the first tendencies towards 'regressive modernization', which were, admittedly, discernible at the same time, are missing out on essential tools for understanding today's crisis of late modernity. For, what is specifically late-modern and traumatic about the current transformation is precisely the radical

Table 5. Modernity as the age of autonomy

First modernity		Second modernity		Third modernity
autonomy of the subject as a legally enshrined right; only limited practical effectiveness	silent revolution	autonomy of the subject as a broad realpolitik demand; practical implementation in the EEP	late modernity	beyond the Kantian subject
autonomy of the subject; analogous modernity				autonomy of AI; digital modernity

clash between the political awakening, the confident aspiration to reform of the EEP, on the one hand, and today's experience (on the eco-emancipatory left) of a comprehensive loss of political agency, efficacy, control, maturity, democracy and future, on the other.

If we turn our attention once again specifically to the guiding and anchor norm of both first and second modernity, that is, to the idea of the autonomous subject as understood by Kant, which underlies this experience of loss, we may now – building on the first interim review in Chapter 3.6 – note that, in first, industrial modernity, freedom, self-determination, the inviolable dignity of human beings, their claim to maturity and universal human rights, were no longer just philosophical ideals, but rights already enshrined in law. In practical terms, however, both the idea of human beings as the individual and collective 'subject' of their own and society's life and the 'autonomy' of this subject remained largely abstract ideals. With the transition from first to second, reflexive modernity, these ideals were transformed into a range of concrete political demands for individual self-determination and collective self-government. They amounted to the emancipatory agenda of the EEP and second modernity. In the face of the seemingly imminent ecological and nuclear apocalypse, which triggered the joint interest in averting the catastrophe and defending society, the conflict between the individual and collective dimensions of the emancipatory project, between the autonomy of the individual and that of the collective subject, initially remained latent. Individual self-realization appeared secondary to the task of collective, rational self-government. Although the new politics of second modernity no longer relied on the old actors and structures, on what Beck described as the 'basic institutions' of first modernity, it very firmly adhered to the 'basic principles', in particular the ideal of the autonomous subject, conceived of in the Kantian sense as collective and being determined by reason. In this respect, second modernity meant a renewal and extension of first modernity, not a radical break.

In late modernity, however, it is precisely this Kantian understanding of the autonomous subject itself that becomes obsolete. And in this respect – as Table 5 indicates – late modernity marks a significant break, indeed. The prevailing ideas of subjectivity and self-determination are being updated in the direction of individual self-realization and interpreted in a way that is no longer primarily aimed at liberation from, or transformation of, the existing order, but rather at opening up new scope for self-realization within this order. In this process, the dimension of individual self-determination gains in importance as compared to the autonomy of the collective subject – this will be explained in greater detail in Chapter 6. At the same time, the commitment to principles and imperatives of a superior reason, to the inclusive common good, loses importance both in the shaping of the individual's own life and in the shaping of societal conditions. However, this does not imply a regression into pre-modern subordination, conformity, acceptance and subjectlessness. Rather, the claim to subjectivity and autonomy, which became generalized and hegemonic with the silent revolution, remains fully intact. However, the idea of the 'identical' subject, that is, the subject as the originator and bearer of an 'identity' – consistent, stable, principled – is individualized (Beck), singularized (Reckwitz) and dynamized (Bauman, Rosa). In turn, the idea of the autonomous subject, that is, the subject as sovereign, as the bearer of a free will and as a decision maker guided by universal reason and responsibility, increasingly appears to be an excessive demand and burden. In the area of both individual and collective decision-making and governance, this burdensome decision-making competence and responsibility, which the NSM and the EEP emphatically claimed, is incrementally delegated to service providers that appear suitable – populist leaders, expert councils, technocratic elites and, very importantly, artificial intelligence. The established progressive understanding of the autonomous subject is thus being overcome in an emancipatory manner: third modernity is a modernity beyond the Kantian subject.

— 6 —

THE EMANCIPATORY CATASTROPHE

Whereas in second modernity the NSM and the EEP were striving for the ecologization of modern society, for the ideal of the free and self-determined subject and for the true democratization of democracy, a completely different scenario has prevailed in late modernity – regardless of the many ecological, emancipatory and democratic advances. And without intending or realizing it, the pioneers of the EEP have themselves made a considerable contribution to this. They fought for the ecological restructuring of industrial society but helped to solidify a society of unsustainability. They campaigned for freedom and self-determination, but instead of realizing a responsible and inclusive civil society, they helped to promote the illiberal and exclusive society of singularization. They fought for true democracy, but rather than accomplishing the ideal of collective self-government, they unknowingly promoted the autocratic-authoritarian turn. It is worth re-emphasizing that none of this was intended; and in none of the three dimensions can the EEP be regarded as the sole – or even the primary – cause of the actual developments. But there is a certain complicity; and this is part of the trauma of late modernity. It raises the question: how did it come about that, instead of the intended goals, the exact opposite transpired in each case? After all, the pioneers of the EEP had always hoped, just as Beck had done, that the impending ecological catastrophe could be turned into an 'emancipatory catastrophe', that is, that by way of a 'social catharsis', it might ultimately actually help to promote the common good (Beck 2016: 115ff; see also Chapter 2.2). Yet, retrospectively, the 'emancipatory catastrophe' rather seems to be that the NSM and the EEP, unknowingly and unintendedly, not only destroyed the latter's own foundations, but also themselves contributed to the emergence of a society that radically contradicts eco-emancipatory values and now formulates, politicizes and negotiates ecological, emancipatory and democratic concerns under significantly different auspices. Again, this raises the question: how exactly did this happen? What are the understandings of ecologization, self-determination and democracy that determine the way that the issues of the EEP are currently repoliticized and negotiated in late-modern societies?

6.1 Reflexivity and dialectics

In trying to answer these questions, the internal contradictions of the EEP and its individual components (cf. Chapter 5.3) are once again crucial. But instead of the concept of 'reflexivity', now the concept of 'dialectics' takes centre stage. The concept of reflexivity is particularly helpful in explaining the disintegration of the EEP. It can shed light on how the EEP erodes its own foundations in the course of its inherent logic. The concept of dialectics, in contrast, is more useful to examine what is newly emerging. It shifts the focus from the goals which the EEP has not managed to achieve to the transformations that have occurred as unforeseen and apparently unpreventable side effects of the EEP. Thus, it offers the conceptual framework for understanding that the EEP is not only a 'gravedigger' but also a 'midwife'. To explain: in pursuing its own logic, this project has made its original goals unattainable and anachronistic, yet this has not led to the end of the world, but – without intending to and without being able to prevent it – the EEP has propelled the emergence of a fundamentally different modernity. According to Horkheimer and Adorno's understanding in their *Dialectic of Enlightenment*, the term 'dialectic' aims to explain how a progressive, emancipatory agenda can unintentionally and unnoticed turn into its opposite: in Horkheimer and Adorno's case, 'enlightenment' into 'barbarism' (Horkheimer & Adorno 1994 [1944]); in the present case, 'ecologization' into 'unsustainability', or 'democratization' into the 'autocratic-authoritarian turn'. If we follow Hegel's understanding, 'dialectics' aims rather to explain how the internal, antithetical and irresolvable contradictions of a particular constellation lead to its untenability, which in turn paves the way for the emergence of a new constellation, a synthesis in which both sides of the contradictions that have been overcome are constitutive parts of the new. Dialectics here is the constructive tension between contradictions, from whose conflict something new emerges: in this case, 'another', a 'third' modernity.

Beck, too, spoke of dialectics. He distinguished between two 'dialectics of modernity': firstly, the 'dialectic of more-modernity', in which the 'basic principles' of modernity are preserved, but the 'basic institutions' must be rebuilt so that they comply with the basic principles. Here Beck saw the dialectical tension between the normative content of the basic principles and the political reality of the institutions in industrial society. Secondly, he saw a 'dialectic of anti-modernity', which was, he noted, about the 'negation' and 'discontinuity' of the basic principles (Beck 2009: 212ff). He described 'self-perpetuating modernization' as anti-modern (ibid.: 223f), if it has detached itself from the 'sacred norms of human existence and civilization' (Beck 2016: 117f), and thus implies the 'radical discontinuity' of the basic principles and a 'constitutional breach within modernity' (Beck 2009: 223).

For Beck, the first dialectic was, clearly, the focal point of interest. However, as was shown in the previous chapter, this modernization does not lead to a truly different modernity, but merely extends and updates the previous one – and its 'sacred' basic principles. At best, as Beck himself said, it paves the way from 'semi-modernity' to a 'more-modernity'. In this respect, the subtitle of the original (German) edition of Beck's *Risk Society* might be misleading: Rather than 'On the way to a different modernity' it should read, more accurately, 'On the way to a more-modernity'. For although Beck always had the possibility of a 'constitutional breach within modernity' in the back of his mind, he was ultimately not interested in the truly different, but only in the 'continuity of basic principles' and the 'enforced enlightenment' (Beck 2009: 47ff), which the risk society, he believed, was able to bring about. He did see the theoretical possibility that modernity and modernization, rather than effecting a transformation of modernity's basic institutions, could also corrode the basic principles themselves, that the 'inviolable basic principles could be qualified or even done away with altogether'. However, he did not pursue this possibility in great depth, instead categorizing the result of this 'unrestricted modernization' as 'anti-modern' (ibid.: 223).

In the late-modern constellation, however, precisely this supposedly 'anti-modern' scenario prevails. In a sense, it does indeed mean 'discontinuity' and a 'constitutional breach', but this discontinuity only relates to the content of the basic modernist principles, not to their name. Concepts such as ecologization, sustainability, democracy, freedom, emancipation or self-determination remain prominent in late-modern societies and may even continue to gain in importance. In the late-modern constellation it is, therefore, imperative to further pursue the dialectic that Beck always neglected because he feared 'unforeseeable moral consequences', if 'the sacrosanct aspect of modernity', the basic principles, were to become 'decidable themselves' (Beck 2009: 379). Interestingly, he saw the negation of modernist basic principles exclusively as anti-modern, not really as a dialectical negation that would produce something new, a truly different modernity, from the tension between antithetical opposites. However, from the perspective of late modernity it is evident that the negation of the basic principles does lead to a truly different modernity – and indeed with 'unforeseeable moral consequences'. For, the reflexive self-undermining of second modernity by no means completely abolishes the traditional basic principles, but only makes their established content anachronistic, transforming them into 'empty signifiers' (Laclau) without any pre-modern, 'holy' or 'sacred' core, initiating the redefining of their content. The self-referential and empty 'code', to borrow from Luhmann's terminology – for example: sustainable/unsustainable, self-determined/externally determined, democratic/non-democratic – remains the same, but the content, the 'programme' of this code, is radically exchanged.

Beck was right to fear 'unforeseeable moral consequences' and an 'anti-modern constitutional breach of modernity', but he was also right in rejecting any prejudicial talk of a 'decline' of values and speaking instead of a 'shift in values in accordance with the demands of the second modernity' (Beck 2009: 221). As a social theorist, he distanced himself from the common cultural criticism that dramatizes 'the decline of values, freedom, democracy, etc., so as to avoid having to acknowledge the catastrophic collapse of our own certainties about the world (though only for ourselves)' (ibid.: 219). This 'posture of cultural criticism', he suspected, is, ultimately only an attempt to avoid 'the conceptual work necessary for understanding the new' (ibid.; cf. Chapters 1.3 and 2.5). But on the threshold of the newly emerging modernity, precisely this conceptual work is essential, particularly with regard to the three big concepts of the EEP – ecologization, emancipation and democratization. Hence, the objective is now to further elaborate how the eco-emancipatory movements themselves have contributed to fundamentally changing the understanding of these terms. And as noted above, in doing this, the contradictions that have always been inherent in these basic principles of the EEP are key. These tensions unfold dialectically in the ongoing process of modernization, and this takes late-modern society – automatically, uncontrollably and as a side effect – beyond Beck's socio-ecological 'more-modernity' into a truly different modernity.

6.2 The dialectic of sustainability

With regard to the first pillar of the EEP, it would actually make sense to speak not of the dialectic of sustainability, but of the dialectic of ecologization or the ecologization project. This would also be appropriate insofar as the contradiction, the built-in dynamic of destabilization and self-transformation, is in fact not specifically linked to the concept of sustainability, which only became hegemonic at the turn of the 1990s, but was inherent in the EEP from the very outset. Hence, the problem of self-undermining also cannot be resolved by abandoning the concept of sustainability, which has often been criticized for being too vague, and replacing it with another, supposedly more radical concept to guide society's ecological transformation. Nevertheless, I am talking here about the dialectic of sustainability. For, firstly, despite all criticism, the term sustainability still dominates the eco-political debate today. Secondly, even if the actual cause of the problem lies deeper and predates the rise of the sustainability concept, the sustainability paradigm has actually played an important role in the destabilization and the – as yet, by no means completed – disintegration of the EEP.

So, how is it that the ecologization of industrial society that the eco-emancipatory movements had set out to achieve, the SET, has never been achieved and also has little prospect of being accomplished in the future? How is it that this project is increasingly falling apart and is itself becoming a target for repoliticization? How is it that late-modern societies, which are actually dealing with the consequences of climate change, species loss, overexploitation of resources, at all levels and with great intensity, and which, in principle, everywhere profess commitment to the goal of sustainability, must ultimately be described as 'societies of unsustainability', which defend the logic of unsustainability by all means, and resolutely pursue a politics of unsustainability? One major reason for this, which has been exhaustively discussed in the literature, is undoubtedly the overwhelming power of capitalist actors and structures, and the fundamental incompatibility of the capitalist logic of expansion and competition with the ecological agenda of collective self-limitation in the name of a good life for all within planetary boundaries. But how can we explain that ecological movements have demonstrated so little persuasive force to oppose this logic of capitalism? How is it that, despite the broad consensus on the urgency of the ecological crisis, which has, time and again, been described as life-threatening, these movements have not been able to summon a political counter-force on a par with capitalist interests?

The reason for this – as already indicated in Chapter 5.2 – is that the project of greening industrial society has never had a reliable normative basis. The belief, the assertion, that there are clear biophysical necessities that make an SET unavoidable, and that politicians only need to listen to 'ecological reason' or follow the findings of natural and Earth system science research, is being reiterated to the present day (cf. Chapter 3.2). Yet this belief has always been an illusion – in some respects a reassuring one – and this has been particularly true since the silent revolution of the 1970s, which gave rise to the EEP in the sense outlined above.

Older nature conservation movements since the end of the nineteenth century were based primarily on religious, aesthetic, romantic, homeland-related and often anti-modernist values and arguments and, therefore, remained rather marginal, with limited mobilization power and political success (cf. e.g. Sieferle 1984; Linse 1986; Rohkrämer 1999). With the eco-emancipatory movements from the early 1970s onwards, environmental issues found much broader societal resonance, but the normative core of these movements – as explained above – was not the extra-societal Other, nature, but the new understandings of autonomy and subjectivity, which gained increasing importance in the late phase of the first modernity – even though these movements explicitly saw themselves as 'environmental' or 'ecological'. Ultimately, these new notions of autonomy and subjectivity were the trigger and motor for the societal mobilization and politicization which, nevertheless, conceived of itself as 'eco'-political. And although the discourses of these movements claimed to relate to the environment and nature, they essentially revolved around cultural constructions of the 'natural' and normative counter-images of the social reality that activists regarded as deficient – or, using Beck's term, semi-modern.

Thus, a fundamental weakness of the EEP was, and is, that it simultaneously aims at the protection of nature, the Other, the objective, the non-societal, the superordinate, and at the centralization of the modernist subject, its autonomy and the realization of its claims to control and management (see Chapter 5.3, Table 3). Ironically, exactly this radical centralization of emancipatory values and concept of the autonomous subject was supposed to finally achieve the protection of nature and the societal transformation that the older nature conservation movements, with their respective driving forces and reference norms, had never been able to achieve. However, protecting the integrity of nature and the environment under the auspices of the autonomy of the Self or the subject – which only constitutes and asserts itself through its emancipation from nature and naturalness (cf. Horkheimer & Adorno 1994 [1944]; Blühdorn 2000: 60–64) – is a contradiction in terms: the integrity of nature requires the limitation and subordination of the subject, whereas the autonomy of the subject requires transgressing supposedly natural boundaries and the domination of nature. The 'political ecology' of the 1970s and early 1980s (cf. e.g. Enzensberger 1973; Die Grünen 1980; Gorz 1978, 1980; Bookchin 1982) – unlike the older 'conservationism' or technology-oriented 'environmental protection' – made emancipatory claims particularly prominent. It was widely referred to as 'ecological fundamentalism'; yet, in the thinking of political ecology, it was never nature that was fundamental, but always the norm of the autonomous subject, which became the benchmark of the 'ecological' critique of industrial modernity and capitalism. All norms of a supposedly objective naturalness, an intrinsic value and the inherent dignity of nature, and all supposedly categorical ecological imperatives always remained subordinate to this 'sacred basic principle'. From a critical-emancipatory perspective, all other norms appeared dubious and potentially ideological, and were incrementally eroded by the logic of emancipatory progress – 'modernized away' as conservative and outdated.

Hence, despite all empirically observable changes and the objective destruction of ecological systems, there has never been a politically resilient normative basis for the ecologization of industrial society, and especially not after the silent revolution had mainstreamed the ideals of the autonomous subject, the responsible citizen and their self-determined life as the highest and inviolable guiding norm. Put differently, just when the change in values in the 1970s had given the ecological issue a level of societal resonance and political significance that it had never achieved before, a threefold dilemma unfolded:

– Firstly, although environmental changes accelerated in the wake of economic development, the ecological and social side effects of industrial modernity became ever more visible, the change in values intensified the social perception of related problems, and new movements mobilized a comprehensive critique of capitalist industrial modernity, this critique and mobilization were – given the 'sacred basic principles' on which they were based – not well equipped to have a much stronger transformative impact on the relationship of modern societies to nature, to the environment, to their biophysical foundations, than the conservative, religious or aesthetic-based movements had had before.

- Secondly, the critique of capitalism, which the discourses of political ecology had made particularly prominent, suggested, already in the early 1980s, an irreconcilable binary choice between the capitalist economy and ecology – which rendered eco-political progress even more difficult. This proclaimed incompatibility of capitalism and ecology conflicted, even within the environmental movements, with the liberation, development and self-realization interests harboured by a broad societal majority, who regarded the 'liberation from capitalism' neither as an absolute prerequisite for their personal self-development nor as a necessary condition for more effective nature and environmental protection.

- And thirdly, the widely perceived violation of the 'sacred norms of human existence and civilization' that had become hegemonic in the wake of the silent revolution called into question the entire model of Western modernity, to whose 'basic principles' the eco-emancipatory movements were, however, themselves deeply committed – despite their criticism. 'The system is bankrupt', wrote the internationally renowned environmental and human rights activist and founding member of the German Green Party Petra Kelly in the early 1980s (Kelly 1984). At the same time, however, the 'sacred norms' of Western modernity were to be maintained, to serve as the basis for a free, open, democratic, ecological world society, and to lead this world society to Kantian 'perpetual peace'.

Against the backdrop of this triple dilemma, the paradigm of 'sustainability' and 'sustainable development' that emerged in the mid-1980s appeared to be the golden solution. It was introduced with the Brundtland Report of the United Nations in 1987 (WCED 1987) and became the hegemonic guiding concept of eco-political debate and practice internationally with the so-called UN Earth Summit in Rio de Janeiro in 1992. Its particular appeal and the reason for its success were that, on the one hand, it held out the prospect of a transformation and ecologization of modern industrial societies, but on the other hand also allowed or promised a continuation of the familiar logic of development and modernization. It built a bridge between (a) the discourse on justice, which regarded further and even accelerated economic development as a precondition for social justice and participation both within Western industrial societies and, in particular, in the so-called Third World, that is, the countries of the Global South; (b) the discourse on limitation, which called for a departure from the logic of infinite growth and a strict limitation on the destruction of nature in favour of its protection and in view of the finiteness of natural resources and the planet; and (c) the emancipatory discourse of democratization and self-determination, which urged the expansion of opportunities for individual and collective participation and decision-making. That it avoided the either/or of anti-capitalist eco-fundamentalism and combined these three agendas rendered the sustainability paradigm irresistibly attractive – especially at a time when, on the one hand, the model of Western modernity was in deep crisis due to its ecological and social side effects but, on the other hand, the end of the Cold War offered a historic opportunity for its globalization. This perspective was equally attractive from an economic, an emancipatory and the ecological point of view.

The hope that the sustainability paradigm could achieve significant eco-political change was primarily based on the fact that it did not demand a departure from capitalism and would therefore generate much broader social acceptance of eco-political agendas than before. In addition, the logic of capitalism and the mechanisms of the market were to be utilized and harnessed specifically as a motor for ecological improvements in all areas of society and life. Instead of confrontation and conflict, the sustainability paradigm also focused on participation, cooperation and understanding between all actors involved. In order to avoid ideological conflicts, the sustainability concept relied heavily on the scientization of eco-political debates and on technological solutions in the sense of 'ecological modernization' (cf. e.g. von Prittwitz 1993; Mol & Sonnenfeld 2000; Jänicke 2007; cf. also Chapter 4.4). Given that there was still no sufficiently integrating, motivating and politically enforceable normative basis for the greening of industrial society, and that this project – especially in its anti-growth and anti-capitalist variants – triggered fears, uncertainty and defensive reactions in large parts of society, the sustainability paradigm explicitly aimed to depoliticize the debate and give practical measures a scientific basis. For, just as in the late-modern present, already in the 1980s, the 'environmental movements and their issues' were stigmatized in parts of society as 'the exalted amusement of civilization deserters infatuated with the Stone Age', as 'mueslis living off public support', and as 'green-tinged left-wing radicals' and 'enemies of the constitution' (Fischer 1989: 8).

The sustainability paradigm was able to calm these fears and defuse eco-political conflicts. It prevailed because it took up many concerns and demands of the NSM, but left behind visions of apocalypse and radical demands for overcoming capitalism. Instead, it was profoundly optimistic about an open, malleable future and the ability of modern societies to solve their problems. What's more, its guiding principle, the concept of sustainability, was completely open in terms of its content. It allowed diverse actors to interpret the term in their own particular way and on the basis of their respective values and interests. For, what is to be sustained, for whom, to what extent, in what quality, for which duration and for what reason – or not – is not defined by the term itself. In this respect, the sustainability paradigm, wherever it sought to set concrete goals and standards, has always been parasitic: it promised to be able to achieve major environmental policy effects, but in its efforts to find consensus through depoliticization, scientization and/or marketization, it always drew on standards that it could not, and did not want to set, justify and enforce itself, but which always had to be adopted, justified and motivated from other sources and contexts. Thus, sustainability can be read as a transformative concept, but also as a stabilizing one. On a discursive surface, it conceals the complexity and contradictions of modern societies – and also of eco-emancipatory movements themselves – which aspire to preserve and further expand their modernist-emancipatory achievements but also see ecological and social side effects that violate 'the sacred norms of human existence and civilization', and therefore demand fundamental change. At the underlying level, however, these contradictions remain unresolved.

Today, the concept of sustainability has seeped into all areas of society and policy fields. Precisely because of its openness in terms of content, it can be applied everywhere, has triggered countless legislative and regulatory initiatives at all political levels, established action programmes and brought about a wide range of reforms. However, it has not initiated a fundamental change in the established logic of modern societies, that is, a structural turning point in the sense of the EEP. Rather, the sustainability paradigm itself can be seen as a major reason for the absence of such structural change and as the midwife for the society of unsustainability that transpired instead. And this is not, as has often been claimed, because in the course of its popularization the term 'sustainability' has become increasingly meaningless and an empty signifier (cf. e.g. Brown 2016) – as signalled above, it has always been this from the very beginning. Much more importantly, the sustainability paradigm, in its effort to depoliticize, has always avoided normative questions and conflicts. It limited itself to researching, counting, measuring, calculating, developing innovative technologies and propagating new market instruments, but always neglected the central role of subjectivity and social norms. Yet, in eco-politics exactly these subjective norms always remain the linchpin. They are what is 'sacred' to society or to those parts of it prevailing in public discourse. Without their perceived violation, environmental changes can never be experienced as problematic nor be politicized, and without these norms no environmental policy goals can be set and implemented either (cf. Chapter 4.4).

But, while it focused on the supposedly non-political, objective dimension, the sustainability paradigm always neglected this subjective, normative aspect and in a liberal manner left it unaddressed. And so, firstly, the hegemony of the sustainability concept led to a situation in which comprehensive knowledge about ecological changes, their causes, their interactions and their consequences is readily available, as well as a wide range of technologies that could be helpful in dealing with them, but the political will to actually apply this knowledge and technology in a targeted, determined and consistent manner is found lacking – because this would require a normative definition that is fundamentally alien to the sustainability paradigm. Secondly, the focus on the objective and the neglect of the subjective created a protected niche in which the liberal values of individualistic self-determination and self-realization were able to develop undisturbed in ways that conflict with the values of restriction, subordination, self-discipline and ecological duty (see Chapter 6.3 for more detail). And this is one of the main reasons why the political will to translate scientific findings and new technologies into effective measures is lacking today. Thus, instead of being truly transformative, the sustainability paradigm has always favoured the development of liberal norms. And this by no means suited only market liberals, but also the self-determination and self-realization interests of eco-emancipatory movements. This said, the sustainability paradigm did help, of course, to achieve a large number of social and ecological reforms. But precisely by attempting to scientize and depoliticize the debate, the sustainability model, ultimately, only extended the logic and structures of the established socio-economic order.

Thirdly, despite the increase in environmental and climate-related knowledge, not only did uncertainty persist regarding the norms for the social use and political implementation of this knowledge, but this increasingly complex knowledge also raised new questions, thereby adding further uncertainty. Beck had already described this effect in the 1980s (Beck 1992: 157). He had also warned early on that in the 'scientized ecology movement, the occasions for and the themes of protest' would 'largely become independent of the agents' of the protests, that is, 'the affected lay people', because ecological dangers were increasingly perceived by scientific means and were 'not only transmitted by science, but in the strict sense scientifically constituted' (ibid.: 162). 'More and more', Beck predicted, 'the centre comes to be occupied by threats that are often neither visible nor tangible to the lay public', and which may 'not even take their toll in the lifetime' of today's citizens or in their respective geographical region (ibid.). In fact, the sustainability paradigm's strategies of scientization increasingly disconnected the eco-political debate from the real-world experiences of citizens' lives, thereby marginalizing those whose values and protests had originally put the ecological issue on the political agenda and diametrically contradicting the NSM's emancipatory claim to political self-determination and self-efficacy. The increasing specialization of science and the ever new, often provisional and contradictory research results undermined trust in science and, as an unavoidable side effect, systematically paved the way for a populist scepticism vis-à-vis science, strategically fomented by interested parties.

In this respect, the boom in 'alternative facts' and 'conspiracy myths' typical of late-modern society is itself a side effect of the scientization of eco-politics driven by the sustainability paradigm. 'Who *believes* in a risk and why', wrote Beck well before these terms became popular in the wake of Donald Trump's first presidency, 'becomes more important than the sophisticated probability scenarios of the experts' (Beck 2009: 196). 'We are witnessing an invasion of politics by culture', he emphasized; the *risk community of fate* is cleaving over the questions of who shares which definitions of risk and how the threats should be dealt with' (ibid.: 196, 197). In late modernity, 'alternative facts', conspiracy myths and populist narratives are putting citizens back at the centre, one might say – or at least they claim to do so. By foregrounding everyday citizens' experiences and what they personally perceive and (want to) believe, they enact a form of re-empowerment that compensates for the loss of control and the decentralization of citizens in the wake of scientization. With their struggle for a 'post-normal science' and the equal recognition of alternative rationalities (Funtowicz & Ravetz 1991, 1992, 1993 are classic examples), emancipatory movements have contributed to this development no less that right-wing campaigns of scepticism towards science, climate change denial or the EU-sceptical demand to 'take back control!'

While it furthered the logic of modernization – scientific, economic, technological, political, cultural – the sustainability paradigm thus bought time for the reflexive modernization of those 'sacred basic principles' that had become hegemonic with the silent revolution and that had initially released considerable political mobilization and transformative energy. The sustainability narrative offered citizens the opportunity to hold on to its promise of being transformative until the reflexive modernization of the supposedly 'sacred' basic principles had eventually exhausted their transformative political mobilization power. After all, reflexive modernization does not refer solely to social institutions and political realities (Beck's 'basic institutions'), but to the social standards for their perception and evaluation as well, that is, the prevailing understandings of freedom, democracy, emancipation, self-determination, identity, and so on (Beck's supposedly 'sacred' basic principles). Hence, not only social institutions were modernized step by step, but these norms, too, incrementally changed. And in late modernity, this process has proceeded so far that the perceived urgency of a transformation is only moderate, at best – at least not strong enough to actually initiate structural changes, even though the social and ecological side effects of the established order are more visible and tangible today than ever. The sustainability paradigm was particularly suitable for this bridging function, precisely because sustainability does not have an essentialist meaning, but as an 'essentially contested concept' (Gallie 1956) is open to continuous redefinition in line with ongoing modernization.

In this sense, the paradigm of sustainability granted modern societies a period of extra time: 'buying time' – to borrow an expression from Wolfgang Streeck (2014), who uses it in a different context (see also Blühdorn 2022a) – as a 'rescue operation for a dying illusion' (Sarkar 2001). It is a concept that can only be properly interpreted and appreciated from the perspective of late modernity or third modernity – and on the basis of the modernization theory approach outlined above in Chapters 4 and 5. In retrospect, this perspective confirms what critics of the sustainability paradigm articulated early on: the sustainability concept has never really been about structural transformation and a turn away from the established logic of unsustainability. First and foremost, it has always been about stabilizing and prolonging capitalism and Western modernity as a whole, which in the 1980s had fallen into a profound crisis. However, the early critics of the sustainability narrative still had a very modernist-normative perspective: they firmly believed in the absolute necessity of an SET and also in the availability of truly catasformative alternatives to the growth- and capitalism-compatible approaches of the sustainability paradigm. Building on the criticism that 'eco-capitalism cannot help us' (Sarkar 2001: 51f), they continued to propose supposedly better, more transformative, eco-socialist, subsistence, post-growth or resilience-oriented approaches.

Today, this criticism is widespread. Many now consider the sustainability paradigm to be exhausted. Very few still see it as a sufficiently concrete, integrating and mobilizing model for a structural social transformation (cf. Benson & Craig 2017; Foster 2015; Gottschlich 2017; Folkers 2022). It has rightly been emphasized that the concept is 'not part of the solution' to the socio-ecological crisis of modern societies, but itself 'a constitutive part of the problem' (Foster 2015: 35). However, this critique is still mostly based on the assumption that a transformation in the sense of the EEP and its sacred norms is inevitable, and on the conviction that a more powerful normative basis for a true SET could be mobilized beyond the sustainability paradigm. In late modernity, however, this assumption and this belief are no longer tenable. They ignore the fact that an alternative guiding norm is only needed as long as, and to the extent that, the EEP and the sacred norms of its SET are really still 'sacred'. Yet, on the threshold to third modernity, this is no longer the case. For, this is the point at which the norms of second modernity become anachronistic and are abandoned.

The 'dying illusion', whose sustainability or 'best-before date' has still not fully expired yet, was therefore, contrary to what Saral Sarkar originally meant by the term, not only that an efficiency revolution would solve the resource problem and enable continued economic growth, that the environmental damage that had already occurred could be eliminated by means of new technologies, and that capitalism could be perpetuated with the help of its ecological modernization (Sarkar 2001). Rather, the illusion was (and is) that the tension between the emancipatory (liberating) and the ecological (constraining-subordinating) dimensions of the EEP could be resolved, that the simultaneity of the opposing interests and values illustrated in Table 3 is possible, that the contradictions of the ecological paradox could be reconciled through the (ecological) reason of the responsible subject (see also Chapter 2.4), and that Western modernity, which had already fallen into a fundamental crisis in the early 1980s, could be stabilized and even globalized, after all. Contrary to what the critics of the sustainability paradigm have often claimed, the illusion is therefore not (only) the tenability of capitalism, but essentially also that of the EEP and Western modernity as a whole. It is the illusion of the open, democratic, ecological, egalitarian, cosmopolitan society. Accordingly, the disillusionment in late modernity is twofold and truly traumatic: not only is there no ecologization of modernity *within* capitalism, but there is none *beyond* capitalism, either. For, the idea of the ecologization of modernity and the values (related to the autonomous subject) that were to be implemented with this project are themselves untenable. Nevertheless, the sustainability paradigm has not failed (see also Blühdorn 2016, 2017, 2022a), but has been highly successful: in bridging the time until the disintegration of the EEP, that is, the time until its ecological problem perceptions, rather than being *solved*, themselves *dissolve(d)*, together with the standards of their perception (cf. Chapter 1.2). And at this point, on the threshold of third modernity, there is no longer any need for a more transformative substitute but, if anything, only for better strategies of adaptation and processing individual and societal grievances of transition – which after an interim period can be expected to gradually subside (cf. Chapter 7.3).

So the dialectic of sustainability lies in the fact that the concept, which it had been assumed and hoped would resolve the dilemmas of modern society and its eco-politics outlined above, and to finally provide a firm normative foundation and an attractive vision for an SET, actually had exactly the opposite effect: it favoured a change in values that hindered the SET and paved the way to the society of unsustainability which, in turn, led to ungovernable repoliticization and polarization and facilitated the metamorphosis from second to third modernity. Based on social and modernization theory, the concept of the dialectic of sustainability offers an interpretation of the enormous success of the sustainability paradigm, an interpretation that goes far beyond the common, 'progressive' criticisms of this approach, and beyond the diagnoses of its exhaustion as an energizing vision for an SET. These criticisms and diagnoses – which is the reason why they can be described as 'progressive' – generally remain caught up in a modernist normativity that in third modernity appears untenable and anachronistic.

6.3 The dialectic of emancipation

But how exactly did this come about? How did the emancipatory values, whose social mainstreaming with the silent revolution initially triggered enormous momentum for eco-political issues and considerable pressure for transformation (midwife), then themselves become the brake and blockade (gravedigger) of the EEP and the midwife of the society of unsustainability and third modernity? The internal contradictions of the emancipation project itself, the tension between its various dimensions, which are equally constitutive for this project but difficult to reconcile, play a central role here. Firstly, this concerns the tension between the liberating, rule-breaking, boundary-transgressing ambition of the emancipation project and the rule-setting, limiting dimension. This tension is not only central to the ecological dimension of the EEP (cf. Table 3), but also in relation to the constitution of subjectivity and identity and the realization of the 'authentic self'. After all, every definition of subjectivity and identity implies a commitment to certain values, rules and principles, and to the detriment of others. Secondly, emancipation is, as already mentioned, a collective and at the same time an individual project: on the one hand, it aims at the collective realization and self-determination of a collective subject, which implies a commitment to certain rules of the general, and on the other hand, it aims at the individual realization and self-determination of an individual subject, which calls such rules into question.

A closer look at these inner tensions sheds light on why the emancipatory change in values and the emancipatory movements since the 1970s have not been able to bring about continuous progress towards a self-determined good life for all within ecological limits, and why in late modernity the logic of liberation, self-determination and self-realization ultimately tips over into the illiberal, authoritarian and exclusive. This tension is the driving force behind an ongoing political struggle between competing interpretations of autonomy and subjectivity. In Beck's words, it is the engine for the reflexive modernization of the emancipation project, because just as with sustainability, emancipation is not an intrinsically meaningful 'sacred basic principle' that is exempt from discussion, but an 'essentially contested concept'. In the search for reasons for the SET's failure (or unexpected outcome), for the disintegration of the EEP, for the emergence of the society of unsustainability and for the metamorphosis from second to third modernity, the changing and at different times prevailing understandings of emancipation are a central parameter. They determine 'the grammar of social struggles and the prospects for the transformation of society' in the sense of the EEP (Fraser in Fraser & Jaeggi 2018: 123).

With the ideal of the 'autonomous subject', Enlightenment philosophy inaugurated the emancipatory project and created the normative reference point, the regulative ideal, for all progressive movements. Since then, emancipatory struggles have revolved around (a) the self-establishment, the constitution, of subjects who distinguish themselves from their context and claim independence from it and their own identity; (b) the self-assertion of these subjects against the

Table 6. Constitutive elements of the emancipatory project

Emancipation			
Liberation from ...		Realization of ...	
self-distinction, demarcation, self-constitution	self-assertion, defence against, struggle against	development of skills and enabling infrastructures	goal, utopia, regulative ideal

forces that restrict, block or oppress their claim to independence, self-development and self-determination; (c) the development of skills and social infrastructures necessary for the practical realization of claims to autonomy; and (d) the ideal, vision or utopia that is the ultimate target and motor of the emancipatory struggle. Following on from the common distinction between 'negative' and 'positive' freedom (Berlin 1969), the first two aspects, the self-distinction and self-assertion of the subject, can be seen as the negative dimension – *liberation from* – of the emancipatory project. The third and fourth aspects, the development of necessary skills and infrastructures as well as the motivating goal, constitute its positive dimension – *realization of*. Translated into the concepts of delimitation and limitation, the first two aspects can be understood as the dimension of the emancipatory project that transcends boundaries and rules, and the other two as the dimension that sets boundaries and provides rules.

The distinction between these four components of the emancipation project – summarized in Table 6 – can be further differentiated, and the respective aspects might be labelled differently (e.g. Ernesto Laclau's distinction between six components of the emancipation project; Laclau 1996: 1–2). However, further elaboration is not necessary at this point, as the aim here is only to outline a purely formal description of emancipation and the emancipatory project, which is open to different interpretations of the concept in terms of content. Put differently, instead of determining minimum content-related criteria or distinguishing the 'legitimate' use of the term emancipation from 'unacceptable' appropriations (e.g. van Dyk & Graefe 2019: 421), the focus is on the formal structure of a term that is initially empty in terms of content. On this basis, it is then possible to examine how the prevailing interpretation of emancipation and the political dispute over autonomy have changed over time.

In terms of content, the 'classic understanding' of emancipation, writes Ernesto Laclau (1996: 4), is the Kantian idea of 'man's emergence from his self-incurred immaturity' (Kant 1970: 54). Although Kant's call for the independent use of reason is primarily directed at the individual and is based on the free will, dignity and inviolable fundamental rights of the individual, he explicitly understands enlightenment or emancipation not as an individual project, but as a collective project of humankind. It aims to realize a potential common to all human beings as rational beings, namely self-determination on the basis of the categorical imperative of reason. And 'those natural capacities' of man 'which are directed towards the use of his reason', Kant emphasizes, can 'be fully developed only in the species, but not in the individual' (Kant 1970: 42). In its constitutive, self-establishing dimension, emancipation here accordingly means the demarcation and self-distinction of rational beings from all those whose actions and will are determined solely by instincts or by emotions and irrational superstition. The claim to autonomy and the status of a subject implies the struggle against the irrational, the instinctive and every form of superstition. The continued effort to use reason, the struggle to adhere to the categorical imperatives of reason – *sapere aude* – and thus the development of maturity is the formative dimension of Kant's understanding of emancipation. And the target and vision is the cosmopolitan society in which the free self-determination of people according to the moral law of reason leads world history to its fulfilment in 'perpetual peace' (Kant 1970: 93–130).

So, the essence, the essential, that was to be liberated and realized in this Kantian idea was the rational being, the maturity, the (theoretical) ability to think and behave individually and collectively in such a way that one could always want the maxim of one's own actions to become general law. Autonomy and subjectivity meant self-determination through universal reason common to all rational beings. In this respect, Kant's concept of autonomy emphasizes the equality of all who participate in universal, transcendental reason. At the same time, it emphasizes the freedom of all who, as rational beings, have a free will and do not have to allow themselves to be determined by instincts and superstition. Very importantly, however, this Kantian notion of freedom also implies the duty of all to make use of reason and acquire maturity.

Kant's concept of enlightenment and maturity, the 'classical understanding' of emancipation, was of course only ever a regulative ideal that was subsequently interpreted and reinterpreted in line with changing historical and societal conditions. In this process, the connection of autonomy to the transcendental reason common to all human beings and the idea of the transcendental subject, which ultimately underlay Kant's concept of autonomy, gradually lost significance. Instead, historically specific understandings of emancipation and the emancipatory project emerged under changing socio-economic conditions. For Laclau, the disintegration of the rationalist-modernist understanding of emancipation marked the beginning of real freedom and the postmodern multiplication of emancipatory agendas (Laclau 1996; cf. also Foucault 1984, 2008). In the present context, however, it is more instructive to imagine the ongoing transformation of the emancipation project – building on the distinction between a *first*, industrial, a *second*, reflexive, and a *third* modernity that leaves behind the Kantian understanding of the autonomous subject – as a three-stage process.

In capitalist industrial society, Marx and the post-Marxist tradition primarily saw the industrial working class as the subject of the emancipatory project. Their claim to autonomy initially meant liberation from their domination, oppression and exploitation by the owners of capital. The development of their own class consciousness, a collective awareness of their own oppression and alienation, the ability to see through the ideological narratives of capital and to organize themselves as a collective political actor were all part of the formative dimension of this emancipatory project. In the face of overwhelming hardship, the improvement of working conditions and material circumstances was the primary goal of the emancipatory struggle. Its horizon, however, was a society liberated from capitalism and ultimately a liberated and pacified world society in which people could individually and collectively develop their potential and their true nature. The idea of a human essence that was no longer determined by rational philosophy and transcendentalism, yet was nonetheless essential, and which for the time being was suppressed and alienated but could be fully realized via the liberation from capitalism, continued to be fundamental here.

With the transition from classical industrial society to post-industrial society, the individual subject and its struggle for individual self-determination, self-realization and social recognition increasingly became the focus of the emancipation project. To a certain extent, the new (eco-)emancipatory movements since the 1970s continued to see themselves as a collective subject and a collective political actor – sometimes even across movements. After all, the protection of the natural environment common to all people and the survival conditions of humanity remained a key concern. But Inglehart, Giddens, Beck and many others have elaborated how, against the backdrop of economic growth, welfare state security systems and educational expansion, the emancipation of the individual now took priority over the emancipation of collective subjectivities (e.g. Inglehart 1977; Giddens 1991; Beck & Beck-Gernsheim 1994; cf. also Chapters 4.3 and 4.4). In the words of Luc Boltanski and Ève Chiapello, 'the artistic critique' of existing social conditions, which aimed at individual particularity and distinctiveness, now became dominant over the 'social critique', which aimed at equality and participation (Boltanski & Chiapello 2017). Thus, older ideals of self-discipline, acceptance of authority and subordination to social norms were replaced by ideals of development, articulation and the experience of the individual's personal authentic self.

Of course, duty, self-limitation, responsibility and moral-rationalist imperatives continued to play an important role in eco-emancipatory thinking, in particular. The Kantian tradition retained great importance there, because eco-emancipatory thinking was about the collective self-determination – and self-limitation – of citizens, society and ultimately global society in accordance with an overarching ecological reason and ecological imperatives. Ecological maturity and responsibility were important guiding principles, whereby this responsibility was expected to extend far beyond individual self-responsibility and relate to society as a whole – ultimately to humanity at large, including future generations. What was required was the citizen, the ecological *citoyen*, not the self-interested private individual, the *bourgeois*. The self-determined acceptance of and rational subordination to obligations; the orientation towards principles of the collective and the aspect of (self-)limitation were, therefore, very present and essential for the understanding of self-determination, which was assumed to follow firm principles of ecological reason. These were precisely what Beck called the 'sacred basic principles' that in second modernity were to become the corrective of first modernity, and without which a reflexive modernization would never be successful.

At the same time, however, the component of personal self-realization was prominent in eco-emancipatory thinking. This striving was in the Romantic tradition of the discovery (self-discovery) and practical development of a personal, authentic, essential self, which was inherent in every individual and had the right to be developed into a unique personality and identity. This self-development was not about subordination to general principles and the acceptance of authorities, of course, but about the development of the individual's special qualities and unique character. Its realization also implied a critique of the purely formal, abstract, ahistorically conceived principles of supposedly universal reason, which ultimately suppress and mutilate the richness and complexity of the self and block its authentic realization. The aim of this critique was to enable more diverse, experimental forms of subjectivity and subjectivation. Here, the element of duty and adherence to principle only retained its significance insofar as the authentic and essential to be realized was conceived as *identitarian*, that is, consistent, reliable and stable over time.

In terms of self-differentiation and self-constitution, emancipation in this understanding therefore increasingly meant the demarcation and distinction of the individual from the social context, the social class, the community, in which they had previously been embedded and by which they had previously been determined in their thinking and lifestyle. Accordingly, the struggle against heteronomy was directed less and less against the ruling class and capitalism but, first and foremost, against standardized mass culture and any form of heteronomy through social constraints and conventions. In the formative dimension, emancipatory movements now focused on the development of individual and collective abilities of self-discovery and the necessary infrastructures for the self-determined realization of one's particularity and identity. And the goal was the authentic self and its individuality. Ronald Inglehart's diagnosis of the 'silent revolution' and Ulrich Beck's talk of 'the age of one's personal life' were aimed at precisely this phase of modernity and this understanding of the emancipatory project (Beck 2001).

In late modernity, or the late phase of second, reflexive modernity, the weighting between the Kantian-rationalist understanding of emancipation (rational, responsible self-determination) and the romantic-individualist understanding (authentic self-realization), which were initially equally present in the EEP, then clearly shifted in favour of the individualist aspect. Not only did the commitment to the general become less important, but also the consistency and stability of the realized self. Any commitment to something stable, permanent, to constitutive principles of a personal identity, comes under suspicion of ideology in late or 'liquid' modernity (Bauman 2000), just as much as the idea of universal and any supposedly superior reason had before. The liberation from the obligatory, the rule-giving, thus spills over from the level of the collective to that of the individual. Subjectivity and identity are getting ever more complex, flexible and fleeting. Any form of commitment to consistent principles becomes an unreasonable restriction and burden (e.g. Sennett 1999; Reckwitz 2020).

This is where Laclau located the final end of the 'classical understanding' of emancipation. It opens up and leaves the field to a variety of 'potential liberation discourses of our postmodern age', which are 'constructed by the movements', but are all 'purely contingent' in their normative justification and can no longer 'be considered as the liberation of any true human essence' (Laclau 1996: 19, 4). Nevertheless, the end of the classical understanding of emancipation was welcomed by many movements, because the norms and assumptions that had hitherto been constitutive of the emancipatory project – categorical imperatives of reason, John Rawls's necessity of public justification, non-negotiable ecological necessities, Habermas's supposedly 'unforced force of the better argument' – had in turn long since become the object of emancipatory criticism, for example from feminist, ecological or postcolonial sides (Davis 1982; Nandy 1983; Fraser 2013; Chakrabarty 2000; Dobson 2022; Pellizzoni 2022). This is precisely why Laclau and these movements saw the 'end of emancipation' of the classical kind as the 'beginning of freedom' (Laclau 1996: 18). In order to prevent the subject whose liberation they were aiming for from immediately being subjected to new rules, restrictions and disciplinary power, emancipatory movements – and critical theory – increasingly focused on removing the obstacles to autonomous self-determination and self-realization and have become increasingly reluctant to define the desired end state in positive terms (see also Foucault 1984, 2008 or Allen 2015). The focus, as Andreas Reckwitz put it, now lay in the struggle against the 'cultural bonds forged by generally held feelings of duty and morality, which characterized the ethos of classical modernity', in the emancipation of 'the subject from the constraints of bourgeois and industrial modernity in favour of a culture that emphasizes the development of individual singularity – a culture of intensive lived experience and emotion' (Reckwitz 2023: 77, 75f).

The emancipatory critique thus pursued and promoted liberation from the exacting demands of (ecological) reason, responsibility and maturity that had been constitutive of the 'classical understanding' of emancipation. It opened up a way out of the rationalist narrowing of this classical concept and the strict demands it implied. It liberated precisely those dimensions of the unique self and individual life – emotion, impulse, spontaneity, alternative rationalities – which this classical concept had excluded. At the same time, however, it diminished the usefulness of emancipation as a key to the ecologization of society and as a guiding norm of reflexive modernization more generally. It reinforced the notorious imbalance between the limiting (rule-setting) and the delimiting (rule-transcending) dimension of the EEP. And by reflexively turning the critical project against itself and successively eroding the normative foundations of their own project – albeit with emancipatory intent – the movements contributed to transforming emancipation into an 'empty signifier', thus facilitating the appropriation of the concept by actors who explicitly reject the principles of emancipatory-progressive movements as traditionally understood.

In terms of identity politics, this gradual reformulation, the reflexive modernization, of the emancipation project leads to a crisis and loss of the self and identity: incrementally, it bid farewell to the essential, the authentic, that was supposed to be liberated and realized. 'If the original modernity was top-heavy', wrote Zygmunt Bauman, 'the present-day modernity is light at the top, having relieved itself from its *emancipatory* duties' (Bauman 2000: 29f). This opens up the abyss that Bauman describes as the central characteristic of late modernity, namely the radical discrepancy between the de jure and de facto autonomy of the late-modern self. While the theoretical claim to freedom, self-determination and authentic self-realization in late-modern societies is more developed than ever before, control over the social conditions of authentic self-determination and self-realization has evaporated, and so has any notion of something truly authentic and essential that could define identity and would not be purely accidental and interchangeable (ibid.: 38ff). Reckwitz therefore diagnoses a 'crisis of self-actualization', Rosa identifies a 'transformation from approximate omnipotence to paralyzing impotence', and Amlinger and Nachtwey describe the syndrome of 'offended freedom' (Reckwitz 2023: 75ff; Rosa 2023: 137; Amlinger & Nachtwey 2025). 'Early modernity', Bauman wrote well before them all, '*disembedded* in order to *reimbed*'. In late modernity, by contrast, uprooting is permanent: 'there is no prospect of re-embeddedment at the end of the road taken by (now chronically) disembedded individuals'. This implies, inter alia, 'the corrosion and slow disintegration of citizenship' (Bauman 2000: 32, 34, 36).

In eco-political terms, this further development of prevailing understandings of autonomy, subjectivity, identity and emancipation leads directly to the 'society of unsustainability', the 'imperial mode of living' and 'life at the expense of others' (Blühdorn 2020b; Brand & Wissen 2017; Lessenich 2019a). This is because it establishes understandings of self-determination and self-realization that are highly individualistic and fixated on the present, resource-intensive and heavily dependent on the consumer goods and entertainment

Table 7. Historicization of the emancipatory project

	Release from ...		Realization of ...		
	Self-distinction from	Struggle against	Acquisition/ development of	Hope for	
Kantian rationalism	animal being, instinct	superstition, irrationality, convenience, laziness	maturity, ability to use reason	collective subject, world society, perpetual peace	Philosophical modernity
Classic industrial society	capitalist power relations, false consciousness, delusive context	ideology, oppression, exploitation, capital owners, capitalism	class consciousness, awareness of alienation, political organizational skills	class subject, socialist personality/new man, liberated international society	First modernity
Post-industrial society	tradition, standardization, mass culture	social norms, predetermined social roles	individual abilities of self-determination and self-realization	individual personality, authentic self-realization	Second modernity
Society of singularities	society, modernist understandings of autonomy and subjectivity	categorical imperatives, restrictive obligations, concepts of the common good	spontaneity, potentials, alternative forms of reason, competitiveness	singularity, optimized self-realization/self-awareness, the entrepreneurial self	Third modernity

industry, and which also deliberately aim for uniqueness and exclusivity. Particularly in view of planetary boundaries, these late-modern forms of self-determination and self-realization are necessarily based on inequality, exclusion and the political control of the marginalized (see Blühdorn 2020b for more details).

Of course, this simplifying sketch of different interpretations of the emancipatory project – summarized schematically in Table 7 – cannot depict the diverse modes in which different social groups and movements articulate the concepts of autonomy and emancipation for their own purposes and mobilize them for their respective struggles for recognition and societal participation. Rather, it outlines and contrasts ideal-typical understandings of autonomy, subjectivity and emancipatory politics that are characteristic of different phases of societal development and modernity. And it attempts to make transparent how, in the course of a 'silent revolution', the demands and expectations regarding self-determination and self-realization have become ever higher, while at the same time the prevailing understanding of these terms has changed considerably.

Many authors regard neoliberalism and the logic of capitalism more generally as the driving force behind this development, which is as such largely undisputed in the social sciences (cf. e.g. Bröckling 2015). Neoliberal capitalism, argues Stefanie Graefe, forces the total malleability and dissolution of traditional understandings of subjectivity and identity, and ultimately only allows autonomy in the sense of self-organization instead of genuine self-determination and authentic self-realization. The 'telos of self-organization', she writes, is no longer 'freedom, equality or authenticity', but only 'the *self-preservation* or survival of the self-organizing entity, which in turn requires its *adaptation* to changing environmental conditions'. 'To put it bluntly', Graefe notes, 'in the [neoliberal] context of subjectivized and flexibilized work, self-determination merges into self-organization, while self-actualization is offered to the subjects as compensation for the burdens associated with the increased demands of self-organization' (Graefe 2019: 82f, 84). Neoliberalism thus appropriates, colonizes and alienates the concept of autonomy in a way that makes 'genuine' autonomy impossible. And the pressure on people to place their entire lives under the categorical imperative of self-optimization and self-marketing at all times results in a syndrome of comprehensive exhaustion (ibid.: 35f).

However, this explanatory approach remains one-sided insofar as it does not take into account that the logic of emancipation itself is also an important driver of change in prevailing understandings of autonomy and subjectivity. For, as explained above, its reflexive modernization is also aimed at opening up new understandings of the subject and the self beyond the disciplined and self-controlled subject of reason, and at mobilizing expanded potentials for self-realization, self-awareness and self-experience beyond the classical notion of autonomy. It seeks relief from the obligations, responsibilities and stringent demands inherent in the Kantian concept of maturity – a temptation which Kant himself had already emphasized when he wrote that 'it is so convenient to be immature' and extremely arduous 'for each separate individual to work his way out of the immaturity which has almost become nature to him' (Kant 1970: 54).

Nancy Fraser's concept of 'progressive neoliberalism' reaches beyond this one-sided criticism of neoliberal capitalism. It emphasizes the interplay between neoliberal deregulation on the one hand and the emancipatory liberation from boundaries and restrictions on the other. 'In this new scenario', Fraser writes, 'marketization has teamed up with emancipation'; 'mainstream liberal currents of emancipatory social movements' have 'adopted thin, meritocratic, market-friendly understandings of equality and freedom', and 'all this has proceeded under the cover of progressive tropes: *multicultural diversity, women's empowerment*, LGBTQ rights' (Fraser in Fraser & Jaeggi 2018: 192f). Here, then, the importance of emancipatory movements is explicitly acknowledged, and Fraser keeps open the horizon for 'richer', 'more authentic' interpretations of equality and freedom. In fact, the problem lies not only in the complicity of some emancipatory movements with the neoliberal agenda, but rather in the fact that the continuous updating, the reflexive modernization, of prevailing understandings of autonomy and emancipation corrodes any notion of a general, authentic and essential. In the search for '*genuine* emancipation' and a 'subject liberated from all power relations', emancipatory movements have systematically eroded the foundations of the emancipation project itself (Allen 2015: 515).

And now that the dimension of the general, the concept of the citizen, has lost its significance in favour of the particular, the singularity, and all notions of the supposedly authentic and essential have become exhausted, the syndrome of disappointment and disillusionment is spreading epidemically, resulting from the contradiction between the promise of autonomy and its systematic unattainability. This syndrome by no means only affects the much-cited losers of modernization, who are much less able than the more privileged echelons of society to make use of the new opportunities of the flexibilized, accelerated and singularized society. Instead, people with very different socio-economic backgrounds and diverse ideological orientations experience the late-modern failure of self-discovery, self-determination and self-realization. In the hope of being able to find some solace and orientation in the sense of self – something authentic, an essence or even 'sacred basic principles' of their identity – climate activists, advocates of wokeness, activists of cancel culture, critical social scientists and right-wing identity movements all turn to the remains of their respective 'tribal fires' (Bauman 2017: 49ff). And the illiberalism, exclusiveness and authoritarianism that in late modernity is characteristic of identity-seeking movements on both the left and the right of the ideological spectrum can essentially be explained by the attempt to counter the depletion of the general and essential and the crisis of self-realization with a new moral fundamentalism.

Elsewhere, I have described the gradual shift of emphasis towards the particular and away from the general, towards the liberating and away from the limiting, as summarized in Table 7, as 'second-order emancipation' and as the 'liberation from maturity' (e.g. Blühdorn 2013: 143ff; Blühdorn & Kalke 2019). Both terms suggest a temporal succession of a first form of emancipation and a subsequent second form. What they also have in common is the emphasis on the proactive, self-determined, creative, intentional aspect of change in prevailing understandings of subjectivity, autonomy and emancipation: the individual itself opens up new possibilities for its self-realization – inter alia, by liberating itself from the high demands and requirements inherent in the classical concept of emancipation and from the burdens and demands also inherent in the concepts of ecological reason, responsibility and maturity. In Beck's words (who was, however, referring to first rather than second modernity), these terms emphasize 'the growing awareness' that – from the perspective of emancipation – second modernity and the EEP have become 'ineffective' and 'counterproductive' (Beck 2007: 55), especially in view of the responsibilities which the NSM and the EEP had placed on themselves and on citizens when they self-confidently proclaimed that they intended to assume responsibility for resolving the crisis of modernity and organizing the good life for all. At the same time, the term 'second-order emancipation' also reflects that the norms of the general, of maturity, of reason, of inclusion, as well as those of the authentic and sacred are essentially something pre-modern that in the long run cannot withstand emancipatory criticism. In this respect, second-order emancipation corresponds to the project of reflexive modernization and means bidding farewell to these remnants of pre-modernity, whose validity and legitimacy are no longer accepted.

Particularly with regard to the EEP, however, it is also helpful to explain the change in prevailing understandings of subjectivity, autonomy and emancipation from the dialectical tension between the equally original and constitutive, but ultimately incompatible, dimensions of this project: the collective, general and thus limiting dimension, which was dominant in first modernity, and the individualistic, particular and delimiting dimension, which became increasingly dominant in second modernity. From this perspective, it would be more accurate to understand the disintegration, the untenability, of the EEP and the metamorphosis of second into third modernity as the result of a 'dialectic of emancipation'. In contrast to the more actor-centred concept of second-order emancipation, talk of the dialectic of emancipation emphasizes the uncontrolled, the unintended, the side effect, the unforeseen and the unpreventable. In the course of this dialectic, the notorious imbalance between the rule- and boundary-crossing and the rule-giving and boundary-setting dimension of the emancipation project becomes ever stronger. Emancipation gradually loses the ability to place a logic of limitation alongside the logic of delimitation – until a reflexive modernization in Beck's sense, that is, a reflexive modernization of society, is ultimately no longer possible, because the reflexive modernization of the 'basic principles' has exhausted its potential and power as a corrective. Furthermore, compared to second-order emancipation, the concept of the dialectic of emancipation also has a broader scope: it refers more strongly to what emerges from the tension – the illiberal, marginalizing and authoritarian (see Blühdorn 2022b and Chapter 6.4).

Regardless of the preferred term, it is now clear how the grammar of political conflict and the prospects for a societal transformation in the sense of the EEP have fundamentally changed in the course of the reflexive modernization of prevailing understandings of autonomy and emancipation. Freedom and self-determination have a radically different meaning in late modernity than in the classical understanding of emancipation. Compared to the Kantian concept of the autonomous subject, the updated understandings are seen as emancipatory progress and a gain. Conversely, the Kantian understanding, which still had considerable significance for the EEP, becomes obsolete and anachronistic, together with Kant's concept of the autonomous subject – as already outlined in Chapter 3.6. In late modernity, autonomy, subjectivity and emancipation have as little to do with imperatives of reason as with the bourgeois idea of maturity or the romantic idea of authenticity. Even if it appears to be pursued collectively in social movements, emancipation is a largely individualized project. Equality and inclusion have taken a back seat to diversity and exclusivity. The transformative and prefigurative dimension, whether with regard to the individual or society as a whole, has largely evaporated. Emancipation aims less and less at a radically different future society and more and more at self-determination, self-realization and self-awareness within the existing order – and at liberation from everything that emancipation was once supposed to mean in the EEP.

At this stage, 'the war of emancipation is not over' (Bauman 2000: 51), of course, and the dialectic of emancipation has not come to a standstill. It is, Bauman continues, 'only the meaning assigned to emancipation under past but no more present conditions that has become obsolete' (ibid.: 48). The goal is still autonomy. And the practice is still emancipation. But these values are understood in a fundamentally different way in late modernity and describe a completely different political programme. From the perspective of progressive movements in the traditional sense, it may be disputed that these late-modern interpretations of autonomy and emancipation can really still be described using these terms. But autonomy and emancipation do not have an essentialist core. Rather, just like sustainability, they are 'essentially contested concepts'. Or to put it differently: just like ecology, emancipation, too, is a 'political chameleon' that can take on very different ideological shades. The 'emancipatory catastrophe' of the EEP, then, lies in the fact that the emancipatory movements and the emancipatory logic themselves have promoted the depletion of their normative foundations and of the concept of emancipation itself, thereby facilitating the reversal of the political thrust of emancipation.

Thus, in late modernity, there is good reason to assume that the end of emancipation in the classical understanding does not mean the beginning of true freedom, but rather the beginning of social conflicts in the sense of Thomas Hobbes. In any case, late-modern societies offer ample evidence of a 'brutalization of social struggles for recognition' (Honneth 2012) and the increasing brutalization of public discourse. Nancy Fraser continues to hope for opportunities for an emancipation project that could be progressive and transformative in the traditional sense (Fraser & Jaeggi 2018: 193). Philipp Staab recognizes signs in the late-modern present that 'collective transformations are gaining in importance', in which 'the common is emphasized over the solitary' (Staab 2022: 71, 107, 28). However, such hopes seem ill-founded, given that late-modern societies glorify 'our freedom, our values and our lifestyle' as an emancipatory achievement, irrespective of its unsustainability and untenability. Such an achievement is defended by 'emancipatory' movements which, according to the conventional understanding of emancipation, can only be described as regressive, that is, exclusive, anti-democratic and anti-ecological (see Jaeggi in Fraser & Jaeggi 2018: 195f).

6.4 The dialectic of democracy

The dialectic of emancipation thus explains how and why the values of freedom and self-determination, which gained such great importance in the course of the silent revolution, have so comprehensively evolved in content and political thrust that they now represent the opposite of their original manifestation, even though the concepts themselves have been retained. It sheds light on what has transpired in the realm of norms, which is of central importance for any ecological transformation of society, but which the paradigm of sustainability, focusing on scientization and striving to depoliticize in order to build consensus, has always deliberately ignored. It thus extends the explanation given in Chapter 6.2 as to why the sustainability paradigm has never been able to achieve its stated goals but has, instead, paved the way for the society of unsustainability. At the same time, the dialectic of emancipation also plays an essential role in explaining why the eco-emancipatory project of democratizing democracy has not led to the ideal of 'true' democracy, and late-modern societies are experiencing what I initially described as the 'post-democratic turn' (Blühdorn 2013), but which can now be more clearly defined as an 'autocratic-authoritarian turn' (cf. Chapter 3.3). The democratization of democracy was the third major pillar of the EEP, alongside the ecologization of industrial society and the realization of the modernist promise of freedom and self-determination (autonomy) – and the 'dialectic of democracy' is the third dimension of the unexpected emancipatory catastrophe.

The concept of the dialectic of democracy is, to begin with, a means to explain the retreat of democracy that has already been mentioned at various points, which can currently be observed even in the most established democratic systems and which, it seems, can hardly be stopped or prevented (cf. Blühdorn 2020e, 2020f). Hence, what has already been discussed in Chapter 3.3, in particular, will be taken up now and further developed. In Chapter 3.3, the crisis and unsustainability of democracy were examined as a distinguishing feature of late modernity. Various explanatory approaches for the 'regression' and possible 'end' of democracy were addressed, which, however, in the sense of traditional critical normativity, mostly amount to attempts to save and revive it (Crouch 2004 is a paradigmatic example). I subsequently suggested that in late modernity such attempts may well be doomed to fundamental failure because democracy is not only threatened and destabilized from the outside, by its enemies, but also by its own logic and internal dynamics, that is, its constant striving for further democratization. Its own logic, according to this reasoning that I will now further elaborate, manoeuvres democracy into a 'multiple dysfunctionality' and even into a 'crisis of legitimacy', which in turn triggers an autocratic-authoritarian turn (e.g. Blühdorn 2020e, 2020f). This is a dialectic process that is, it seems, uncontrollable and unstoppable. Not only does it destroy faith in democracy and democratization as crucial means of an SET, but it actually threatens to transform democracy into an instrumental vehicle for the politics of unsustainability.

Both the question of the unsustainability of democracy itself and the possible untenability of democracy as a means of sustainability policy and transformation are still largely ignored in the social science literature on sustainability. This is even more true of the consideration that democracy in late modernity may not only have developed into a 'glass ceiling' for a fundamental sustainability transformation (Hausknost 2020, 2022) but may even have become an instrument for legitimating the politics of unsustainability. Although there is a comprehensive literature on the relationship between democracy and sustainability, this is still primarily devoted to the question of how a transformation to sustainability could be democratically shaped and promoted through measures of democratization. In this literature, the dual assumption is, firstly, that such an SET must and, eventually, will take place and, secondly, that it must and will be compatible with democratic principles. This literature takes little account of the reality that there is not much evidence for a structural transformation of modern societies and their natural relations, despite the many measures of ecological-democratic modernization, and that, from a social theory perspective, there is little prospect of this changing any time soon. Moreover, democracies are disintegrating everywhere, being undermined and replaced by autocratic-authoritarian forms of government. And the idea that democracy and the project of its democratization themselves may not only have contributed to this autocratic-authoritarian turn, but also to the consolidation of unsustainability and its legitimization, is even further beyond the normative horizon of the social science sustainability literature.

However, the perspective of reflexive modernization, the focus on the unintended side effects of modernity itself and, in particular, societal attempts to deal with these side effects, bring these questions to the fore. Philip Manow's reflections on the '(de-)democratization of democracy' are instructive in this regard (Manow 2020; see Chapter 3.3). Manow does not deal directly with the relationship between democracy and sustainability, nor with eco-emancipatory movements and the EEP. However, he sees the self-endangerment, even 'self-destruction' of democracy as the 'fundamental conflict that seems to characterize our time' (ibid.: 25). He diagnoses a 'de-democratization' that is, he suggests, paradoxically, inextricably linked to the moves towards a 'democratization of democracy' (ibid.: 23). In fact, Manow explicitly speaks of a 'dialectic of the democratization and de-democratization of democracy' (ibid.: 55). And in line with Beck's view of the crisis of first modernity, Manow attributes the destabilization of the democratic order to the 'complete victory' of liberal democracy and its 'unqualified success' (ibid.: 20, 24, 145). It is to be understood, he notes, 'as a paradoxical consequence of the enforcement of democracy without alternative' (ibid.: 20).

Manow sees the central problem in the democratizing erosion of the principle of representation. Liberal representative democracy, he writes, drawing on Jacques Rancière, John Dunn and others, was never democratic in the sense of the sovereignty of the people, but always meant the rule of an elite based on the principle of 'repression through representation' (ibid.: 45f). The people were excluded by installing procedures for their representation, and it was this exclusion that stabilized the supposed rule of the people. However, democracy became increasingly inclusive. An increasing number of social groups and minorities fought for ever more far-reaching participation. And this constant expansion of participation, Manow suggests, gradually eroded the stabilizing principle of representation. The current problem of democracy, he believes, lies in 'the constant expansion of this participation, it is *the problem of the democratization of democracy*'. 'In essence', Manow notes, 'the thesis is that the [. . .] expansion of opportunities for participation, described as the democratization of democracy, seems to threaten the institutional conditions under which democracy functions' (ibid.: 52, 171).

Strategies of depoliticization through the transfer of political decisions and responsibilities to non-majoritarian institutions within and beyond the nation state are an attempt to counter this threat and stabilize overburdened democracies. However, such strategies once again imply a de-democratization, which ultimately only fuels the discontent of the excluded and their struggle for the democratization of democracy. According to Manow, this struggle for direct participation is particularly destabilizing because it challenges the 'mediating bodies' such as political parties and erodes 'their filter function'. The crucial factor is that the 'massive expansion of opportunities for political participation and communication' is bypassing and eliminating the 'established control functions of representative institutions'. It is 'the extreme positions', in particular, 'the outsider preferences that were previously reliably filtered out by established mechanisms, well-established procedures and intermediary bodies', Manow notes, that gain a prominent place in the media and the public sphere. Thus, articulate minorities obtain 'control of the topic agenda', and officially constituted politics can 'often only be reactive' (ibid.: 111, 58, 113, 115).

Manow's considerations relate primarily to (right-wing) populism, which he explains as 'the breaking open of an exclusion' and the 'return of the unrepresented', and which he sees as the main self-threat and self-destruction of democracy in late modernity (ibid.: 50, 51). However, what he says about populist movements may also be applied to the eco-emancipatory movements since the 1970s. At the time, these movements rebelled against representative, liberal democracy just as much as the populist right is doing today. The eco-emancipatory movements also demanded entry into the system of representation, which, they insisted, did not take sufficient account of them and the concerns they raised. The eco-emancipatory movements, too, saw the principle of representation and the elite rule that it conceals as the central problem. Just like right-wing populists today, they called for grassroots democracy and direct participation. In calling for a democratization of democracy, they targeted both the principle of representation, which they saw as exclusionary, and liberalism, which they saw as too one-sided in its emphasis on individual rights. Both also apply to today's populists – who, however, no longer understand the principle of participation in the same way as the NSM of the 1970s and 1980s did, and who, in view of today's prevailing understandings of freedom, subjectivity, self-determination and self-realization, also have a different understanding of 'true', or fully democratized, democracy.

The starting point for the criticism of the eco-emancipatory movements had been that liberal, representative democracy satisfied neither the ideal of democratic self-determination nor the requirements of the ecological restructuring of modern (industrial) society. In eco-political terms, many even saw a complicity between liberalism and the system of industrial exploitation and destruction of nature, because liberalism declares the freedom, rights and private property of the individual to be inviolable, while the ecological agenda places a higher value on ecological imperatives and safeguarding the common good (cf. e.g. Wissenburg 1998; Barry & Wissenburg 2001). Liberal representative democracy was, therefore, explicitly considered to be a major cause of the social and ecological crisis. Today, as citizens are called upon everywhere to defend liberal democracy with all determination against alleged or actual internal and external threats, this is easily forgotten. Yet, in key respects, liberal democracy was regarded as deficient and dysfunctional. This was the very reason for the call to modernize and democratize it. Ideals of a better democracy included, inter alia, 'grassroots' democracy, 'direct' democracy, 'participatory' democracy and 'deliberative' democracy (e.g. Macpherson

1977; Dryzek 2000). In all cases, however, the democratization of democracy aspired to extend democratic rights to previously excluded or marginalized groups, to deepen existing and newly created opportunities for participation, and to expand the range of topics open to democratic negotiation and decision-making. According to the principle that even the private sphere is political, many issues that had been previously treated as private matters and attributed to individual freedom in the name of liberalism were now to be placed under democratic control and accountability. At the same time, the established institutions of political decision-making were to be replaced as far as possible by alternative, self-determined institutions. This applied not only to the established parties, but also to the media, educational institutions, scientific research and all kinds of social institutions – with the unambiguous aim to circumvent and eliminate the filter function of the established mediating bodies.

Thus, the eco-emancipatory movements pursued exactly what Manow describes today as the primary problem of late-modern democracies and what he blames, above all, on right-wing populism (Manow 2020: 58). With their project of democratizing democracy, the NSM aimed for a structural change in the political public sphere, attempted to wrest political discourse from the control of the established parties and media, and fought to redefine the political agenda in their own terms. In doing so, they assumed that the cause of the problem, the ecological and social irrationality and irresponsibility, lay primarily in the inherent logic of the economic and administrative system and in the elites of capital and political power, while citizens and civil society were assumed to be the actors of reason, responsibility, maturity and the true common interest. The economic-administrative system and the political elites, on the other hand, were seen as disconnected from the citizens and their true needs and had – as right-wing populists are saying today – become detached from them. Accordingly, the aim was to reconnect the economy, administration, politics and technology to the citizens' real needs, true values and reason instead of allowing them to continue to follow their own destructive logic. Exactly this had been the aim of the democratization of democracy.

This project was based on the assumption that, after sufficient democratic negotiation, the politically enlightened citizenry would always opt for what was ecologically necessary because it was ecologically sensible, morally right and responsible to the common good, and because it would also ensure true prosperity and social satisfaction. Some of these beliefs live on to the present day (e.g. Paech

2012; Folkers & Paech 2020; Jackson 2011, 2021). Thus, democratic self-determination was expected to reverse the filter function of the established institutions, to filter out the individualistic and economic irrationality that had prevailed thus far and bring the responsible, reasonable and mature to the fore. The democratization of democracy was believed to give full weight, putting it in Ulrich Beck's words again, to the 'sacred basic principles' of modernity – not least because participatory and deliberative democracy would have an enlightening and educational effect on citizens. It would transform private individuals who had, thus far, primarily followed their individualistic interests into responsible citizens who would now feel much more obliged by ecological imperatives and the common good and would more fully commit themselves to their implementation, making optimal use of the expanded and deepened means of democratized democracy.

However, this was the fatal error in eco-emancipatory thinking – and the reason why the democratization of democracy never achieved the aspired goal. In fact, it was not only that the newly created opportunities for democratic participation were used very unequally by different sections of society and therefore unintentionally distorted political equality in favour of the educated and articulate middle classes. The eco-emancipatory movements also did not take into account that reflexive modernization reconfigures the 'basic principles' according to which democracy was to be democratized. However, as described in Chapter 6.3, these reference norms – the prevailing understandings of freedom, subjectivity, self-determination and self-realization – have changed in a way that suddenly makes democracy appear dysfunctional in several respects.

In late modernity, in the neo-Biedermeier retreat to the private and personal (cf. Chapter 6.3), ecological reason, responsibility and maturity, subordination to general principles or a commitment to the common good play at most a casual role. It is ever more difficult to believe in the 'true fulfilment' that supposedly lies in self-limitation – especially in the face of excessive new uncertainties. The diversification of social groups, the singularization of late-modern individuals and the pluralization and flexibilization of personal identities increasingly limit the ability of democratic institutions to make substantial and stable decisions and thus their ability to deal effectively with pressing social problems. In addition, democracy is also losing its emancipatory efficiency: it appears less and less as an essential prerequisite and guarantee of freedom, self-determination and self-realization, which are predominantly understood in an individualistic manner today. Instead, democratic decisions are increasingly perceived as interference in private affairs, as a restriction of personal rights and an obstacle to full self-development. This is especially true when self-determination and self-realization explicitly claim singularity and exclusivity, and when planetary ecological boundaries require the effective exclusion of (global) social majorities from the favoured understandings of a good and fulfilling life. Against this backdrop, confidence in the alternative and supposedly better forms of democracy – direct, egalitarian, participatory, deliberative – has largely evaporated. In the course of the modernization of reference norms, they are also becoming dysfunctional because personal values and interests are ever more complex, contradictory and changeable. Furthermore, there is no common reason any more that might facilitate 'reasonable' democratic negotiation and binding decisions.

In late modernity, this multiple dysfunctionality of democracy (see also Blühdorn 2020c, 2020d, 2020e) is leading to a comprehensive loss of trust, which affects not only the existing democratic institutions, but also faith in democracy per se. And the democratization of democracy pursued by the eco-emancipatory movements has clearly contributed to this. It has further strengthened the effect of the change in prevailing understandings of freedom, self-determination and a good life: democracy democratized in the sense described above is even more dysfunctional than before, both in terms of its ability to solve problems and in terms of its suitability as a political means for today's patterns of self-realization.

Thus, what Manow writes about late-modern (right-wing) populism may also be applied to the eco-emancipatory movements. In ecological terms, their democratization of democracy led to a sclerotic constellation, which in Chapter 3 has been described as 'ecological ungovernability'. And any further democratization may well exacerbate rather than improve this dysfunctionality. In any case, in view of late-modern value preferences and foreseeable losses of prosperity and comfort, what is required for an SET is likely to be highly unpopular – and downright unreasonable. Democratic achievements such as environmental impact assessments or public participation procedures become additional obstacles for projects such as the expansion of renewable energies. Philipp Staab rightly observes: 'Civil society activism' is 'frustrated by its own success' in late modernity, because the urgent problems cannot be dealt with 'by a subpolitically clogged democracy at the required speed'. Instead of democratizing democracy, Staab observes, the widely perceived lack of political capacity now is to be countered 'by means of a primacy of state control, which is based on specialist expertise, is not slowed down by deliberative processes or representation obligations and which enforces sensible rules with sanctions if necessary' (Staab 2022: 132, 176). When today's climate movements demand 'listen to the science!', this not only goes against the older demand of eco-emancipatory movements to democratize science and knowledge, but, borrowing Manow's words, it is an 'invitation to disregard majorities, and thus evidence of an at best half-hearted attitude towards democracy – which appears legitimate [only] as long as it functions as a wish-fulfilment machine for a liberal middle class that does not find it difficult to make friends with another form of rule if it promises to deliver roughly the same thing' (Manow 2020: 170).

Conversely, when former German Chancellor Olaf Scholz said that 'anyone who wants to make climate policy' must 'be confident that every single legal regulation would find a majority in a referendum',[1] this may sound like a commitment to grassroots democracy. In reality, however, this professed commitment to democracy, firstly, is a pretext for governments to shirk their leadership responsibilities and, secondly, turns democracy into a legitimation instrument for a kind of politics that is predictably limited to stabilizing the unsustainable status quo. Whereas previously, when the movements were still demanding 'listen to the people!', governments insisted that clear scientific evidence was needed before they could act decisively from an informed position, the constellation has now reversed: in view of the comprehensive scientific data and the 'historical disappointment about the lack of effectiveness of sub-political forms of addressing the problems' (Staab 2022: 178), the movements demand 'listen to the science!', and actors who at best half-heartedly support the SET are demanding 'listen to the people!' as a reliable strategy to block any significant transformation.

Manow is undoubtedly right in suggesting that the democratization of democracy threatens to become counterproductive in late modernity. However, he narrows the perspective too much to the political-institutional dimension and neglects the sociocultural dimension, which is at least as important. In particular, the reflexive modernization of democratic reference norms – above all that of the autonomous subject – makes democracy dysfunctional both as a liberal and as a representative form of government: democracy can no longer be liberal in late modernity because the apparently

---

[1] Scholz on 14 July 2023 in his summer press conference: Anna Lehman, 'The Chancellor's Summer Balance Sheet: Scholz's Imperative', taz.de, 14 July 2023. https://taz.de/Sommer bilanz-des-Bundeskanzlers/!5947357/. See also: https://www.youtube.com/watch?v=qZ _qMWi2aa0 (from 1:03:42).

non-negotiable claim to today's understandings of freedom and self-realization necessarily implies the radical limitation of those entitled to it (see Lessenich 2019a, 2019b). It can no longer be representative because the multilayered and fleeting subject of late modernity can no longer be represented in the sense that the eco-emancipatory movements had once imagined, namely in the sense of reflecting its values and interests as authentically as possible (cf. Blühdorn 2013: 203–215). In fact, it is the modernization of the 'basic principles' that makes the democratization of democracy a serious problem, because it reverses the interpretation of the content and political thrust of the concept of democracy and radically redefines what the democratization of social institutions implies.

The dysfunctionality and deficits of liberal, representative democracy, which already formed the starting point of the EEP and provided the impetus for the project to democratize democracy, were therefore not eliminated in the implementation of this project, but rather reinforced – while the alternative forms of democracy that were once considered better have lost the foundations on which they were based. Instead, the autocratic-authoritarian turn is unfolding, driven by the interests of a diversity of social actors who are united in their scepticism towards democracy: elites who have always been against democracy in favour of their own interests; ecological activists who have lost confidence in democratization and now prefer to rely on a combination of science (for the facts), moral fundamentalism (for the norms) and strict regulation (for the policy effectiveness); over-burdened citizens who find democratic participation too exhausting, time-consuming or burdensome; and all those who, in the face of planetary boundaries, are trying to secure their values, freedom and lifestyle by drawing borders and demanding exclusion. What they all have in common is that they no longer believe in the democratization of democracy. Or to quote Philipp Staab: 'Democratization in the sense of an expansion of deliberative forms of participation [. . .] is not the envisaged programme' any longer (Staab 2022: 174). This is the emancipatory catastrophe that has irrevocably undermined the democratic pillar of the EEP.

6.5 Emancipation from the EEP

So with regard to the democratic pillar, too, the EEP does not simply fail because capitalism and its elites block and suppress it, but essentially owing to its own internal logic of maximal politicization and participation. In the third pillar of the EEP, we again see what Beck described as a crisis of success or victory: the 'reinvention of politics' and the democratization of democracy initially promoted individual and collective political self-determination considerably, but at the same time produced side effects that lead to democratic sclerosis and ungovernability and threaten to suffocate democracy. Just like the emancipation from emancipation and the emergence of the society of unsustainability in the wake of the sustainability paradigm, the exhaustion and replacement of democracy in the course of the attempt to democratize it, too, is a crisis of victory. In all three dimensions, after resounding successes, the exact opposite of what was originally intended was ultimately brought about, or emerged as a side effect despite all good intentions.

In sum, the dialectic of sustainability, the dialectic of emancipation and the dialectic of democracy, which, as we have seen, are directly linked to each other, act as the gravedigger of the EEP and the SET – and at the same time as the midwife of a next society and a different modernity, in which the EEP becomes anachronistic. The analysis of the threefold dialectic reveals how its three supporting pillars are disintegrating, why the EEP is no longer tenable, and to what extent the emancipatory logic itself is a major driving force behind this. Contrary to the hope that Beck places in this concept, from a late-modern perspective, precisely this traumatic experience is the 'emancipatory catastrophe'. The society of unsustainability has already largely abandoned the emancipatory-transformative ideals of the EEP. It struggles – in the name of its own updated understandings of emancipation, autonomy and subjectivity – to maintain the status quo; to stabilize what from the perspective of the EEP appears as the order of unsustainability. This struggle once again means a reinvention of politics, one that no longer constitutes and implements the eco-emancipatory project, but which attacks it, turns it into a political target and repoliticizes it. And while the EEP is losing its power because reflexive modernization has eroded its foundations, instead of the 'counter-hegemonic bloc' that Nancy Fraser and others are still hoping for (Fraser 2019, 2023; see also Chapter 3.3), new discourse alliances and forms of complicity are emerging, united – whether explicitly or tacitly – by a post-ecologist consensus to defend the established order.

Nevertheless, it would be wrong and undialectical to regard merely as a disaster and loss that which, from the perspective of second modernity, initially appears to be a comprehensive failure and catastrophe. For, the third pillar of the EEP, too, that is, the dialectic of

190

democracy, concerns, in Beck's words, 'the growing awareness of the inefficiency' of second modernity and the EEP, 'indeed of the counterproductivity of its measures'. In his time, Beck was referring to the inefficiency of first modernity and its institutions. From the perspective of late modernity, however, the norms and institutions of second modernity fall prey to the same verdict. The ambivalence towards democracy and, above all, towards its further democratization, clearly indicates this. In fact, the suggestion that the EEP 'is collapsing' due to its inherent contradictions and that this might be described as an 'emancipatory catastrophe' accords too little attention to this inefficiency and counterproductivity. From the perspective of second modernity, these suggestions may seem appropriate, for, from this point of view, the prospects are gloomy and defeatist, indeed. Yet, this assessment not only neglects that considerable progress has been made, too – both ecologically and in terms of self-determination and the democratization of democracy – but the EEP has actually been overcome in an emancipatory manner, that is, driven by the logic of emancipation itself. Accordingly, from the perspective of third modernity, the relief and liberation from its outdated assumptions, norms and obligations appear as an emancipatory gain. One may decide, of course, to regard the normative standards of second modernity as absolute and to reject those of third modernity. In this case, the diagnosis presented here may be described as gloomy and pessimistic. Yet, this kind of thinking would fail to grasp the distinctive and specifically late-modern quality of the late-modern condition.

When Beck wrote of the 'emancipatory catastrophe', he hoped that the catastrophe, regardless of whether it had already occurred or was still imminent, would have an emancipatory effect by setting in motion counter-efforts that would advance the emancipatory project. To a certain extent, this hope has come true. Ultimately, however, the (impending) catastrophe is emancipatory not insofar as it would lead to a 'more-modernity' in which Beck's 'sacred basic principles' are more fully implemented, but insofar as it overcomes the earlier interpretation of these basic principles in an emancipatory manner and thus leads to a truly different modernity. This adjusted use of Beck's term initially suggests the exact opposite of what Beck meant by it: emancipatory efforts towards ecologization, greater self-determination and more democracy bring about stabilized unsustainability, the abandonment of the autonomous subject and the dysfunctionality of democracy. In some respects, however, the above analysis leads back to Beck's understanding of the emancipatory catastrophe: for the abandonment of the EEP is an emancipatory advance and gain – not in the sense that it would promote the 'sacred basic principles', but in the sense that it overcomes their previous burdensome interpretation. Just as it is sociologically inadequate to interpret right-wing populism one-dimensionally as a regression (Manow 2020; Lütjen 2022), it is also wrong to understand the untenability of the EEP exclusively as a failure. Rather, late modernity gives reason to assume that emancipation itself has rendered it anachronistic.

INTERREGNUM

The triple dialectic of the EEP at last fulfils Beck's prophecy of the 'other modernity'. The reflexive modernization of Beck's 'basic principles' takes late-modern societies beyond the condition Beck called 'more-modernity' into a truly different modernity. And only if this reflexive modernization is interpreted in this way can the distinctiveness of contemporary Western societies – which have long since evolved well beyond Beck's 'second modernity' – be grasped. The criticism of Beck's theory of reflexive modernization formulated at the beginning of Chapter 5.3 could therefore also be formulated differently: in retrospect, his theory of a 'halved' or 'truncated' modernity proves to be a halved or truncated theory of the metamorphosis of modernity. The triple dialectic means that, rather than the 'sacred basic principles' of humanity reshaping the unsustainable basic institutions of society, the reflexively modernized basic principles stabilize the basic institutions of unsustainability which have themselves become sacrosanct. The triple dialectic determines the conditions under which ecological issues are now formulated and negotiated and under which the assumptions, certainties and demands of the EEP are repoliticized in late modernity. From the perspective of the EEP, this metamorphosis of the normative foundations and this repoliticization appear traumatic. But perhaps this is just a transitional phenomenon.

Late-modern societies find themselves in an intermediate stage in which, on the one hand, the results of the threefold dialectic are clearly recognizable, but in which, on the other hand, the metamorphosis to third modernity is only partially complete. And it is not actually third modernity itself that is traumatic but primarily this intermediate stage, the *interregnum*. For as long as late-modern societies are still *on the way* to the new modernity, the old basic principles resonate and their violation is painful – especially for those who have always understood the interregnum, that is, the phase when 'the old is dying' but the new 'cannot be born' yet (Gramsci 1971: 276), as the preliminary stage of a more democratic, fairer, more ecological and more emancipated society and world. Such intermediate phases, the pioneers of the SET keep assuring us to the present day, are 'episodes of relatively emphatic freedom, when we can contemplate changing the rules of the game' because the existing 'regime begins to unravel' and 'newly radicalized social actors put forth a broad array of competing ideas about what should replace it' (Fraser & Monticelli 2021: 7; see also Chapter 2.2). But in late modernity, such narratives of hope seem ever less plausible.

Beck himself did not explicitly speak of an *interregnum*, yet he, too, saw a situation in which 'we are witnessing the destruction of the certainties' of industrial modernity, but that 'a new order has not (yet) emerged' (Beck 2009: 219). Ultimately, he failed to meet his own demand that in this situation we have 'to think beyond apocalypses or the salvation of the world' and instead 'focus on its metamorphosis', that is, on 'what is now emerging – future structures, norms and new beginnings' (Beck 2016: 36, 39; see also Chapters 4.2 and 4.5). But he provided important tools that, throughout this book, have proved especially useful for describing and explaining late-modern societies and their crises and transformations.

Regarding the further development of Beck's approach outlined above, there are, of course, at least two caveats: firstly, my view of the path to the next modernity focuses primarily on two dimensions of metamorphosis, the ecological and the emancipatory. In addition to the dynamics of emancipation and ecological change, other dynamics, too, play an important role in the great transformation of late-modern societies, such as the steady increase in complexity, capitalist expansion, marketization and concentration of power, and the dynamics of the digital revolution and artificial intelligence. In their own ways – as signalled in Chapter 3 – they all confirm and reinforce the disintegration or transformation of the modernist central norm of the EEP, that is, the idea of the subject and its claim to autonomy. The fact that they remained in the background here does not imply that they are insignificant, but here the focus has been specifically on the eco-emancipatory dynamic, which has received far too little attention in the relevant literature to date.

Secondly, my analysis of the transformation of late-modern societies and their eco-political discourses is based in various respects on simplifying constructions. This concerns the concept of the EEP, which, as emphasized in the very first chapter, is a homogenizing abstraction, as well as the model of the three modernities, which is no less abstract, homogenizing and, above all, rather static and seemingly closed. However, both have proved to be extremely helpful in the attempt to understand the eco-political turning point and the specifically late-modern features of the current constellation. Such abstractions have always been indispensable in the telling of history(ies), that is, in the attempt to make societal developments comprehensible. The *Enlightenment*, *Romanticism* or the German *Vormärz* have never existed in the singular, either. It is important to remember that (hi)stories can always also be told differently and that each perspective makes certain dimensions particularly visible, while others remain in the background. Multi-perspectivity is indispensable, and beyond second modernity, more so than ever.

By way of conclusion, I will now return to five sets of questions that have already been touched upon at various points and pursue them in more detail. Firstly, the question of whether the thesis of the dual untenability – of the late-modern order of unsustainability and the EEP – is not excessively pessimistic, deterministic and, in fact, anti-emancipatory or even outright reactionary. Secondly: what exactly is to be gained from this kind of analysis? Rather than investigating irresolvable problems and dilemmas, wouldn't it be much simpler and also more constructive to continue the search for possible solutions and the familiar narratives of hope? Thirdly, how do late-modern societies practically cope with their problem of double untenability? How do they process and deal with the experience of the disintegration of their traditional self-descriptions and self-understandings? Fourth, is the new third modernity diagnosed here, suitably conceptualized as postliberal modernity? How does this diagnosis relate to recent debates on postliberalism? And finally: what does the analysis of the dual untenability and the metamorphosis to postliberal modernity mean for critical sociology, transformative sustainability research and (eco-)political education?

7.1 Pessimistic, deterministic, reactionary?

The analytical approach that I have been pursuing throughout previous books and again in this volume has often been criticized as overly pessimistic, deterministic, affirmative or even reactionary (e.g. Neckel 2020; K.W. Brand 2021). Hence, it seems necessary to re-emphasize: none of this really applies to the argument put forward here! The analysis of the dual untenability can only be described in this way from a perspective that I am explicitly trying to avoid here so as to capture the specifically late-modern and the *other* modernity. Or put differently: this critique is based on reference norms that the present analysis does not share without reflection, but which it makes the object of investigation. Those raising such objections do not want to engage in this experiment; they deliberately close themselves off from what this book is about – the contingency, the dissolution, the reconfiguration of eco-emancipatory norms – and retreat into the (eco-) political comfort zone (cf. Blühdorn 2022c), to the (eco-)sociological 'tribal fire' or, using the words of Rockström and colleagues (2009a), into the 'safe operating space' of familiar patterns of eco-political thinking and debate that provide security, orientation and reassurance. This is a legitimate decision, but not one that is conducive to the sociological agenda of this book – understanding late modernity and its untenability.

Furthermore, the objection that the analysis presented here is disturbingly pessimistic itself testifies to a dubious understanding of social science and places questionable expectations on it. For, unlike religion, for example, social science is not primarily about generating optimism and hope but about increasing knowledge about the understanding of late-modern society. This includes exploring whether and to what extent traditional ideas of autonomy, emancipation, subjectivity, self-realization and a good life (for all) still resonate within society today – and why this may no longer be the case. Thus, the aim here is to go beyond the familiar discourses of pessimism and their counterparts, the discourses of optimism. Both are backward-looking and – seemingly in opposition to each other but still jointly – obscure the view of specifically late-modern society's metamorphosis. They hold on to basic principles that fade in late modernity and are blind to the newly emerging, the truly different. Anyone seeking to comprehend late modernity must, therefore, as indicated above, guard against both reinforcing pessimism and the impulse to foster optimism (cf. Chapter 5.1). It is for this reason that Beck rejected the doomsday scenarios of older, mostly conservative cultural criticism: 'In lamenting the end of *the* world', he wrote, 'it remains silent concerning the decline of its own unreflected certainties about the world' (Beck 2009: 219). From today's perspective, this can be applied to all those contemporary diagnostic, social-theoretical and cultural-critical approaches that remain more or less visibly trapped in the normativity of the lost or at least closing era of second modernity. As a matter of fact, although late-modern society is not especially optimistic with regard to the implementation of the EEP, it is also not particularly pessimistic in terms of the apocalypse being imminent. The younger generation, in particular, no longer believes in the 1.5 degree Celsius climate target agreed at the 2016 UN Climate Summit in Paris or in the good life for all. Yet young people are still mainly positive about their own personal prospects for the future (e.g. Albert et al. 2019; Habich 2023).

With regard to the objection that the diagnosis is deterministic, one might add: it is true that the disintegration of the specifically modernist positioning of the supposedly autonomous subject vis-à-vis the world, and of the modernist belief in the subject's control over the world, is seen here as an essential characteristic of late modernity. Indeed, in the literature on late modernity and the Anthropocene as a whole, both are widely regarded as central characteristics of the current condition. Yet this does not imply any kind of determinism. Rather, this diagnosis is precisely about the return of uncertainty, unpredictability, coincidences and the dominance of unforeseen side effects – which as long ago as the 1980s Ulrich Beck had placed at the centre of his concept of the risk society. Accordingly, there is no reason to conceive of third modernity as an unchangeable final state. It is the condition we currently have to reckon with and understand, but quite clearly, the three-stage model used here – and history – remains open.

As to the suspicion that my theory of late modernity is anti-emancipatory, conservative or reactionary, it could be added: this theory does not propagate any kind of return – neither to conservative values nor to the Kantian understanding of autonomy and emancipation (cf. the criticism by Amlinger & Nachtwey 2025: 282). In fact, it does not make normative demands about *what should be* or happen, at all, but rather attempts to grasp *what is* (no longer) the case in late modernity in contrast to previous phases – whereby such attempts are of course always based on certain patterns of perception and underlying values. The notion of an *emancipatory catastrophe* understood in the sense of the EEP, in implementing its own logic, effecting the opposite of what it originally wanted to achieve, could of course be misunderstood as anti-emancipatory. But for this kind of assessment, the *sacred basic principles* of second modernity would have to be taken as a basis and regarded as unchangeable. However, the theory of late modernity is precisely about grasping the transformation of the emancipatory basic principles, and this is a task that critical sociology must face up to, even if this means normative uncertainty and a loss of orientation.

This loss of orientation triggers reflex-like attempts to compensate for and restabilize the uncertainty and unsustainability through radicalized and fundamentalist black-and-white or friend–foe positioning. Pessimistic! Affirmative! Reactionary! Such categorizations, more than anything, are attempts to reassure oneself of one's correct attitude and moral judgement. Particularly in late modernity, when the established critical standards, the critical orthodoxies, are disintegrating (cf. Chapter 2.5), when the emancipatory logic itself erodes them, such practices of reassurance and self-orientation are understandable. To a certain extent, they are part of late-modern palliative care. The less one's own normative position can be justified as *correct*, the more important it becomes to adopt strategies of self-affirmation and self-assurance, such as the emphatic distancing from perceived oppositional viewpoints. Indeed, this need for self-assurance, which no longer has a reliable point of reference, is the driving force behind the late-modern tendency towards political polarization.

However, such forms of demarcation in no way diminish, let alone reverse, the untenability discussed here; they simply deny it. As with the criticism mentioned above that the approach developed here relies on abstractions and simplifications, such normative demarcations are used to justify disengaging with the hypotheses outlined, in order not to allow for their disturbing and unsettling implications. Similarly, the suggestion that the primarily culturalist approach pursued here not only gives too little weight to the biophysical facts but also ignores the capitalist structures and power relations in present societies, opens up possible escape routes to the established certainties. However, these defensive reflexes fail to recognize that the analysis undertaken here is neither about denying biophysical facts or capitalist power relations, nor about disputing the emancipatory successes of the EEP, and certainly not about calling for or defending anti-ecological, anti-democratic or anti-emancipatory positions. The late-modern concepts of freedom, subjectivity and self-realization are not affirmed or justified here. Biophysical realities, changes and causal relationships are in no way disputed or relativized. There is also expressly no intention to exonerate the structures and power relations of capitalism. Rather, the aspiration is to grasp the traumatic nature of the unintended side effects of the EEP, which is, from the perspective of the analytical model presented here, the distinguishing feature of late modernity. This traumatic aspect must be confronted, rather than categorizing it as reactionary and ignoring it. Sociological theory of all fields has the task of confronting it and making it comprehensible. A (self-)critical theory of late modernity is thereby required not to reproduce the familiar strategies of self-reassurance, but to expose them as the defensive reflexes and immunization strategies that they are. This kind of theory is critical precisely insofar as it attempts to show how, why and with what consequences in late modernity the traditional distinction between progressive and regressive politics has become untenable but also – precisely for this reason – why it is defended with such fierce determination.

7.2 What is the benefit?

But what – and who – is helped by all this? What is the point of analysing the dual untenability? Wouldn't it be better and easier to continue to offer narratives of hope and deliver what is demanded everywhere from sustainability research: constructive and pragmatic solutions to concrete problems? In Chapter 1.4, I noted that the dual aim of this book is to make a contribution to the theory of late modernity from the perspective of the sociology of sustainability and a contribution to the sociology of sustainability from the perspective of social theory. I pointed to deficits both in the sociology of sustainability and in the theory of late modernity. In its commitment to its transformation agenda, the former deals far too little with the realities of late-modern society and its politics of unsustainability. The latter, meanwhile, takes too little account of the significance of the great eco-political awakening of the 1970s, which forms the backdrop to the great depression of late modernity. Both are very much enmeshed in fading norms, and being fully focused on the transformation they want to bring about, they run the risk of losing sight of what is actually observable. However, Beck rightly emphasized that a 'sociology that unreflectedly succumbs to the premises of its research object, and is in this sense uncritical, fails to fulfil its most basic task': it does not break with 'the fixations of society's self-descriptions and thus remains incapable of registering either empirically or analytically what drives social and political reality and splits it apart' (Beck 2009: 210). This is precisely why current environmental sociology, which to a large extent continues to see itself as a transformative sociology of sustainability, fails to make the leap into the sociology of unsustainability and why large parts of critical sociology find it difficult to grasp the essence of late modernity.

In a sense, my approach, which aims beyond pessimism and optimism and is primarily oriented towards sociological analysis, is aptly described by Beck's statement that the dialectic of modernization is giving rise to '*another* society, *another* modernity, which is perhaps not a whit better in any sense of the word', but 'so different that it arouses and stimulates the sociologist's curiosity and business' (Beck 1993: 66; cf. also Beck 2009: 212ff). This statement clearly points beyond Beck's own work on what he called second modernity. But it can well be applied to the sociological investigation of the untenability and metamorphosis of late modernity. For, after the crisis of the EEP, which had sought to renew, update and ecologically ground the ideals of the Enlightenment, the social sciences no longer have any reliable criteria by which they could characterize the emerging third modernity as 'better in any sense of the word'. From the perspective of second modernity and the EEP, the observable metamorphosis of late-modern societies is, of course, an abyss. In terms of social theory, however, the emerging new modernity is, more than anything, *different*. And this arouses the curiosity and interest of the sociologist – whose 'business', in view of the late-modern erosion of norms, is increasingly restricted to the descriptive, analytical and explanatory dimension.

Beyond sociological curiosity and the attempt to conceptualize and understand the late-modern *Zeitenwende*, however, the analysis of the dual untenability may also help to appease and perhaps even break out of the spiral of conflict in which late-modern societies are trapped: a considerable threat for these societies lies not only in the rapid destruction of biophysical systems, but also in the fact that all norms available for evaluating the late-modern transformation are – more visibly than ever – mere unfounded, contingent fundamentalisms. This is precisely what makes late modernity so uncertain, irritable, polarizing and explosive. Radical, self-referential fundamentalism takes the place of rational reasoning and justification – but is notoriously hypersensitive and precarious. In this constellation, the climate issue and the EEP, too, have become a matter of faith, a culture war, a radically divisive issue and a jarring, ideologized confrontation. With its reflexes of defence and sociologically unfounded narratives of hope, environmental sociology itself further fuels this firestorm of conflict. The constant renewal of emancipatory promises, hope and solutions creates ever new potential for disappointment and frustration (see also Berlant 2011).

Especially against the backdrop of the eco-emancipatory belief in rationality, reason and empowerment, in the activists' moral and cognitive superiority and their role as a responsible avant-garde, the disillusionment weighs heavily on the pioneers of the EEP. They had been convinced that they had to bring a recalcitrant (world) society to eco-emancipatory reason. In late modernity, however, this self-understanding collapses and disillusionment leads, at least in parts of society, to a further intensification of the campaign – and correspondingly to an intensification of the counter-reactions. A perspective of increasing polarization, conflict and violence is opening up. Against this backdrop, the added value of the analysis undertaken here perhaps lies not least in the fact that it makes the late-modern traumatization visible and explains its causes. It might contribute to an understanding of the late-modern condition and dilemma. The uncomfortable thought, the concession, that eco-emancipatory movements themselves had made a range of untenable assumptions, and that their activism has triggered unexpected side effects, may help to defuse the conflict. At the same time, the analysis opens up a new perspective from which these polarizations and other phenomena characteristic of late modernity can be recognized and interpreted as coping strategies for the dual untenability.

7.3 Coping with the trauma

These coping strategies include, first and foremost, the distraction and diversion industry already mentioned in Chapter 1. Smartphones and social media, in particular, most effectively ensure that opportunities to reflect on the unsustainability(ies) of late modernity do not arise in the first place. Secondly, the complexity-reducing withdrawal from the public and political sphere and the neo-Biedermeier retreat into the family, the private sphere or some kind of identitarian community are important. Moreover, the defensive reflexes described above suppress the perception and reflection of the double untenability. They block out the 'fatal consequences' of reflexive modernization and the threefold dialectic that Beck had already warned of. The 'firewall' of hope- and consolation-narratives serves the same purpose. Their constructors tirelessly assure us that the necessary understanding, the required criteria, the effective technologies and the political will are now available, that the right path has already been taken and now only needs to be pursued with greater determination and accelerated pace – and in doing so, attempt to stabilize the crumbling certainties and self-perceptions of second modernity.

Furthermore, these coping strategies include the adoption of conspiracy theories, which in late modernity have a huge resonance. As the belief collapses that the human subject is distinct from and superior to nature and can shape and control the world – or at least its respective lifeworld – according to its will and principles, and instead the loss of control, ungovernability and the predominance of the unexpected become paramount, conspiracy theories gain traction. Amlinger and Nachtwey aptly describe them as an attempt at 'epistemic resovereignization, which is intended to heal the insult of the late-modern subject'. Conspiracy narratives 'compensate for the reality of barriers and deprivations', they explain, 'by constituting a phantasm of sovereignty over exclusive bodies of knowledge' (Amlinger & Nachtwey 2021: 17). In fact, these narratives and the movements in which they are cultivated are coping strategies in an even broader sense: they reconfirm the modernist belief in the ability to shape and control – but only ascribe this ability to the elites. Ordinary citizens, in contrast, are portrayed as powerless, at the mercy of others, disenfranchized and therefore – in a thoroughly emancipatory sense – also relieved of any obligation to and responsibility for what the elites seek to define and impose as the general interest. Here, then, the modernist belief in the autonomy of the subject, which is, however, only attributed to the elites, is combined with the late-modern liberation from this ideal and the obligations associated with it. What is performatively addressed in the conspiracy discourses is therefore not simply the 'reality of barriers and deprivations', but also the late-modern contradiction between the defence and the emancipatory divestment of modernist understandings of the subject and autonomy.

At the same time, these discourses offer their critics the opportunity to reassure themselves of their own normative position and judgement. For them, the strong demarcation from the supporters of such theories, whom they categorize as irrational and disoriented, becomes evidence of their own righteousness and moral superiority. Thus, the adherents of conspiracy theories and those rejecting the 'flood of conspiracy thinking' as 'dangerous in terms of democratic politics', as a 'regressive form [. . .] of post-traditional community formation' and as an 'aggressive' and 'destructive' threat to the 'social order' (Amlinger & Nachtwey 2021: 19, 18; Amlinger & Nachtwey 2025: 230ff, 237ff), collaborate – from opposing sides – to reinforce or performatively restore the normative categories that are disintegrating in late modernity. Within the space of radical disorientation, they need each other as a point of reference in order to sustain their defence- or simulation-project and thus overcome the dilemma of late modernity.

In a similar sense, social movements and their 'new politics' may be understood from the perspective developed here. Large segments of social movement research and environmental sociology still portray the movements and their practices as avant-gardes and pioneers of a more liberated, democratic and socio-ecologically sustainable society. In late modernity, however, such interpretations are increasingly losing their plausibility: it is becoming increasingly obvious that these diverse, mostly urban movements and initiatives are not primarily testing out and practising – prefiguring – alternative forms of life and coexistence that will eventually replace the established order of unsustainability in society at large (cf. e.g. Deflorian 2021 or Dannemann et al. 2024). In light of the dual untenability investigated here, these initiatives rather appear as rearguard actions, as administrators of second modernity's legacy and as arenas for coping with the syndrome of *offended freedom*. The subpolitical niches for experiments for a sustainable future metamorphose into places of retreat and experience for the *dying illusion*. The pioneers of the SET have become the avant-garde of life in the social, political, ecological and cultural ruins of liberalism, the EEP and Western modernity.

Harriet Bulkeley, too, portrays experimental politics as a coping strategy (e.g. Bulkeley 2023). She does not refer specifically to subpolitics in Beck's sense but sees a turn towards the experimental in institutionalized, official politics. Bulkeley argues that the comprehensive uncertainty following the collapse of the modernist understanding of politics is forcing this turn. This modernist understanding had assumed that a problem is first clearly defined, then suitable solutions are sought, which are ultimately implemented in a targeted and coordinated manner. Yet, as the modernist certainties evaporate, Bulkeley no longer sees experimental politics as the optimistic testing of alternative, sustainable forms of life and society by avant-gardes, but rather as an attempt by political decision makers to navigate the increasing lack of clarity about problem definitions, solution formulas and policy objectives. In the face of this ambiguity, Bulkeley suggests, late-modern societies simply have no other option; they are condemned to fiddle around and experiment (cf. e.g. Bulkeley 2023; in a more affirmative sense also see Overdevest et al. 2010).

Going one step further, the experimental politics of civil society movements and initiatives can also be understood as a way of coping with the collapse of the beliefs and self-perceptions of the EEP and with the late-modern contradiction between the demand for greater autonomy, participation, creative power and self-efficacy, on the one hand, and their emancipatory and relieving denial, on the other. Experimental politics is, then, not so much the search for solutions, for alternatives, but rather a simulation to demonstrate the supposed relevance and feasibility of the questions posed by the EEP: *how do we want to live? What kind of world do we want to live in?* In a society that, to paraphrase Philipp Staab, has bid farewell to the 'modern concept of emancipation' and replaced it with the guiding principle of 'adaptation', in the Anthropocene, which renders the modernist subject–world relationship increasingly anachronistic (cf. Chapter 3.2), it actually no longer makes sense to ask these questions, and there is no longer a reliable basis on which a collective answer can be found and implemented. Experimental politics, however, creates a space for discourse and experience in which the meaningfulness of these questions can be reconstituted and made tangible. Especially in the interregnum, social movements and their experimental politics are, thus, not least, an experiential space for the performative restoration, the simulation (cf. Blühdorn 2007b, 2013), of the ability to shape and control in the sense of the EEP, and of the willingness to actually do so. Beyond the future-oriented and transformative self-descriptions that the movements cultivate, they can be understood as *regenerative* in a double sense: they bring the obsolete back to life again, making it tangible; and they offer a 'time-out' from normality, an alternative experience of the world, that fulfils specifically modernist needs, but neither can nor is intended to become permanent, because that would threaten emancipatory achievements which are non-negotiable (cf. Blühdorn 2006, 2023). In the interregnum, in particular, late-modern society self-critically accuses itself. It recognizes, for example, that these emancipatory achievements are exclusive to some and based on the premise that they are denied to others (see Lessenich 2019b). Hence, discursive spaces are required in which such contradictions can be reconciled.

Finally, the conspicuous prominence of the term 'resilience' can also be interpreted as a response to the trauma of late modernity. As second modernity has become recognizable as an extension- rather than a transformation-project, as the belief in the ability to shape and control things, which the EEP had refreshed and reinforced as the modernist idea of the autonomous subject, has proven to be an illusion or has been overcome in the course of reflexive modernization, the side effects of first and second modernity are increasingly inescapable. *There is no alternative*, especially because these side effects have arisen not least in the course of emancipatory logic itself. Social inequality and exclusion are just as unavoidable a part of the new modernity as the untenability of democracy and increasingly frequent ecological disasters. This is a reality that late-modern citizens have to come to terms with. While second modernity had still aimed for a great transformation and correction, the primary goal in third modernity is, therefore, to optimize resilience.

It is even truer of resilience than it is of sustainability, that it is concerned with 'securing what exists despite perennial crises' (Folkers 2022: 250). Above all, its aim is 'to ensure the continuity of the present in the face of ever new threats' (ibid.). The new prominence of the resilience agenda therefore signals a clear shift away from the EEP. This agenda is no longer about opening up new emancipatory spaces for the progressive realization of equality and self-determination, but rather about increasing the capacity to withstand, to absorb and to adapt. On the one hand, this refers to the system of society as a whole, which is to be enabled to restore its previous form and functionality as quickly and comprehensively as possible after external shocks. Yet the individual dimension might be even more important. The sustainability discourse has long placed great emphasis on the responsibility of the individual, on individual behaviour and on individual decisions. It embraced the eco-emancipatory belief in individual self-determination, creative power and self-realization. The resilience project is now essentially about the late-modern individual acquiring a reserve of resilience, the metaphorical equivalent of a 'thick skin'. While the environmental movement of the 1980s still practised a 'cult of personal affectedness' (Stephan 1993), late modernity is all about keeping the inevitable exteriorities at a safe distance. And in this respect, it is helpful to remember that environmental problems are never objectively problematic anyway, but always subjectively perceived violations of norms. Accordingly, this is precisely where the starting point for effective countermeasures is located: overcoming problems not by changing social or biophysical conditions, but by changing their subjective perception. Resilience, therefore, means individual and collective desensitization to the violation of the norms which once underpinned the EEP (see also Graefe 2019).

In the literature, the striking new focus on resilience has often – and quite rightly – been traced back to the hegemony of neoliberalism and its ideology of self-responsibility. Quite commonly, this then leads to calls for emancipation and transformation as counter-strategies (e.g. Graefe 2019). Yet this approach ignores the fact that the late-modern demand for resilience is not only due to the hegemony of neoliberalism, but also to the unexpected side effects, the victory-crisis, of the EEP itself. Those who, in third modernity, in the society of inequality and exclusion, are on the 'losing side', can practise resilience if they do not allow themselves to be thrown off course by their marginalization and offended freedom, but rather try to come to terms – materially and psychologically – with the inevitable. Those on the 'winning side', in turn, must make themselves insensitive and impervious to the social and ecological devastation that is inextricably linked to their freedom, values and lifestyle. Here, resilience means learning to live with cognitive and ethical dissonance. In both respects, eco-social movements and civil society initiatives can make a substantial contribution (cf. e.g. Wakefield 2018; MacGregor 2019).

7.4 Beyond dystopia

As noted above, coping strategies, be they escapist, denialist or simulative in nature, may be required only temporarily – in the interregnum. For those holding on to eco-emancipatory values, the collapse of the EEP is traumatic, but others are celebrating the 'end of the green hegemony' (e.g. Rödder 2024) and the liberation from what they perceive as suffocating woke dogmatism and ideology. The newly emerging modernity – autocratic and technocratic, saturated by artificial intelligence and conceivably under the global leadership of China – is not in itself pessimistic, defeatist or dystopian. It is neither progressive and emancipatory in the established sense, nor, as outlined above, would it be appropriate to describe it as regressive, for it dialectically overcomes and suspends the normative yardstick required for such an assessment – the autonomous subject. Hence, the triple dialectic takes late-modern societies beyond the practices of simulation (Blühdorn 2007, 2013b) which accompany the departure from the values, self-descriptions and institutions of second modernity. And contrary to the EEP's dualistic imaginary of SET vs apocalypse, this does not mean the end of humanity and the uninhabitability of the planet (cf. Chapter 1). For the time being at least it means, first and foremost, that – even in Europe and the Western world – the EEP's utopia is no longer attractive and its dystopias are no longer dystopian.

Extending Beck's distinction between first and second modernity, I have so far referred to the new modernity emerging from the dialectic of the EEP as third modernity. This suggested a neat three-stage model (see Table 4) which helps to recognize the significance of the EEP for the definition, crisis and metamorphosis of late modernity. From today's perspective, however, Beck's second or reflexive modernity appears as a rather short phase, barely on a par with its predecessor. Undoubtedly, the silent revolution and reflexive modernization have had a major transformative impact on modern societies, yet, ultimately, Beck's second modernity – and the EEP, too – remained a project that was derailed and superseded rather soon. Furthermore, reflexive modernization and second modernity were not really guided by 'sacred norms' distinct from those guiding first modernity, but in seeking to address the unforeseen side effects of first modernity and fulfil the promises which it had left unfulfilled, they held on to the same regulative ideals. As noted above, Beck himself referred to his first modernity as a 'halved' or 'truncated' modernity (Beck 1992: 153) and to its successor as a 'radicalized' and '*hyper*-modernity' (Beck 2009: 55), again suggesting that his second modernity is not categorically different and new, but the corrective continuation of first modernity. And as regards third modernity, the contours of which have, since the beginning of Donald Trump's second presidency in particular, become blatantly visible, this concept now appears unduly vague.

It may, therefore, be appropriate to move away now from the three-stage model and zoom in on the key feature distinguishing this new modernity from both its predecessors. Given that the Kantian idea of the autonomous subject is, undoubtedly, the most sacred basic norm of Western modernity; given, furthermore, the centrality of this norm in all three dimensions of the EEP (see Table 1); and given that in late modernity exactly this norm – or at least the Kantian understanding of it – has become outdated and is being renegotiated, this new modernity may suitably be referred to as *postliberal modernity* as opposed to the *liberal modernity* that preceded it, comprising both Beck's first and his second modernity.

This term takes up a concept, postliberalism, that has recently been much debated (e.g. Deneen 2018, 2023; Pabst 2018, 2021). It captures the distinctive feature of the new era, but it has its own weaknesses. In particular, in its currently prevailing use, the term postliberalism is highly ideologically charged. It stands for a reactionary political agenda that militates against the progressive left and demands a 'regime change' (Deneen 2023) to restore traditional family values, the religious justification of the social hierarchies and the authority of supposedly *natural* elites. Also, relying on the prefix 'post', the term postliberal modernity is not much more specific about the new era than the term third modernity. It still fails to make explicit that this is an exclusive, autocratic, authoritarian modernity that – for the further self-aggrandizement of a privileged elite – overtly abandons the values and institutions of equality, democracy, human rights, the rule of law or a good life for all, and instead relies ever more openly on the right of the strongest – politically, militarily, technologically, financially – as Donald Trump's authoritarian coup or Israel's genocide against the Palestinians dramatically illustrate. Furthermore, the existing literature on postliberalism does not reflect that the EEP and second modernity had themselves been deeply critical of liberal thinking, most notably its Cartesian dualism and its commitment to individualism. Nor do postliberals acknowledge that in the EEP, too, the stabilization and regeneration of the foundations of social life had been a central concern, and they fail to demonstrate why their own agenda should be more promising than earlier attempts.

This said, postliberal thinking focuses specifically on the cultural transformation of late-modern societies that has been a central interest throughout this book. Its proponents share the above diagnosis that 'the modern liberal ordering of the world is exhausted' (Borg 2024: 8). And although the EEP itself does not figure prominently in this debate, their explanation for this exhaustion very strongly resembles the argument that has been made above. In this literature, the autonomy- and identity-agendas of the progressive (liberal) left are the very centre of attention, and in line with Beck's notion of the 'victory-crisis', many proponents of postliberalism believe that liberal modernity 'has failed because liberalism has succeeded' (Deneen 2018: 3, 179). Mirroring what has been said above about the EEP, they argue that liberal modernity has run into problems not just because liberal ideals have 'been realized incompletely or captured by special interests of big business, but rather because its inner logic tends to undermine its core aims' (Borg 2024: 10). And corresponding to the above analysis of the EEP's triple dialectic, they argue that liberalism – because of its inherent contradictions – 'erodes the values' which it 'purportedly defends' and 'tends to lead to its own undoing' (ibid.: 3, 4). In fact, theorists of postliberalism have explicitly conceptualized the rise of the new era as the 'dialectical response to a liberalism that is increasingly exposing its own contradictions' (ibid.: 12): 'A political philosophy that was launched to foster greater equity, defend a pluralist tapestry of different cultures and beliefs, protect human dignity, and, of course, expand liberty', Deneen has argued, 'in practice generates titanic inequality, enforces uniformity and homogeneity, fosters material and spiritual degradation, and undermines freedom' (Deneen 2018: 3). And this is not, as Borg suggests, 'because of some nefarious design' of liberal thinking, but 'due to the steady erosion of all sources of authority deemed as external to the individual will' (Borg 2024: 10). Just as I have noted with regard to eco-emancipatory thinking (see Chapter 6.3), postliberal thinkers, too, have argued that 'liberalism has abandoned any substantive vision of the good', and 'what has happened then, is, at least in part due to the failure of liberalism to accept any boundaries to itself' (ibid.: 9, 13).

So the parallels between postliberal thinking and the argument developed throughout this book are obvious. But the literature on postliberalism is primarily political and activist rather than sociological. The term postliberal modernity, in contrast, is not about any normative agenda, but stripped of its reactionary ideological baggage, the term is adopted here as a sociological descriptor for a modernity that moves beyond the core values shared by Beck's first and second modernities. While the proponents of postliberal thinking undertake 'a critique of liberalism', hoping to find 'remedies for its perceived deficiencies', most notably its unrestricted individualism (Borg 2024: 13), while they set out again 'in search of the common good' (ibid.), hope for a 'coming era of renewal' (Pabst 2021) and fail to recognize that just this is what the EEP and reflexive modernization had already attempted, the new modernity emerging from the triple dialectic moves beyond such hopes and the values underpinning them. Indeed, the factual transformation that empirically occurs in late-modern societies provides scant evidence of such renewal – and the theorists of postliberal politics offer little in terms of sociological analysis that might support their hopes. Instead, the new modernity moves beyond dystopia and the imaginary in which much of postliberal thinking remains stuck. Hence, the term postliberal modernity is used here in a more radical sense. For if social theory wants to understand the metamorphosis of late modernity, it needs to overcome the backward-oriented perspective and its attempts to secure or retrieve what the logic of emancipation has rendered obsolete.

7.5 Critical sociology, transformative sustainability research and (eco-)political education

Thus, the analytical framework developed in this book opens up innovative perspectives on a number of phenomena and debates in late-modern society. For critical sociology, transformative sustainability research and also political (sustainability) education, however, the thesis of the dual untenability of late-modern society and the eco-emancipatory project poses fundamental problems. If it is true that the basic principles of first and second modernity have become exhausted and are being abandoned in the emerging postliberal modernity, critical sociology no longer has any reliable standards of criticism; environmental sociology no clear transformation perspectives; and political education no pedagogical objectives. 'In comparison to the horizon opened up by the negation of the basic principles of modernity', said Beck, 'most cultural criticism looks outdated and *idyllic* [. . .] or even downright affirmative' (Beck 2009: 229). This is even more true when what is at stake is not just the 'negation' of the basic principles of modernity, which Beck saw as a step towards 'anti-modernity' (ibid.: 233f), but their emancipatory rejection, which rather than anti-modernity leads to postliberal modernity. What Beck called an 'idyll' corresponds to what in earlier sections I have referred to as critical sociology's 'tribal fire'. And what Beck wrote about cultural criticism applies to significant parts of the eco-sociological literature, too: it claims to be critical and progressive, pretends to have normative standards by which society can be criticized and transformed, but ultimately, more than anything, reinforces the order of unsustainability.

Critical sociology finds itself in the dilemma that, in order to do justice to its diagnostic self-commitment, it would have to face up to the emancipatory abandonment (or radical reframing) of the modernist idea of the autonomous subject. Yet, if it does so, it loses the normative basis for its critical and transformative agenda – to which it feels equally committed. Or to put it another way: in the face of reflexive modernization and the triple dialectic, critical sociology can no longer adhere to its (untenable) emancipatory-critical standards. If it does so anyway, it runs the risk of further reinforcing unsustainability. It then becomes – while perceiving of itself as critical – affirmative and complicit with the established order. As early as the 1940s, Horkheimer and Adorno wrote: 'it is characteristic of the sickness that even the best-intentioned reformer who uses an impoverished and debased language to recommend renewal, by his adoption of the insidious mode of categorization and the bad philosophy it conceals, strengthens the very power of the established order he is trying to break' (Horkheimer & Adorno 1994 [1944]: xiv). Following the silent revolution of the 1970s – as explained in detail in Chapter 4 – there was hope that the ecological crisis would provide a new, reliable, ecological point of reference for societal critique and transformation. While before the 'supremacy of Marxist theory' had led to a 'petrification of critique', Beck believed, social critique could 'now draw new breath' (Beck 1993: 53f). And while previously only intellectual elites could 'apply more or less well justified standards to society and then judge and condemn it (and often against the self-image of those affected)', reflexive modernity was supposed to facilitate a 'democratization of criticism' and 'social self-criticism' (ibid.: 54, 53).

In late modernity, exactly this democratization has undermined the normative power of critique. A critical sociology that simply holds on to its traditional categories can contribute little to the understanding of late modernity and the *next society*. It is then – to extend the metaphor used previously – more than anything, part of the palliative care team that organizes late-modern society's pain therapy. But if it shifts its focus from the transformative to the analytical side of its critical business and endeavours to explain why, for example, the narratives of the degrowth movements, post-capitalism or experimental politics are built on sand in terms of social theory, it could also reduce the potential for disappointment and frustration. By making transparent what normative assumptions underlie the warnings and promises that play a central role in eco-emancipatory mobilization discourses; by clarifying what kind of understandings of social structures and dynamics of change such warnings and promises are based on, and to what extent such understandings are justified, it could help to address the syndrome of *offended freedom* from the side of prevention – but it would then run the risk of being perceived as purely affirmative.

Transformative sustainability research faces the same dilemma. It wants to induce change, signpost perspectives and proffer hope. It provides introductions 'to the art of social change', formulates guidelines for the 'departure into the world of tomorrow' and develops ideas on 'how societies could become sustainable' (Schneidewind 2018; Göpel 2022; Luks 2023). But today, late-modern societies look back on more than five decades of such hopeful narratives, and by now the limits of this approach have become abundantly clear. In the face of the authoritarian, exclusive, inhumane and brutal reality of postliberal modernity, their constant renewal is becoming increasingly cruel (see Berlant 2011). Their supposed optimism ultimately produces frustration, because what is presented as a transformation strategy in fact prolongs and deepens unsustainability. At least for those parts of this literature that aspire to offer more than bestselling narratives of hope, those that claim to be serious about social science and are prepared to reflect on their own entanglement in sustained unsustainability, it is therefore time to put aside the transformative ambitions and first take a much closer look at the reality of late-modern societies. The task at hand is to illuminate much more thoroughly – and also beyond the well-trodden explanatory paths – how and why unsustainability comes about, how and why these societies maintain their policies of unsustainability, what price they pay for this approach, and how the implications of sustained unsustainability are managed in practice. Instead of presenting ever more studies promising an SET that are largely disconnected from the reality of late-modern societies, the aim should be to develop a sociology of untenability.

Even more than the transformative sustainability literature, the theory and practice of political education and sustainability education persist in Beck's *idyll*. With almost touching simplicity, much of the relevant literature reproduces the values and beliefs of the EEP and shows little awareness that in late modernity these once sacred principles may have become anachronistic (Chapter 3), reflexively modernized (Chapter 5), overtaken by the emancipatory dynamic (Chapter 6) and counterproductive in terms of social and ecological sustainability. According to its own understanding, political education aims for maturity, autonomy, independent personal development etc. (cf. for example, the Frankfurt Declaration on Political Education from 2015). It aims to open up spaces for thought and development, promote plurality, tolerance and openness, and create space for utopias of sustainability. In reality, however, much of this literature is neither utopian nor open, but completely caught up in the normativity and agenda of the EEP and second modernity. It speaks of a 'participatory and emancipatory education', is convinced that the sustainability transformation must be 'democratic and participatory', and views 'young citizens', in particular, 'as change agents' (Kenner & Nagel 2022: 102f). This literature reflects neither on the dialectic of democracy nor on the dilemmas of second-order emancipation – and therefore has no access to the reality of late modernity. It campaigns against the shift to the populist right, but barely explores to what extent – and why – this shift also affects those whom political educationalists regard as the primary 'agents of change' (see e.g. Decker et al. 2022). It has no criteria to distinguish the *good* political engagement that it wants to strengthen from the *bad*, which it simply categorizes as 'populist political surrogates' (Kolleck 2020: 16). And it shows little awareness of the close connection between *emancipatory* politicization and those forms of activism which established social science continues to describe as *regressive*.

None of this is surprising or reproachable, because it is in fact unclear what a political education that moves beyond these beliefs or reflects on their untenability might look like. There is no obvious substitute for them. The theory of political education therefore frames its own abysses and dilemmas simply as 'welcome learning opportunities'. Civic education, Kenner and Nagel note, should contribute to making a society more 'resilient' to the forces of political destabilization (2022: 108, 113). However, it can probably only achieve this in the sense of resilience sketched above. Given that the order of unsustainability has been brought about and is sustained, inter alia, by emancipatory agendas, there is no reason to assume that political education could change this order – inequality, exclusion, division, polarization, demarcation, deportation – nor slow down or even reverse the social developments it aims to avert. However, theorists and practitioners of political education do open up discursive spaces in which the commitment to the values that are aborted in postliberal modernity – a good life for all within ecological limits, ethics of inclusion, democracy, responsibility – can be cultivated and experienced, while elsewhere the opposite logic rules. Once again, this is all about the simultaneity of the contradictory. Discourses and practices of simulation are coping strategies for the cognitive and ethical dissonances of late modernity and, at the same time, have a pacifying effect on the excluded, in whose real inclusion those who seek to secure their emancipatory achievements can have no genuine interest. In this way, political education, too, becomes – against its will and without being able to avoid it – affirmative and complicit.

Hence, critical sociology, transformative sustainability research and political education all suffer from the syndrome that, in late modernity and beyond, the distinction between critical and affirmative, progressive and regressive, transformative and stabilizing is becoming increasingly problematic. For all three of them, reflexive modernization and the threefold dialectic lead to an irresolvable dilemma: whether they take a critical-emancipatory stance against the metamorphosis of modernity or limit themselves to understanding and explaining its unsustainability(ies), in both cases they become accomplices to unsustainability and affirmative pioneers of postliberal modernity. In the face of this dilemma, the striking sustainability of the unsustainable, which progressives have always resolutely fought, suddenly turns into a source of hope: in the interregnum, the hard to extinguish – but ultimately still unsustainable – discourses of simulation and the debates at the idyllic tribal fire(s) of critical sociology, transformative sustainability research and political education offer relief and consolation. They can no longer promote the EEP and an SET; and they will hardly arrest the advance of postliberal modernity. Yet, on the way to this new modernity, they can alleviate the trauma of liberal modernity's untenability – until such time as the pain slowly subsides and eventually, perhaps, fully disappears.

REFERENCES

Agamben, Giorgio. 2004. *State of Exception*. Chicago: Chicago University Press.

Agamben, Giorgio. 2021. *Where Are We Now?: The Epidemic as Politics*. London: ERIS.

Albert, Mathias, Hurrelmann, Klaus and Quenzel, Gudrun. 2019. *Die 18. Shell Jugendstudie: Jugend 2019: Eine Generation meldet sich zu Wort*. Munich: Beltz Verlag.

Allen, Amy. 2015. 'Emancipation without Utopia: Subjection, Modernity, and the Normative Claims of Feminist Critical Theory'. *Hypatia* 30(3).

Amlinger, Carolin and Nachtwey, Oliver. 2021. 'Sozialer Wandel, Sozialcharakter und Verschwörungsdenken in der Spätmoderne'. *Aus Politik und Zeitgeschichte* 35–36.

Amlinger, Carolin and Nachtwey, Oliver. 2025. *Offended Freedom: The Rise of Libertarian Authoritarianism*. Cambridge: Polity.

Augstein, Jakob (ed.). 2017. *Reclaim Autonomy: Selbstermächtigung in der digitalen Weltordnung*. Berlin: Suhrkamp.

Aulenbacher, Brigitte, Bärnthaler, Richard and Novi, Andreas. 2019. 'Karl Polanyi, "The Great Transformation" and Contemporary Capitalism'. Special issue, *Österreichische Zeitschrift für Soziologie* 44(2).

Baecker, Dirk. 2007. *Studien zur nächsten Gesellschaft*. Frankfurt am Main: Suhrkamp.

Baecker, Dirk. 2018. *4.0 oder Die Lücke die der Rechner lässt*. Leipzig: Merve.

Barry, John and Wissenburg, Marcel (eds). 2001. *Sustaining Liberal Democracy: Ecological Challenges and Opportunities*. New York: Palgrave.

Bauman, Zygmunt. 1999. *In Search of Politics*. Cambridge: Polity.

Bauman, Zygmunt. 2000. *Liquid Modernity*. Cambridge: Polity.

Bauman, Zygmunt. 2017. *Retrotopia*. Cambridge: Polity.

Beck, Ulrich. 1986. *Risikogesellschaft: Auf dem Weg in eine andere Moderne*. Frankfurt am Main: Suhrkamp.

Beck, Ulrich. 1988. *Gegengifte: Die organisierte Unverantwortlichkeit*. Frankfurt am Main: Suhrkamp.

Beck, Ulrich. 1992. *Risk Society*. London: Sage.

Beck, Ulrich. 1993. *Die Erfindung des Politischen*. Frankfurt am Main: Suhrkamp.

REFERENCES

Beck, Ulrich. 1997. *The Reinvention of Politics: Rethinking Modernity in the Global Social Order*. Cambridge: Polity.

Beck, Ulrich. 1998. *Democracy without Enemies*. Cambridge: Polity.

Beck, Ulrich. 2001. 'Das Zeitalter des "eigenen Lebens": Individualisierung als "paradoxe Sozialstruktur" und andere offene Fragen'. *Aus Politik und Zeitgeschichte* B29.

Beck, Ulrich. 2007. *Weltrisikogesellschaft*. Berlin: Suhrkamp.

Beck, Ulrich. 2009. *World at Risk*. Cambridge: Polity.

Beck, Ulrich. 2016. *The Metamorphosis of the World*. Cambridge: Polity.

Beck, Ulrich and Beck-Gernsheim, Elisabeth (eds). 1994. *Riskante Freiheiten: Individualisierung in modernen Gesellschaften*. Frankfurt am Main: Suhrkamp.

Bell, Daniel. 1974. *The Coming of Post-Industrial Society: A Venture in Social Forecasting*. New York: Harper Colophon Books

Benson, Melinda H. and Craig, Robin K. 2017. *The End of Sustainability: Resilience and the Future of Environmental Governance in the Anthropocene*. Lawrence, KS: University Press of Kansas.

Berlant, Laurent. 2011. *Cruel Optimism*. Durham, NC: Duke University Press.

Berlin, Isaiah. 1969. *Four Essays on Liberty*. Oxford: Oxford University Press.

Biermann, Frank. 2014. *Earth System Governance: World Politics in the Anthropocene*. Cambridge, MA: MIT Press.

Biermann, Frank. 2021. 'The Future of "Environmental Policy" in the Anthropocene: Time for a Paradigm Shift'. *Environmental Politics* 30(1–2).

Block, Katharina and Dickel, Sascha. 2020. 'Jenseits der Autonomie: Die De/Problematisierung des Subjekts in Zeiten der Digitalisierung'. *Behemoth: A Journal of Civilisation* 13(1).

Blühdorn, Ingolfur. 2000a. *Post-Ecologist Politics: Social Theory and the Abdication of the Ecologist Paradigm*. London, New York: Routledge.

Blühdorn, Ingolfur. 2000b. 'An Offer One Might Prefer to Refuse: The Systems Theoretical Legacy of Niklas Luhmann'. *European Journal of Social Theory* 3(3).

Blühdorn, Ingolfur. 2006. 'Self-Experience in the Theme Park of Radical Action?: Social Movements and Political Articulation in the Late-Modern Condition'. *European Journal of Social Theory* 9(1).

Blühdorn, Ingolfur. 2007a. 'Self-Description, Self-Deception, Simulation: A Systems-Theoretical Perspective on Contemporary Discourses of Radical Change'. *Social Movement Studies* 6(1).

Blühdorn, Ingolfur. 2007b. 'Sustaining the Unsustainable: Symbolic Politics and the Politics of Simulation'. *Environmental Politics* 16(2).

Blühdorn, Ingolfur. 2011. 'The Politics of Unsustainability: COP15, Post-Ecologism, and the Ecological Paradox'. *Organization & Environment* 24(1).

Blühdorn, Ingolfur. 2013. *Simulative Demokratie: Neue Politik nach der post-demokratischen Wende*. Berlin: Suhrkamp.

Blühdorn, Ingolfur. 2016. 'Sustainability – Post-Sustainability – Unsustainability', in Teena Gabrielson, Cheryl Hall, John M. Meyer and David Schlosberg (eds), *The Oxford Handbook of Environmental Political Theory*. Oxford: Oxford University Press.

Blühdorn, Ingolfur. 2017. 'Post-Capitalism, Post-Growth, Post-Consumerism? Eco-political Hopes beyond Sustainability'. *Global Discourse* 7(1).

Blühdorn, Ingolfur. 2018. 'Nicht-Nachhaltigkeit auf der Suche nach einer politischen Form: Konturen der demokratischen Postwachstumsgesellschaft'. *Berliner Journal für Soziologie* 28.

Blühdorn, Ingolfur (ed.). 2020a. *Nachhaltige Nicht-Nachhaltigkeit: Warum die ökologische Transformation der Gesellschaft nicht stattfindet.* Bielefeld: transcript.

Blühdorn, Ingolfur. 2020b. 'Die Gesellschaft der Nicht-Nachhaltigkeit: Skizze einer umweltsoziologischen Gegenwartsdiagnose', in Ingolfur Blühdorn (ed.), *Nachhaltige Nicht-Nachhaltigkeit: Warum die ökologische Transformation der Gesellschaft nicht stattfindet*, Bielefeld: transcript.

Blühdorn, Ingolfur. 2020c. 'Demokratie der Nicht-Nachhaltigkeit: Begehung eines umweltpolitischen Minenfelds', in Ingolfur Blühdorn (ed.), *Nachhaltige Nicht-Nachhaltigkeit: Warum die ökologische Transformation der Gesellschaft nicht stattfindet*, Bielefeld: transcript.

Blühdorn, Ingolfur. 2020d. 'Kein gutes Leben für Alle! Annäherungen an einen Paradigmenwechsel', in Ingolfur Blühdorn (ed.), *Nachhaltige Nicht-Nachhaltigkeit: Warum die ökologische Transformation der Gesellschaft nicht stattfindet.* Bielefeld: transcript.

Blühdorn, Ingolfur. 2020e. 'The Legitimation Crisis of Democracy: Emancipatory Politics, the Environmental State and the Glass Ceiling to Socio-ecological Transformation'. *Environmental Politics* 29(1).

Blühdorn, Ingolfur. 2020f. 'The Dialectic of Democracy: Modernization, Emancipation and the Great Regression'. *Democratization* 27(3).

Blühdorn, Ingolfur. 2022a. 'Sustainability: Buying Time for Consumer Capitalism', in Luigi Pellizzoni, Emanuele Leonardi and Viviana Asara (eds), *Handbook of Critical Environmental Politics.* Cheltenham: Edward Elgar.

Blühdorn, Ingolfur. 2022b. 'Liberation and Limitation: The Emancipatory Project and the Grammar of the Autocratic-Authoritarian Turn'. *European Journal of Social Theory* 25(1).

Blühdorn, Ingolfur. 2022c. 'Planetary Boundaries, Societal Boundaries, and Collective Self-Limitation: Moving Beyond the Post-Marxist Comfort Zone'. *Sustainability: Science, Practice, and Policy* 18(1).

Blühdorn, Ingolfur. 2023. 'Recreational Experientialism at "the Abyss": Rethinking the Sustainability Crisis and Experimental Politics'. *Sustainability: Science, Practice, and Policy* 19(1).

Blühdorn, Ingolfur. 2025. 'Ecological Ungovernability and the Transition to Postliberal Modernity: On the Triple Dialectic of the Eco-emancipatory Project'. *European Journal of Social Theory* 28(4).

Blühdorn, Ingolfur and Dannemann, Hauke. 2019. 'Der post-ökologische Verteidigungskonsens: Nachhaltigkeitsforschung im Verdacht der Komplizenschaft', in Carolin Bohn, Doris Fuchs, Antonius Kerkhoff and Christian Müller (eds), *Gegenwart und Zukunft sozial-ökologischer Transformation.* Baden-Baden: Nomos.

Blühdorn, Ingolfur and Deflorian, Michael. 2021. 'Politicisation beyond Post-Politics: New Social Activism and the Reconfiguration of Political Discourse'. *Social Movement Studies* 20(3).

Blühdorn, Ingolfur and Kalke, Karoline. 2019. 'Befreiung aus der Mü(n)digkeit: Demokratische Krise, flüchtiges Subjekt und digitale Revolution', in NÖ

Forschungs- und Bildungsges.m.b.H. (NFB) and Donau-Universität Krems (eds), *Demokratie! Zumutung oder Zukunft: Tagungsband zum Symposion Dürnstein*. Hamburg: tredition.

Böhme, Gernot. 1992. *Natürlich Natur: Über Natur im Zeitalter ihrer technischen Reproduzierbarkeit*. Frankfurt am Main: Suhrkamp.

Boltanski, Luc and Chiapello, Ève. 2017. *The New Spirit of Capitalism*. London, New York: Verso.

Bookchin, Murray. 1982. *The Ecology of Freedom: The Emergence and Dissolution of Hierarchy*. Palo Alto: Cheshire Books.

Borg, Stefan. 2024. 'In Search of the Common Good: The Postliberal Project Left and Right'. *European Journal of Social Theory* 27(1).

Brand, Karl Werner (ed.). 2017. *Die sozial-ökologische Transformation der Welt*. Frankfurt am Main: Campus.

Brand, Karl Werner. 2021. 'Das schwarze Loch der Nicht-Nachhaltigkeit: Eine kritische Auseinandersetzung mit Ingolfur Blühdorns Forschungsansatz'. *Berliner Journal für Soziologie* 31.

Brand, Karl Werner, Büsser, Detlef and Rucht, Dieter. 1983. *Aufbruch in eine andere Gesellschaft: Neue soziale Bewegungen in der Bundesrepublik*. Frankfurt am Main: Campus.

Brand, Ulrich. 2009. *Die Multiple Krise: Dynamik und Zusammenhang der Krisendimensionen, Anforderungen an politische Institutionen und Chancen progressiver Politik*. Berlin: Heinrich-Böll-Stiftung.

Brand, Ulrich. 2016. 'Transformation as a New Critical Orthodoxy: The Strategic Use of the Term *Transformation* Does Not Prevent Multiple Crises'. *GAIA* 25(1).

Brand, Ulrich, Görg, Christoph and Wissen, Markus. 2019. 'Overcoming Neoliberal Globalization: Social-Ecological Transformation from a Polanyian Perspective and Beyond'. *Globalizations* 17(1).

Brand, Ulrich et al. 2021. 'From Planetary to Societal Boundaries: An Argument for Collectively Defined Self-Limitation'. *Sustainability: Science, Practice and Policy* 17(1).

Brand, Ulrich and Wissen, Markus. 2021. *The Imperial Mode of Living: Everyday Life and the Ecological Crisis of Capitalism*. London: Verso.

Brennan, Jason. 2016. *Against Democracy*. Princeton, Oxford: Princeton University Press.

Bröckling, Ulrich. 2015. *The Entrepreneurial Self: Fabricating a New Type of Subject*. Frankfurt am Main: SAGE.

Brown, Trent. 2016. 'Sustainability as Empty Signifier: Its Rise, Fall, and Radical Potential'. *Antipode* 48(1).

Brown, Wendy. 2012. 'Wir sind jetzt alle Demokraten . . .', in Giorgio Agamben, Alain Badiou, Slavoj Žižek, Jacques Rancière, Jean-Luc Nancy, Wendy Brown, Daniel Bensaïd and Kristin Ross (eds), *Demokratie? Eine Debatte*. Berlin: Suhrkamp.

Bulkeley, Harriet. 2023. 'The Condition of Urban Climate Experimentation'. *Sustainability: Science, Practice and Policy* 19(1).

Butterwegge, Christoph. 1999. 'Folgen der "regressiven Modernisierung" bzw. "Amerikanisierung" des deutschen Sozialstaates', in Christoph Butterwegge (ed.), *Wohlfahrtsstaat im Wandel: Probleme und Perspektiven der Sozialpolitik*. Wiesbaden: VS Verlag.

REFERENCES

Cassegard, Carl and Thörn, Hakan. 2018. 'Toward a Postapocalyptic Environmentalism? Responses to Loss and Visions of the Future in Climate Activism'. *Environment and Planning E: Nature and Space* 1(4).

Chakrabarty, Dipesh. 2000. *Provincializing Europe: Postcolonial Thought and Historical Difference*. Princeton: Princeton University Press.

Chakrabarty, Dipesh. 2002. 'Europa provinzialisieren: Postkolonialität und die Kritik der Geschichte', in Sebastian Conrad, Shalini Randeria and Regina Römhild (eds), *Jenseits des Eurozentrismus: Postkoloniale Perspektiven in den Geschichts- und Kulturwissenschaften*. Frankfurt am Main: Campus.

Crouch, Colin. 2004. *Post-Democracy*. Cambridge: Polity.

Crouch, Colin. 2015. *The Knowledge Corrupters: Hidden Consequences of the Financial Takeover of Public Life*. Cambridge: Polity.

Crozier, Michel, Huntington, Samuel P. and Watanuki, Joji. 1975. *The Crisis of Democracy: Report on the Governability of Democracies to the Trilateral Commission*. New York: New York University Press.

Crutzen, Paul J. 2002. 'Geology of Mankind'. *Nature* 415.

Crutzen, Paul J. and Steffen, Will. 2003. 'How Long Have We Been in the Anthropocene Era?'. *Climatic Change* 61.

Crutzen, Paul J. and Stoermer, Eugene F. 2000. 'The Anthropocene'. *Global Change Newsletter* 41.

Dannemann, Hauke, Haderer, Margaret and Blühdorn, Ingolfur (2024). 'Why Now? Questioning the Confidence in Eco-political Experimentation in Civil Society'. *Environment and Planning E: Nature and Space* 7(6).

Davis, Angela Y. 1982. *Women, Race and Class*. New York: Vintage Books.

de Moor, Joost. 2022. 'Postapocalyptic Narratives in Climate Activism: Their Place and Impact in Five European Cities'. *Environmental Politics* 31(6).

Decker, Oliver, Kiess, Johannes, Heller, Ayline and Brähler, Elmar (eds). 2022. *Autoritäre Dynamiken in unsicheren Zeiten: Neue Herausforderungen – alte Reaktionen?*. Giessen: Pyschosozial-Verlag.

Deflorian, Michael. 2021. 'Refigurative Politics: Understanding the Volatile Participation of Critical Creatives in Community Gardens, Repair Cafés and Clothing Swaps'. *Social Movement Studies* 20(2).

Degele, Nina and Dries, Christian. 2005. *Modernisierungstheorie: Eine Einführung*. Munich: Fink.

Delanty, Gerard. 2024. 'Social Theory and the Idea of the Future'. *European Journal of Social Theory* 27(2).

Demirović, Alex, Dück, Julia, Becker, Florian and Bader, Pauline (eds). 2011. *Vielfachkrise im finanzmarktdominierten Kapitalismus*. Hamburg: VSA.

Deneen, Patrick J. 2018. *Why Liberalism Failed*. New Haven, London: Yale University Press.

Deneen, Patrick J. 2023. *Regime Change: Toward a Postliberal Future*. New York: Sentinel.

Die Grünen-Bundesgeschäftsstelle (ed.). 1980. *Das Bundesprogramm*.

Dimbath, Oliver. 2020. 'Zeitdiagnostik statt Gesellschaftstheorie? Ulrich Becks Begriffe der Individualisierung, der reflexiven Modernisierung und der Kosmopolitisierung zwischen Feuilleton und Soziologie', in Oliver Römer, Clemens Boehncke and Markus Holzinger (eds), *Soziologische Phantasie und kosmopolitisches Gemeinwesen: Perspektiven einer Weiterführung der Soziologie Ulrich Becks*. Baden-Baden: Nomos.

REFERENCES

Djeffal, Christian. 2018. 'Normative Leitlinien für künstliche Intelligenz in Regierung und öffentlicher Verwaltung', in Resa Mohabat Kar, Basanta E. Thapa and Peter Parycek (eds), *(Un)berechenbar? Algorithmen und Automatisierung in Staat und Gesellschaft*. Berlin: Fraunhofer-Institut für Offene Kommunikationssysteme FOKUS.

do Mar Castro Varela, Maria and Dhawan, Nikita. 2020. *Postkoloniale Theorie: Eine kritische Einführung*. Bielefeld: transcript Verlag.

Dobson, Andrew. 1990. *Green Political Thought*. London: Unwin Hyman.

Dobson, Andrew. 2022. 'Emancipation in the Anthropocene: Taking the Dialectic Seriously'. *European Journal of Social Theory* 25(1).

Dörre, Klaus. 2021. 'Kampf um die Öffentlichkeit: Kapitalistische Landnahme und die Zerstörung von Vernunft', in Nils S. Borchers, Selma Güney, Uwe Krüger and Kerem Schamberger (eds), *Transformation der Medien: Medien der Transformation*. Frankfurt am Main: Westend.

Dörre, Klaus, Rosa, Hartmut, Becker, Karina, Bose, Sophie and Seyd, Benjamin (eds). 2019. *Große Transformation? Zur Zukunft moderner Gesellschaften*. Wiesbaden: Springer.

Dryzek, John. 2000. *Deliberative Democracy and Beyond: Liberals, Critics, Contestations*. Oxford: Oxford University Press.

Eisenstadt, Shmuel. 2000. *Die Vielfalt der Moderne*. Weilerswist: Velbrück.

Elsässer, Lea, Hense, Svenja and Schäfer, Armin. 2021. 'Not Just Money: Unequal Responsiveness in Egalitarian Democracies'. *Journal of European Public Policy* 28(12).

Enzensberger, Hans M. 1973. 'Zur Kritik der politischen Ökologie'. *Kursbuch* 33.

Eppler, Erhart. 1975. *Ende oder Wende: Von der Machbarkeit des Notwendigen*. Munich: dtv.

European Commission. 2022. *Ethische Leitlinien für Lehrkräfte über die Nutzung von KI und Daten für Lehr- und Lernzwecke*. Luxembourg: Amt für Veröffentlichungen der Europäischen Union.

Fians, Guilherme. 2022. 'Prefigurative Politics', in Felix Stein (ed.), *The Cambridge Encyclopedia of Anthropology*. https://www.anthroencyclopedia .com/entry/prefigurative-politics

Fischer, Joschka. 1989. *Der Umbau der Industriegesellschaft: Plädoyer wider die herrschende Umweltlüge*. Frankfurt am Main: Eichborn.

Fisher, Mark. 2009. *Capitalist Realism: Is there no Alternative?* Winchester, Washington: Zero Books.

Folkers, Andreas. 2022. 'Nach der Nachhaltigkeit: Resilienz und Revolte in der dritten Moderne'. *Leviathan* 50(2).

Folkers, Manfred and Paech, Niko. 2020. *All You Need Is Less: Eine Kultur des Genug aus ökonomischer und buddhistischer Sicht*. Munich: oekom.

Foster, John. 2015. *After Sustainability*. Abingdon: Earthscan.

Foucault, Michel. 1984. 'What Is Enlightenment?', in Paul Rabinow (ed.), *The Foucault Reader*. New York: Pantheon Books.

Foucault, Michel. 2008. *The Birth of Biopolitics: Lectures at the Collège de France 1978–1979*. Basingstoke, New York: Palgrave Macmillan.

Frankfurter Erklärung. 2015. *Für eine kritisch-emanzipatorische Politische Bildung*. https://uol.de/f/1/inst/sowi/ag/politische_bildung/Frankfurter_Erklae rung_aktualisiert27.07.15.pdf

Fraser, Nancy. 2013. *Fortunes of Feminism: From State-Managed Capitalism to Neoliberal Crisis*. London: Verso.

Fraser, Nancy. 2015a. 'Krise, Kritik und Kapitalismus'. *Transit: Europäische Revue 46*.

Fraser, Nancy. 2015b. 'Legitimation Crisis? On the Political Contradictions of Financialized Capitalism'. *Critical Historical Studies* 2(2).

Fraser, Nancy. 2017. 'Vom Regen des progressiven Neoliberalismus in die Traufe des reaktionären Populismus', in Heinrich Geisenberger (ed.), *Die Große Regression*. Berlin: Suhrkamp.

Fraser, Nancy. 2019. *The Old Is Dying and the New Cannot Be Born*. London: Verso.

Fraser, Nancy. 2022. *Cannibal Capitalism: How Our System Is Devouring Democracy, Care, and the Planet – and What We Can Do about It*. London: Verso.

Fraser, Nancy and Jaeggi, Rahel. 2018. *Capitalism: A Conversation in Critical Theory*. Cambridge: Polity.

Fraser, Nancy and Monticelli, Lara. 2021. 'Progressive Neoliberalism Isn't the Solution. We Need a Radical Counter-Hegemonic and Anti-Capitalist Alliance: A Conversation with Nancy Fraser'. *Emancipations: A Journal of Critical Social Analysis* 1(1).

Friedrichs, Werner. 2022. 'Vom erschöpfenden Verteidigen zum entschiedenen Anstecken: Zur Zukunft der Demokratie in der neuen Kosmologie des Anthropozäns', in Ilka Maria, Tonio Oeftering and Nikolaj Schulte-Wörmann (eds), *Angegriffen und erschöpft!? Demokratie(n) und Politische Bildung*. Frankfurt am Main: Wochenschau Verlag.

Funtowicz, Silvio and Ravetz, Jerome. 1991. 'A New Scientific Methodology for Global Environmental Issues', in Robert Costanza (ed.), *Ecological Economics: The Science and Management of Sustainability*. New York: Columbia University Press.

Funtowicz, Silvio and Ravetz, Jerome. 1992. 'Three Types of Risk Assessment and the Emergence of Postnormal Science', in Sheldon Krimsky and Dominic Golding (eds), *Social Theories of Risk*. Westport, CT: Greenwood.

Funtowicz, Silvio and Ravetz, Jerome. 1993. 'Science for the Post-Normal Age'. *Futures* 25(7).

Gallie, Walter Bryce. 1956. 'Essentially Contested Concepts'. *Proceedings of the Aristotelian Society 56*.

Geiselberger, Heinrich (ed.). 2017. *The Great Regression*. Cambridge: Polity.

Giddens, Anthony. 1991. *Modernity and Self-Identity: Self and Society in the Late Modern Age*. Cambridge: Polity.

Göpel, Maja. 2022. *Wir können auch anders: Aufbruch in die Welt von morgen*. Berlin: Ullstein.

Goldsmith, Edward. 1972. *A Blueprint for Survival*. London: Penguin.

Gorz, André. 1978. *Ökologie und Politik: Beiträge zur Wachstumskrise*. Reinbek bei Hamburg: Rowohlt.

Gorz, André. 1980. *Ökologie und Freiheit*. Reinbek bei Hamburg: Rowohlt.

Gottschlich, Daniela. 2017. *Kommende Nachhaltigkeit: Nachhaltige Entwicklung aus kritisch-emanzipatorischer Perspektive*. Baden-Baden: Nomos.

Gough, Ian. 2020. 'Defining Floors and Ceilings: The Contribution of Human Needs Theory'. *Sustainability: Science, Practice and Policy* 16(1).

Graefe, Stefanie. 2019. *Resilienz im Krisenkapitalismus: Wider das Lob der Anpassungsfähigkeit*. Bielefeld: transcript.

Gramsci, Antonio. 1971. *Selections from the Prison Notebooks of Antonio Gramsci*, ed. and trans. Quintin Hoare and Geoffrey Nowell-Smith. London: Lawrence & Wishart.

Gramsci, Antonio. 2012. *Gefängnishefte: Gesamtausgabe in 10 Bänden*. Hamburg: Argument Verlag.

Guterres, António. 2021. Speech at the UN General Assembly in New York, September 2021. https://www.un.org/sg/en/content/sg/speeches/2021-09-21/address-the-76th-session-of-general-assembly

Guterres, António. 2022. Speech at the UN Climate Summit (COP 27) in Sharm El-Sheikh, November 2022. https://www.un.org/sg/en/content/sg/speeches/2022-11-07/secretary-generals-remarks-high-level-opening-of-cop27

Habermas, Jürgen. 1976. *Legitimation Crisis*. Cambridge: Polity.

Habermas, Jürgen. 1980. 'Die Moderne – ein unvollendetes Projekt', in Jürgen Habermas (1990), *Die Moderne – ein unvollendetes Projekt: Philosophisch-politische Aufsätze*. Stuttgart: Reclam.

Habermas, Jürgen. 2021. 'Überlegungen und Hypothesen zu einem erneuten Strukturwandel der politischen Öffentlichkeit', in Martin Seelinger and Sebastian Sevignani (eds), *Ein neuer Strukturwandel der Öffentlichkeit? Leviathan* (37). Baden-Baden: Nomos.

Habich, Jörg. 2023. 'Einstellungen und Sorgen der jungen Generation Deutschlands 2023'. https://www.bertelsmann-stiftung.de/de/publikationen/publikation/did/einstellungen-und-sorgen-der-jungen-generation-deutschlands-2023

Haderer, Margaret. 2023. 'Experimental Climate Governance as Organized Irresponsibility? A Case for Revamping Governing (Also) through Government'. *Sustainability: Science, Practice and Policy* 19(1).

Hausknost, Daniel. 2020. 'Die gläserne Decke der Transformation: Strukturelle Blockaden im demokratischen Staat', in Ingolfur Blühdorn (ed.), *Nachhaltige Nicht-Nachhaltigkeit: Warum die ökologische Transformation der Gesellschaft nicht stattfindet*. Bielefeld: transcript.

Hausknost, Daniel. 2022. 'Zur Zukunft der Umweltpolitik: Die gläserne Decke der Transformation'. *Politische Ökologie* 1/2022(168).

Helbrecht, Ilse. 1996. 'Die Wiederkehr der Innenstädte: Zur Rolle von Kultur, Kapital und Konsum in der Gentrification'. *Geographische Zeitschrift* 84(1).

Herrmann, Ulrike. 2022. *The End of Capitalism: Why Growth and Climate Protection Are Incompatible – And How We Will Live in the Future*. Melbourne: Scribe.

Hobbes, Thomas. 1970 [1651]. *Leviathan*. Stuttgart: Reclam.

Hofmann, Jeanette. 2022. 'Demokratie und Künstliche Intelligenz'. https://digid.jff.de/demokratie-und-ki/

Hofstetter, Yvonne. 2014. *Sie wissen alles: Wie intelligente Maschinen in unser Leben eindringen und warum wir für unsere Freiheit kämpfen müssen*. Munich: Bertelsmann.

Hofstetter, Yvonne. 2016. *Das Ende der Demokratie: Wie die künstliche Intelligenz die Politik übernimmt und uns entmündigt*. Munich: Bertelsmann.

Holm, Andrej. 2010. 'Gentrifizierung und Kultur: Zur Logik kulturell vermittelter Aufwertungsprozesse'. *Jahrbuch StadtRegion 2009/10: Stadtkultur und Kreativität*.

REFERENCES

Honneth, Axel. 2012. 'Brutalization of the Social Conflict: Struggles for Recognition in the Early 21st Century'. *Distinktion: Scandinavian Journal of Social Theory* 13(1).

Horkheimer, Max and Adorno, Theodor W. 1994 [1944]. *Dialectic of Enlightenment*. New York: Continuum.

Hradil, Stefan. 2002. 'Vom Wandel des Wertewandels: Die Individualisierung und eine ihrer Gegenbewegungen', in Wolfgang Glatzer, Roland Habich and Karl Ulrich Mayer (eds), *Sozialer Wandel und gesellschaftliche Dauerbeobachtung*. Opladen: Leske + Budrich.

Inglehart, Ronald. 1977. *The Silent Revolution: Changing Values and Political Styles among Western Publics*. Princeton: Princeton University Press.

Inglehart, Ronald. 1997. *Modernization and Postmodernization: Cultural, Economic, and Political Change in 43 Societies*. Princeton: Princeton University Press.

Inglehart, Ronald and Welzel, Christian. 2005. *Modernization, Cultural Change, and Democracy: The Human Development Sequence*. Cambridge: Cambridge University Press.

Inglis, David. 2024. 'Better Late than Modern? Between "Late Capitalism" and "Late Modernity"'. *European Journal of Social Theory* 27(4).

Jackson, Tim. 2011. *Prosperity without Growth: Economics for a Finite Planet*. Abingdon: Earthscan.

Jackson, Tim. 2021. *Post Growth: Life after Capitalism*. Cambridge: Polity.

Jaeggi, Rahel. 2013. 'Was (wenn überhaupt etwas) ist falsch am Kapitalismus? Drei Wege der Kapitalismuskritik', in Rahel Jaeggi and Daniel Loick (eds), *Nach Marx*. Frankfurt am Main: Suhrkamp.

Jäger, Anton. 2023. *Hyperpolitik: Extreme Politisierung ohne politische Folgen*. Berlin: Suhrkamp.

Jänicke, Martin. 2007. *Megatrend Umweltinnovation: Zur ökologischen Modernisierung von Wirtschaft und Staat*. Munich: oekom.

Jasansky, Simon, Lieber, Mirko, Giljum, Stefan and Maus, Victor. 2023. 'An Open Database on Global Coal and Metal Mine Production'. *Scientific Data* 10(1).

Jonas, Hans. 1984. *The Imperative of Responsibility: In Search of an Ethics for the Technological Age*. Chicago: University of Chicago Press.

Jonas, Hans. 1993. *Dem bösen Ende näher: Gespräche über das Verhältnis des Menschen zur Natur*. Frankfurt am Main: Suhrkamp.

Jörke, Dirk. 2019. *Die Größe der Demokratie: Über die räumliche Dimension von Herrschaft und Partizipation*. Berlin: Suhrkamp.

Kaase, Max. 1982. 'Partizipatorische Revolution – Ende der Parteien?', in Joachim Raschke (ed.), *Bürger und Parteien: Ansichten und Analysen einer schwierigen Beziehung*. Bonn: Bundeszentrale für politische Bildung.

Kaase, Max. 1984. 'The Challenge of the 'Participatory Revolution' in Pluralist Democracies'. *International Political Science Review* 5(3).

Kant, Immanuel. 1970. *Political Writings*. Cambridge: Cambridge University Press.

Kelly, Petra. 1984. *Fighting for Hope*. London: Chatto & Windus, Hogarth Press.

Kenner, Steve and Nagel, Michael. 2022. 'Große Transformation mit jungen Change Agents? Partizipative politische Bildung für nachhaltige Entwicklung als Antwort auf multiple Krisen der Gegenwart'. *Zeitschrift für Didaktik der Gesellschaftswissenschaften* 13(2).

King, Anthony. 1975. 'Overload: Problems of Governing in the 1970s'. *Political Studies* 23(2–3).

Klein, Naomi. 2015. *This Changes Everything: Capitalism vs. the Climate*. New York: Simon & Schuster.

Kleinhückelkotten, Silke, Nietzke, Peter H. and Mose, Stephanie. 2016. *Repräsentative Erhebung von Pro-Kopf-Verbräuchen natürlicher Ressourcen in Deutschland (nach Bevölkerungsgruppen)*, 39/2016. Dessau-Roßlau: Umweltbundesamt.

Knöbl, Wolfgang. 2007. *Die Kontingenz der Moderne: Wege in Europa, Asien und Amerika*. Frankfurt am Main: Campus.

Knöbl, Wolfgang. 2013. 'Aufstieg und Fall der Modernisierungstheorie und des säkularen Bildes "moderner Gesellschaften"', in Ulrich Willems, Detlef Pollack, Helene Basu, Thomas Gutmann and Ulrike Spohn (eds), *Moderne und Religion: Kontroversen um Modernität und Säkularisierung*. Bielefeld: transcript.

Kolleck, Nina. 2020. 'Bildung für die Zukunft in Zeiten globaler Krisen? Chancen und Dilemmata in der demokratischen und (trans)kulturellen Bildung sowie der Bildung für nachhaltige Entwicklung'. *Zeitschrift für Schul- und Professionsentwicklung* 2(6).

Kuhn, Berthold. 2019. *Ecological Civilization in China*. Berlin: Dialogue of Civilizations Research Institute.

Laclau, Ernesto. 1996. *Emancipation(s)*. London, New York: Verso.

Latour, Bruno. 2017. *Facing Gaia: Eight Lectures on the New Climatic Regime*. Cambridge: Polity.

Latour, Bruno. 2018. *Down to Earth: Politics in the New Climatic Regime*. Cambridge: Polity.

Latour, Bruno and Schultz, Nikolaj. 2022. *On the Emergence of an Ecological Class*. Cambridge: Polity.

Lessenich, Stephan. 2019a. *Living Well at Others' Expense: The Hidden Cost of Western Prosperity*. Cambridge: Polity.

Lessenich, Stephan. 2019b. *Grenzen der Demokratie: Teilhabe als Verteilungsproblem*. Stuttgart: Reclam.

Lessenich, Stephan. 2022. *Nicht mehr normal: Gesellschaft am Rande des Nervenzusammenbruchs*. Berlin: Hanser.

Levitsky, Steven and Ziblatt, Daniel. 2018. *Wie Demokratien sterben: Und was wir dagegen tun können*. Munich: Deutsche Verlags-Anstalt.

Linse, Ulrich. 1986. *Ökopax und Anarchie: Eine Geschichte der ökologischen – Bewegungen in Deutschland*. Munich: dtv.

Lipset, Seymour M. 1959. 'Some Social Requisites of Democracy: Economic Development and Political Legitimacy'. *American Political Science Review* 53(1).

Lipset, Seymour M. 1960. *Political Man; The Social Bases of Politics*. New York: Doubleday.

Liu, Chen, Chen, Lily, Vanderbeck, Robert M., Valentin, Gill, Zhan, Mei, Diprose, Kristina and McQuaid, Katie. 2018. 'A Chinese Route to Sustainability: Postsocialist Transitions and the Construction of Ecological Civilization'. *Sustainable Development* 26(6).

Luhmann, Niklas. 1995. *Social Systems*. Redwood City, CA: Stanford University Press.

Luhmann, Niklas. 1986a. *Ökologische Kommunikation*. Opladen: Westdeutscher Verlag.

Luhmann, Niklas. 1986b. 'Das Trojanische Pferd: Ein Interview', in Kai-Uwe Hellmann (ed.), *Protest*. Frankfurt am Main: Suhrkamp.

Luhmann, Niklas. 1989. *Ecological Communication*. Cambridge: Polity.

Lührmann, Anna and Lindberg, Staffan I. 2019. 'A Third Wave of Autocratization Is Here: What Is New about It?'. *Democratization* 26(7).

Luks, Fred. 2019. '(Große) Transformation – die neue große Nachhaltigkeits-erzählung?', in Fred Luks (ed.), *Chancen und Grenzen der Nachhaltigkeits-transformation*. Wiesbaden: Springer Gabler.

Luks, Fred. 2023. *Ökonomie der Großzügigkeit: Wie Gesellschaften nachhaltig werden*. Bielefeld: transcript.

Lütjen, Torben. 2022. 'The Anti-Authoritarian Revolt: Right-Wing Populism as Self-Empowerment?'. *European Journal of Social Theory* 25(1).

Lyotard, Jean-François. 1984. *The Postmodern Condition: A Report on Knowledge*. Manchester: Manchester University Press.

Lyotard, Jean-François. 1988. *The Differend: Phrases in Dispute*. Minneapolis: University of Minnesota Press.

MacGregor, Sherilyn. 2019. 'Finding Transformative Potential in the Cracks? The Ambiguities of Urban Environmental Activism in a Neoliberal City'. *Social Movement Studies* 20(3).

Macpherson, Crawford B. 1977. *The Life and Times of Liberal Democracy*. Oxford: Oxford University Press.

Malm, Andreas. 2016. *Fossil Capital: The Rise of Steam Power and the Roots of Global Warming*. London: Verso.

Manow, Philip. 2020. *(Ent-)Demokratisierung der Demokratie*. Berlin: Suhrkamp.

Marcuse, Herbert. 1964. *Der eindimensionale Mensch*. Munich: dtv.

Mason, Paul. 2016. *Postcapitalism: A Guide to Our Future*. London: Penguin.

McKibben, Bill. 1990. *The End of Nature*. London: Penguin.

Meadows, Dennis, Meadows, Donella and Randers, Jorgen. 1972. *Die Grenzen des Wachstums*. Stuttgart: Deutsche Verlags-Anstalt.

Merchant, Carolyne. 1980. *The Death of Nature: Women, Ecology and the Scientific Revolution*. San Francisco: Harper & Row.

Mitchell, Timothy. 2011. *Carbon Democracy: Political Power in the Age of Oil*. London: Verso.

Mol, Arthur and Sonnenfeld, David (eds). 2000. *Ecological Modernisation around the World*. London: Frank Cass.

Monticelli, Lara. 2022. *The Future Is Now: An Introduction to Prefigurative Politics*. Bristol: Bristol University Press.

Moser, Stephanie and Kleinhückelkotten, Silke. 2018. 'Good Intents, but Low Impacts: Diverging Importance of Motivational and Socioeconomic Determinants Explaining Pro-Environmental Behaviour, Energy Use, and Carbon Footprint'. *Environment and Behaviour* 50(6).

Mouffe, Chantal. 2018. *Für einen linken Populismus*. Berlin: Suhrkamp.

Mouffe, Chantal. 2023. *Towards a Green Democratic Revolution: Left Populism and the Power of Affects*. London: Verso.

Mounk, Yascha. 2018. *The People vs. Democracy: Why Our Freedom Is in Danger and How to Save It*. Cambridge, MA: Harvard University Press.

REFERENCES

Nachtwey, Oliver. 2016. *Die Abstiegsgesellschaft: Über das Aufbegehren in der regressiven Moderne*. Berlin: Suhrkamp.

Nachtwey, Oliver. 2018. *Germany's Hidden Crisis: Social Decline in the Heart of Europe*, trans. Loren Balhorn and David Fernbach. London: Verso.

Nandy, Ashis. 1983. *The Intimate Enemy: Loss and Recovery of Self under Colonialism*. Oxford: Oxford University Press.

Nassehi, Armin. 2020. 'Die Ästhetik der Erreichbarkeit und Benennbarkeit: Eine unsachliche Kritik', in Angelika Poferl and Natan Sznaider (eds), *Ulrich Becks kosmopolitisches Projekt*. Baden-Baden: Nomos.

Nassehi, Armin. 2021. *Unbehagen: Theorie der überforderten Gesellschaft*. Munich: C.H. Beck.

Nassehi, Armin. 2022a. 'Die Rückkehr des Feindes'. *Zeit Online*, 25 February 2022. https://www.zeit.de/kultur/2022-02/demokratie-bedrohung-russland-ukraine-krieg-wladimir-putin.

Nassehi, Armin. 2022b. 'Nichts ist mehr selbstverständlich'. *Der Spiegel*, 2 April 2022.

Neckel, Sighard. 2020. 'Der Streit um die Lebensführung: Nachhaltigkeit als sozialer Konflikt'. *Mittelweg* 36(6).

Neyrat, Frédéric. 2019. *The Unconstructable Earth: An Ecology of Separation*. New York: Fordham University Press.

Noelle-Neumann, Elisabeth and Petersen, Thomas. 2001. 'Zeitenwende: Der Wertewandel 30 Jahre später'. *Aus Politik und Zeitgeschichte* B29.

Offe, Claus. 1972. *Strukturprobleme des kapitalistischen Staates: Aufsätze zur Politischen Soziologie*. Frankfurt am Main: Suhrkamp.

Overdevest, Christine, Bleicher, Alena and Gross, Matthias. 2010. 'The Experimental Turn in Environmental Sociology: Pragmatism and New Forms of Governance', in Matthias Gross and Harald Heinrichs (eds), *Environmental Sociology: European Perspectives and Interdisciplinary Challenges*. Dordrecht: Springer.

Pabst, Adrian. 2018. *Liberal World Order and Its Critics: Civilisational States and Cultural Commonwealths*. Abingdon, New York: Routledge.

Pabst, Adrian. 2021. *Postliberal Politics: The Coming Era of Renewal*. Cambridge: Polity.

Paech, Niko. 2012. *Liberation from Excess: The Road to a Post-Growth Economy*. Munich: oekom.

Parsons, Talcott. 1971. 'Evolutionäre Universalien in der Gesellschaft', in Wolfgang Zapf (ed.), *Theorien des sozialen Wandels*. Cologne: Kiepenheuer & Witsch.

Pellizzoni, Luigi. 2022. 'A Different Kind of Emancipation? From Lifestyle to Form-of-Life'. *European Journal of Social Theory* 25(1).

Polanyi, Karl. 1957 [1944]. *The Great Transformation: The Political and Economic Origins of Our Time*. Boston: Beacon.

Reckwitz, Andreas. 2020. *The Society of Singularities*. Cambridge: Polity.

Reckwitz, Andreas. 2021. *The End of Illusions: Politics, Economy, and Culture in Late Modernity*. Cambridge: Polity.

Reckwitz, Andreas. 2023. 'The Theory of Society as a Tool', in Andreas Reckwitz and Hartmut Rosa (eds), *Late Modernity in Crisis: Why We Need a Theory of Society*. Cambridge: Polity.

Reckwitz, Andreas and Rosa, Hartmut. 2023. *Late Modernity in Crisis: Why We Need a Theory of Society*. Cambridge: Polity.

REFERENCES

Rockström, Johann et al. 2009a. 'A Safe Operating Space for Humanity'. *Nature* 461.

Rockström, Johann et al. 2009b. 'Planetary Boundaries: Exploring the Safe Operating Space for Humanity'. *Ecology and Society* 14(2).

Rockström, Johann et al. 2021. 'Identifying a Safe and Just Corridor for People and the Planet'. *Earth's Future* 9(4).

Rödder, Andreas. 2024. 'Das Ende der grünen Hegemonie'. *Frankfurter Allgemeine Zeitung*, 7 January 2024.

Rohkrämer, Thomas. 1999. *Eine andere Moderne? Zivilisationskritik, Natur und Technik in Deutschland 1880–1933*. Paderborn: Schöningh.

Römer, Oliver, Boehncke, Clemens and Holzinger, Markus (eds). 2020. *Soziologische Phantasie und kosmopolitisches Gemeinwesen: Perspektiven einer Weiterführung der Soziologie Ulrich Becks*. Baden-Baden: Nomos.

Rosa, Hartmut. 2015. *Social Acceleration: A New Theory of Modernity*. New York: Columbia University Press.

Rosa, Hartmut. 2023. 'Best Account: Outlining a Systematic Theory of Modern Society', in Andreas Reckwitz and Hartmut Rosa (eds), *Late Modernity in Crisis: Why We Need a Theory of Society*. Cambridge: Polity.

Rosa, Hartmut, Strecker, David and Kottmann, Andrea. 2007. *Soziologische Theorien*. Stuttgart: UTB.

Roth, Roland. 1994. *Demokratie von unten: Neue soziale Bewegungen auf dem Wege zur politischen Institution*. Cologne: bund Verlag.

Rucht, Dieter. 1994. *Modernisierung und neue soziale Bewegungen: Deutschland, Frankreich und USA im Vergleich*. Frankfurt am Main, New York: Campus.

Sarkar, Saral. 2001. 'Sustainable Development: Rescue Operation for a Dying Illusion', in Veronika Bennholdt-Thomsen, Nicholas Faraclas and Claudia von Werlhof (eds), *There Is an Alternative: Subsistence and Worldwide Resistance to Corporate Globalization*. London: ZED Books.

Schäfer, Armin and Zürn, Michael. 2021. *Die demokratische Regression*. Berlin: Suhrkamp.

Schellnhuber, Hans Joachim. 1999. '"Earth System" Analysis and the Second Copernican Revolution'. *Nature* 402(S6761).

Schneidewind, Uwe. 2018. *Die Große Transformation: Eine Einführung in die Kunst gesellschaftlichen Wandels*. Frankfurt am Main: Fischer.

Sennett, Richard. 1999. *The Corrosion of Character: The Personal Consequences of Work in the New Capitalism*. New York: Norton.

Shearman, David and Smith, Joseph W. 2007. *Climate Change Challenge and the Failure of Democracy*. Westport, CT: Praeger.

Sieferle, Rolf-Peter. 1984. *Fortschrittsfeinde? Opposition gegen Technik und Industrie von der Romantik bis zur Gegenwart*. Munich: C.H. Beck.

Spaargaren, Gert and Mol, Arthur. 1992. 'Sociology, Environment, and Modernity: Ecological Modernization as a Theory of Social Change'. *Society & Natural Resources* 5(4).

Spengler, Oswald. 1991 [1922]. *The Decline of the West*. Oxford: Oxford University Press.

Staab, Philipp. 2022. *Anpassung: Leitmotiv der nächsten Gesellschaft*. Berlin: Suhrkamp.

Steffen, Will et al. 2015. 'Planetary Boundaries: Guiding Human Development on a Changing Planet'. *Science* 347(6223).

Steffen, Will et al. 2018. 'Trajectories of the Earth System in the Anthropocene'. *Proceedings of the National Academy of Sciences of the United States of America* 115(33).

Stephan, Cora. 1993. *Der Betroffenheitskult: Eine politische Sittengeschichte.* Reinbek bei Hamburg: Rowohlt.

Streeck, Wolfgang. 2014. *Buying Time: The Delayed Crisis of Democratic Capitalism.* London: Verso.

Streeck, Wolfgang. 2016. *How Will Capitalism End? Essays on a Failing System.* London: Verso.

Tauss, Aaron (ed.). 2016. *Sozial-ökologische Transformation: Das Ende des Kapitalismus denken.* Hamburg: VSA.

Touraine, Alain. 1971. *The Post-Industrial Society. Tomorrow's Social History: Classes, Conflicts and Culture in the Programmed Society.* New York: Random House.

Tsing, Anna. 2016. *The Mushroom at the End of the World: On the Possibility of Life in Capitalist Ruins.* Princeton: Princeton University Press.

Tyfield, David. 2021. 'Will China Deliver Urban "Ecological Civilization"', in Janette Webb, Faye Wade and Margaret Tingey (eds), *Research Handbook on Energy and Society.* Cheltenham: Edward Elgar Publishing.

Tyfield, David and Rodríguez, Fabricio. 2022. 'Against and For China's Ecological Civilisation: Economising the *Bios* or "Life-ising" Transition?' *International Quarterly for Asian Studies* 53(3).

Ulbricht, Lena. 2020. 'Scraping the Demos: Digitalization, Web Scraping and the Democratic Project'. *Democratization* 27(3).

van der Loo, Hans and van Reijen, Willem. 1992. *Modernisierung: Projekt und Paradox.* Munich: dtv.

van Dyk, Silke and Graefe, Stefanie. 2019. 'Wer ist Schuld am Rechtspopulismus? Zur Vereinnahmung der Vereinnahmungsdiagnose'. *Leviathan* 49(4).

Van Reybrouck, David. 2016. *Against Elections: The Case for Democracy.* London: The Bodley Head.

von Prittwitz, Volker (ed.). 1993. *Umweltpolitik als Modernisierungsprozess.* Opladen: Leske+Budrich.

United Nations. 2015. 'Transforming Our World: The 2030 Agenda for Sustainable Development'. New York: United Nations.

Wagenknecht, Sahra. 2022. *Die Selbstgerechten: Mein Gegenprogramm – für Gemeinsinn und Zusammenhalt.* Frankfurt am Main: Campus.

Wainwright, Joel and Mann, Geoff. 2020. *Climate Leviathan: A Political Theory of Our Planetary Future.* London: Verso.

Wakefield, Stephanie. 2018. 'Infrastructures of Liberal Life: From Modernity and Progress to Resilience and Ruins'. *Geography Compass* 12(7).

Wakefield, Stephanie. 2021. 'Experimental Government in the Anthropocene', in David Chandler, Franziska Müller and Delf Rothe (eds), *International Relations in the Anthropocene: New Agendas, New Agencies and New Approaches.* New York: Palgrave.

WBGU (German Advisory Council on Global Change). 2011. *World in Transition: A Social Contract for Sustainability.* Berlin: WBGU.

WCED (World Commission on Environment and Development). 1987. *Our Common Future.* Oxford: Oxford University Press.

Welsch, Wolfgang. 1987. *Unsere postmoderne Moderne.* Weinheim: Acta humaniora.

Welzer, Harald. 2017. *Die smarte Diktatur: Der Angriff auf unsere Freiheit.* Frankfurt am Main: S. Fischer.

Wiest, Karin and Hill, André. 2004. 'Sanfte Gentrifizierung, Studentifizierung und Inseln ethnischer Konzentration in ostdeutschen Innenstadtrandgebieten'. *Raumforschung und Raumordnung, Spatial Research and Planning* 62(6).

Wilson, Japhy and Swyngedouw, Erik (eds). 2014. *The Post-Political and Its Discontents: Spaces of Depoliticisation, Spectres of Radical Politics.* Edinburgh: Edinburgh University Press.

Wissenburg, Marcel. 1998. *Green Liberalism: The Free and the Green Society.* London: UCL Press.

Zapf, Wolfgang. 1975. 'Die soziologische Theorie der Modernisierung'. *Soziale Welt* 26(2).

Zapf, Wolfgang. 1991. 'Modernisierung und Modernisierungstheorien', in Wolfgang Zapf (ed.), *Die Modernisierung moderner Gesellschaften: Verhandlungen des 25. Deutschen Soziologentages in Frankfurt am Main 1990.* Frankfurt am Main: Campus.

Zuboff, Shoshana. 2018. *Das Zeitalter des Überwachungskapitalismus.* Frankfurt am Main: Campus.

Zuboff, Shoshana. 2019. *The Age of Surveillance Capitalism.* London: Profile Books.